THE
GREAT WESTERN'S
LAST YEAR

THE GREAT WESTERN'S LAST YEAR

EFFICIENCY IN ADVERSITY

ADRIAN VAUGHAN

The History Press

Cover illustrations: Front: GW6 by H.N. James. (Colour-Rail) *Back*:
Examples from the *Great Western Railway Magazine*.

First published 2013

The History Press
The Mill, Brimscombe Port
Stroud, Gloucestershire, GL5 2QG
www.thehistorypress.co.uk

British Library Cataloguing in Publication Data.
A catalogue record for this book is available from the British Library.

ISBN 978 0 7524 6532 6

Typesetting and origination by The History Press
Printed in Great Britain

CONTENTS

ACKNOWLEDGEMENTS

Kind permission to scan images in the *Great Western Staff Magazine* was granted by British Rail (Residuary) Ltd, for which I am very grateful. The Trustees of Pendon Museum of the Vale of the White Horse very kindly sent me the full set of 1947 *Great Western Railway Magazines*, enabling the best possible results of 1947 paper and newsprint images. The use of these images was vital to the authenticity and relevance of the book's illustrations. I must acknowledge the kind assistance I have received from some friends: Allan Pym, still a mechanical signalman on Network Rail, who helped me with diagrams of track layouts; Mike Christensen OBE for his help with financial

No 2931 *Arlington Court* at Platform 2 Exeter St David's on 13 September 1947. (R.C. Riley, Transport Treasury. Ref: RCR 1473)

matters on the GWR; Mr Michael Page, ex-Western Region Cardiff Divisional Signal & Telegraph Engineer, for his information regarding his father, F.H.D. Page, Chief Signal & Telegraph Engineer of the GWR; David Collins, last Chief Signal & Telegraph Engineer of Western Region for his replies to my questions. I must also gratefully acknowledge the help I received from Mr Chris Turner of Didcot and from Mr Steve Cooper, a Trustee of the Great Western Society, who took the photograph of the 1942-1947 GWR coat of arms used on the front cover. And finally, I must acknowledge my debt to my editor, Christine McMorris, for her care in helping me prepare this book.

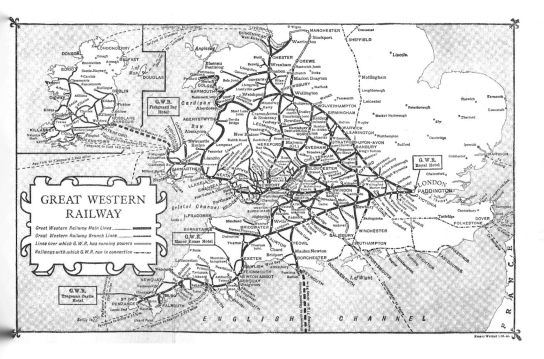

THE TRANSPORT BILL

The Railway Companies' Statement

The Bill for the Act of Nationalisation of the British railway system passed its second reading on 18 December 1946. There was the final reading to come but the Labour government had an overwhelming majority of seats in parliament, nationalisation of transport having been the policy of the Labour Party since 1900, and that policy forming part of the election manifesto of 1945 so overwhelmingly voted for by the electors – nationalisation was a foregone conclusion. The headline on the first page of the *Great Western Railway Magazine* for January 1947 was:

The Transport Bill

All four companies opposed the Bill, and as it also proposed the nationalisation of road freight and passenger haulage, the Road Haulage Association became an unlikely ally of the railways.

Some of the points of objection noted in the Statement were:

i. The Bill provides for the nationalization of transport with no assurance that a practical scheme will be evolved by the (British Transport) Commission which will provide a more adequate, efficient and co-ordinated service than can otherwise be given and which will meet the needs of industry and the travelling public and be acceptable to them.

ii. The Bill makes no provision for the co-ordination of transport. The scheme submitted to the Government by the railways and road hauliers for the co-ordination of freight traffic throughout the country has not received the attention it deserves. It ensures for traders to use any form of transport, including their own. It avoids the dangers and abuses of monopoly and it safeguards the nation's transport from the dangers of political pressure.

iii. The Commission are to be subject to general direction by the Minister. This means political interference when political expediency demands it. The Commission are subject to direction by the Minister on nearly every matter. They are not to have independence or freedom.

v. The Commission will not have to prove annually before a Statutory Tribunal – as the Railways have had to do since 1921 – that their management is economical and efficient.

ix. The financial terms for the acquisition of the Railways put forward in the Bill are unjust and would cause widespread hardship to the many people who depend for their livelihood on the income from railway stocks. In 1945 £42 million was paid in interest and dividends. Even between the years 1928 to 1938 which included many years of acute depression, the average annual amount paid in interest and dividends was £35 million. Compare these figures with the £23 million which is the annual amount payable if the stock to be issued by the government in exchange for railway stock carries 2.5% interest.

The Statement was brought to a proud and defiant conclusion as follows:

When presenting the Transport Bill to the House of Commons on 16 December 1946, the Minister of Transport rejected the request for a public inquiry and after three days debate the Bill was approved and committed to a Standing Committee. Although the Minister of Transport paid tribute to the magnificent work done by the railways during the war, the Chancellor of the Exchequer – having stated that he would devote himself to the financial side of the measure – went out of his way to make an unwarranted attack upon the railways, which he described as 'a disgrace to the country and a poor bag of assets'. Railwaymen throughout the country cannot but resent these disparaging remarks. Prior to the war the British railways compared favourably with those of any country in the world. It was the efficiency of their pre-war organizations and the high standard at which their lines and rolling stock had been maintained despite long periods of trade depression, that enabled the railways to meet the heavy demands of war.

It is no fault of the railway that their permanent way and their locomotive stock, which, prior to the war, were the finest in the world, are now suffering from the effects of war strain. To make good the wartime depreciation of their assets the railways have set aside £148 million which represent the cost of making good the difference in the amount of maintenance work carried out during the war compared with a corresponding pre-war period, and that is without any allowance for abnormal wear and tear for which they are claiming a further £40 million from the Government.

But while the necessary financial provision has been made by the railway companies to restore the railways to their pre-war standard, it has not been possible to obtain sufficient materials and labour – and if there is any suggestion that more work should have been done, the responsibility for it not having been done rests with the government.

It may be assumed that the Government will make every effort to get the Bill passed during the present session of Parliament and, if eventually the railways are nationalized, there will be many members of staff who will feel sad that they will no longer be associated with a Company of whose achievements and traditions they may feel proud.

The *Financial Times* editorial of 3 September 1946 was in favour of nationalisation:

Open competition is too costly to contemplate and it is likely to lead to the breakdown of public services, and no effective middle course appears possible without subsidies. The complete co-ordination of transport by means of a scheme of unification is the only way to get the best possible service at the lowest economic cost.

There had not been 'open competition' between the companies since the 1921 Transport Act. From 1930 they were moving towards co-ordination and co-operation. Income from freight traffic was pooled, two companies with stations side by side, as at Oxford, would have one Station Master between them. Locomotive shed facilities would be shared should the need arise. The GWR had joint ownership of local bus companies: GWR and Southern or LMS and the original company; Thames Valley; Western National; Western Welsh. The companies were developing a co-operation with road collection and delivery services. These policies were still being acted upon and extended in 1947.

The Great Western was in a surprisingly good financial condition – given the abuse the company had suffered from various governments since 1914. The government took control of the railways during the Great War under an Act of 1871 which bound the government to pay compensation for all wear and tear caused by wartime use. Railway charges were not allowed to rise in line with inflation and, towards the end, the companies were spending 100 per cent of their entire government rent on operating. Sir William Plender, famous accountant appointed by the government in 1919 to investigate the railway companies' claims, stated that, in return for the guarantee of full compensation, the companies had given land transport service to the government worth £112,043,808. On the sea and canals the railways had given a further ten to fifteen million pounds' worth of transport. The total amount paid to the railways during the Great War was £95,313,607 which included an amount for renewals. This took no account of 'extra wear and tear', nor the cost of replacing all the additional fuel and materials used, nor for all the munitions that railway factories had turned out – all to be bought at heavily inflated post-war prices. Lord Plender's report stated that 'it is not possible to calculate what is owed to the companies but it is not less than £150,000,000'. (Command 1132 of 1921)

Then the 1921 Transport Act was passed, which obliged 120 railway companies to amalgamate into four groups. The Great Western therefore was obliged to take over sixty smaller companies, many of them insolvent or almost in that financial state. This meant re-laying their tracks and supplying them with modern locomotives and carriages. As all rates and fares were controlled by a court of law – the Railway Rates

Tribunal – to raise or lower fares was a time-consuming process. This made price competition with the road haulier very difficult: road hauliers could quote any price they liked – on the spot – without reference to anyone. Section 58 of the Act stated that railway charges would be: 'Such as will yield the Standard Revenue equivalent to the net combined revenue of 1913 together with a sum equal to 5% on capital expenditure.' In spite of having 'one hand tied behind our back and our ankles hobbled' and being loaded with the costs of taking over impecunious railways, the Great Western managed surprisingly well.

In 1939 the railways came under government control again, for a fixed sum – a rent. This was insufficient and in fact they never received the full amount they were promised. But – as in the Great War – the companies served the nation admirably and by 1947 the GWR's track, locomotives and rolling stock – along with the same assets that belonged to the other companies – were seriously in need of restoration and renewal.

The Minister of Transport, Mr Barnes, in bringing forward the Labour Party's Bill for nationalisation on 16 December 1946 said:

If we allowed these separate undertakings to continue after the war in the scramble for capital, (they) would probably be handicapped. We cannot afford a continuance of situations of that kind. Capital must go where it is most needed, and where it will best serve our national resources. That applies to material, and manpower as well. Before I conclude this part of my remarks, in which I reject the demand for an inquiry, I emphasise that transport is not, of itself, a productive service. It is an overhead cost on the whole of British trade and industry. Parliament, in my view, in looking at transport, should look at it as a major overhead cost, and its organisation should be directed entirely from that angle.

Further, the Labour Party, the Trades Union Congress, the Co-operative Congress – [Laughter.] After all, these three bodies represent the majority of the people of these islands and in any case they are entitled to express their views like any other organisations. The point I was about to make was that these three great major organisations who have been speaking for the organised workers and consumers of this country for many years – [HON. MEMBERS: 'Consumers?'] – Yes, consumers – have stated quite clearly in published documents, and in many other ways, their firm conviction that these transport services should come under national ownership. I am satisfied that every candidate of the Labour Party stated this issue at the last General Election. The Conservative Party have never laid their programme so clearly before the electorate as the Labour Party has been in the habit of doing. I do not consider that anybody can dispute that, as far as we are concerned, both the principle of nationalisation, and our clear intention, have been submitted to the electorate, and have received their endorsement.[1]

Mr W.S. Morrison, Member for Tewkesbury and Cirencester, opened the second day of debate on the Transport Bill on 17 December 1946. He pointed out that the Treasury took as the true value of the railway companies' property the value of their shares on the stock market in 1946. Morrison showed up the fraud of taking share price because share value depends on the volume of trading, and relatively few railway shares were ever traded over the previous twenty-five years. The vast majority were held steadily by great organisations, such as hospitals, insurance companies and pension funds. The railway companies kept their dividends low in order to plough money back into the restoration of the business; the share value was also low. The actual value of the railway companies was in the land, ships, docks and harbours, the hotels, and all the other assets they held.

Morrison continued:

But having valued the railways we have to pay for them. We are told in Clause 93 (2), that 'The British transport stock which is to be created and issued under paragraph (b) of subsection (1) of this section in satisfaction of a claim to compensation of any amount shall be such stock as is, in the opinion of the Treasury, equal in value at the date of the issue to that amount, regard being had to the market value of government securities at that date.' 'Regard being had to the value of Government securities at that date' – we are completely away now from any regard to the value of the property that is being acquired – and the time when we shall calculate what is actually to be paid will not be the time when the undertaking is purchased, but will be after the Chancellor of the Exchequer has had a further undisclosed period for rigging the market in Government securities. In the absence of some further information from the Chancellor today, the recipients of this stock are being promised for their property no more than a pig in a poke. What sort of animal it will turn out to be when the bag is opened remains to be seen.

Returning to my main argument, which is the effect on the people concerned, I am assuming that the yield of this stock will be 2½ per cent. I have to assume that that is so. In round figures, the effect will be this. In 1945 the total yield of the four main line railways in interest and dividends was £41,499,262. The annual interest on the British Transport Stock which they will receive will be £22,694,593. The recipients then will lose of their income on the whole, £18,804,669. There are, of course, different reductions in different stocks, which I think is very unjust in itself, but the average overall reduction of income for the holders of these stocks – trustee stocks, a great number of them – is 45.3 per cent, very nearly half the income on the whole. This is a grave slice of the income of many a humble home. It is also a big slice of the resources of trusts, and I think it should further make hon. Gentlemen opposite question whether this bitter fruit can possibly grow from a sound tree. All the railway shareholders will suffer, but it is a further vice of this method of compensation that they do not suffer equally. By this 'hit or miss' method of valuation, grave inequalities are introduced as between the different classes of stockholders. They are all in the tumbrel together, but comparing one with another some get a first-class ride as opposed to a third-class ride in that gloomy vehicle. I will give some examples.

Southern Railways 5 per cent. deferred ordinary stock, which has paid its dividends constantly—with, I think, one slight diminution one year—as a result of rumours and fears was depressed into the 70s. If we take 75, the return was about £6 13s 6d per cent. The Government's terms for this stock are £77 12s 6d, which at 2½ per cent. will give a yield of £1 18s 6d per cent; three-quarters of the yield is taken away and the holders are left to whistle for it. Take the holder of £1,000 of London Midland and Scottish 4 per cent debenture stock. The present income on that is £40. Under this Bill he will get £1,180, which at 2½ per cent. gives him £29 10s, a loss of 26 per cent of his income. On the other hand, £1,000 of L.M.S. 4 per cent. first preference stock has a present yield of £40, the holder gets £850, which at 2½ per cent. brings in £21 5s, a loss of 46 per cent of his income. Here are these three good stocks; the holder of one loses 75 per cent, the second 26 per cent, and the third 46 per cent. Surely, if nothing else will, this should demonstrate the inequalities which flow from taking six days' Stock Exchange prices as the datum line for a transaction of this magnitude. [2]

The interest paid on British Transport Commission Stock was fixed at 3 per cent before the Bill became law.

The Labour government had stated in the party manifesto that transport nationalisation was their policy and the majority of voters had voted for that so there could only be one outcome. The *de facto* nationalisation of the railways from 1939 onwards enabled more traffic to be shifted than ever before and under extreme conditions, and so the policy seemed to a great many people to be a sound one. The government had had the benefit of free transport by taking over the railways but in so doing it had worn out four previously magnificently well maintained and managed railways. The renewals funds of the four disappeared into the Treasury. Private capital was not to be forthcoming to rebuild the private railways – only taxpayers' money could be used to rebuild the nationalised railways – and that, the Labour government would be as reluctant to provide as the Conservatives.

The Great Western directors, knowing that the GWR would be taken into public ownership at the end of 1947, loyally and honestly continued to manage their railway with the same care and concern as if it would still be a private company in a hundred years. And they paid out a good dividend – also constrained by law – at the end of the year.

Notes

1   House of Commons, *Hansard, vol. 431*, col. 1617.
2   House of Commons, *Hansard, vol. 431*, col. 1785.

GREAT WESTERN RAILWAY
MAGAZINE

JANUARY · 1947

VOL. 59 · NO. 1

THE GREAT WESTERN: "Hooray! Never even blew me cap off!"

A 1922 Cartoon. (See Page 2)

PRICE ONE PENNY

JANUARY

The Board of Directors of the Great Western Railway gathered in the Grand Boardroom at Paddington on 24 January. There were seventeen members of the Board[1] and twelve were present: Deputy Chairman, the 3rd Earl of Dudley, the Hon. A.W. Baldwin, J.J. Astor, W.M. Codrington, Sir William Fraser, Charles Hambro, Cyril E. Lloyd, Geoffrey F. Luttrell, James V. Rank, Sir W. Reardon-Smith Bt, Sir George Harvie-Watt, Col Sir W. Charles Wright Bt. Five Members were missing: Viscount Wyndham Portal, Lord Dulverton, Captain Hugh Vivian, the Hon. Edward Cadogan and Mr Maurice Harold Macmillan. Viscount Portal is shown as 'Chairman' on the Directors' Fees Ledger but he was not formally elected to that post until March.

At this meeting the fourth resolution to be passed was that, as there was £4,016, 8s 7d of directors' fees unclaimed from the preceding year, 'that money would be paid to the Chairman and utilised in the manner which was indicated by the Directors'. This was an annual ritual going back to 1922 when the decision was taken that directors' unclaimed fees would go to the 'Helping Hand' fund for the employees. The Chairman's annual fee in 1947 was £6,000. This fee had not changed since 1922. The Deputy Chairman was entitled to £3,000 p.a., also a sum unchanged since the same year.

The total gross remuneration allowed to the seventeen GWR directors in 1947, was £22,660. All fees had income tax deducted before being paid. No bonuses were paid to any board member.[2] They worked for such small amounts as to be – almost – volunteers. These men attended board meetings regularly and divided themselves into sub-committees for 'Finance', 'Labour', 'Locomotive & Carriage', 'Engineering', and 'Law & Parliamentary'. They directed a railway network and railway operation far more onerous, and far more complex, than that in use today, and they ran it at a profit in spite of receiving *less* money than they were entitled to as rent under the wartime Government Control Agreement.

In 1929 the four railway companies in partnership had obtained parliamentary powers to operate passenger air services. The Great Western Railway inaugurated their first flights on 11 April 1933. The following year the GWR service was taken over by 'Railway Air Services' owned by all four railway companies. In 1946 the government brought into being the nationalised 'British European Airways' (BEA) and the railways' liquid and physical assets were taken into BEA ownership as from 31 January 1947. At the January meeting of the GWR Board, the directors accepted the government's offer of £550,000 for the liquid and physical assets of the Railway Air Services.

On staff matters, the directors noted that the General Manager, Sir James Milne, had met the representatives of the National Union of Railwaymen (NUR), the Railway

Clerks Association (RCA) and the Associated Society of Locomotive Engineers and Fireman (ASLEF) and had agreed that the War Bonus be 'consolidated into the ordinary weekly wage'. This was a technicality, adopted on 1 July 1946, which guaranteed that the amount an employee received each week/month would not go down. The Minute stated: 'In the case of male adults the maximum rate of War Bonus is £73 p.a. for salaried staff and 28/ a week for the wages grades *with appropriately lower rates for women* and juniors.'[3]

All four railway companies were finding it difficult to recruit and retain clerical staff. The general managers of the four companies met and decided that, as from 1 January, the pay scales for clerical staff would be increased to a maximum of £293 p.a. (112s 6d per week) for males and 90s a week for females. And as a further improvement it was resolved that the maximum rate would be paid when the clerk reached the age of 28, rather than thirty-two as previously. The curious thing about lower pay for women was that they did not receive an equal reduction in the price of a bus ticket or a pound of tea.

'Heads of Departments' were awarded increases up to a maximum of £438 p.a. and they could apply to the Directors' Finance Committee for consideration for higher pay up to £573 p.a.

Men working in the dozens of locomotive running & maintenance depots (R&M) asked to be put on a system of bonus payments – 'payments by results' – for faster repairs and maintenance. The precise method of working such a system was still being studied but while this was being worked out so that a satisfactory conclusion could be reached, the R&M men were to be paid 33½ per cent more on their existing wages as from 27 January.

The civil police were given a pay rise as from November 1946 and so the Railway Police Federation put in a claim for a rise. This was still under discussion in January.

Directors Lloyd, Baldwin, Hambro and Luttrell formed the Engineering Committee. Cyril Lloyd was the Chairman. They scrutinised and authorised Signal & Telegraph and Civil Engineering expenditure. In January the Signal & Telegraph Department spent £8,830 on maintenance or improvements throughout the vast network of the Great Western Railway. Bramley level crossing gates and three signals were replaced for £1,460; the telegraph poles and wires between Newent and Dymock and between Stow-on-the-Wold and Bourton-on-the-Water were renewed for £4,100. At Newport (Monmouthshire) a house, No 148 Caerleon Road, was purchased to accommodate a member of staff for £1,500.

On 4 April 1944 the bridge over the Wye at Chepstow had suffered severe buckling of one section of a plate girder in the land-span. The bridge was carrying a continuous stream of the heaviest traffic it had ever carried – and would ever carry – due to the wartime work of the South Wales steelworks. The bridge had a 'fore and aft' movement in it when 90-ton locomotives rolled to it at either end. The chains had to be wedged down tight against the upright supports, large wedges of oak had to be hammered in to maintain the tension of the chains, but with the extreme traffic some slack developed and the forward thrust – created by each heavy train moving onto the bridge at the permitted 25mph – exerted a sudden, fierce, end-on pressure on the web plates of the land-spans until finally one large sheet plate buckled inwards towards the track. The metal was by then 92 years old. A 15mph speed restriction was applied. In January 1947 a 'partial reconstruction' of the bridge was authorised at a cost of £68,000.

A total of £101,000 was voted to be spent on civil engineering projects, ranging from large projects like Chepstow, to £1,250 for the repair of a culvert at Dauntsey. However, there was such a great shortage of labour and materials that many of the works could not be started.

The winter period from December 1946, through January and well into March 1947 became increasingly arctic to the point where domestic houses and railway trains could be buried under drifting snow. Everything looked bleak and appeared to be grey or almost black. By this time I had started going to school, and remember the bitter cold and the darkness indoors because of the electricity power cuts, and have memories of our kitchen being illuminated by just a couple of candles, accompanied by the blue gas flame under a saucepan of cooking potatoes.

Lorry drivers employed by London-based haulage companies had gone on an unofficial strike as early as 5 January. This ensured that food supplies to the capital and food distribution throughout the capital were disrupted. Mr Attlee brought in the Grenadier Guards to move food from the docks to cold stores and to Smithfield meat market. This caused the Smithfield and Billingsgate meat and fish porters to go on strike. The staff of all four railway companies stayed at work throughout the entire winter – three shifts around the clock – and, as a matter of fact, there were no official strikes by railwaymen from 14 May 1926 until 30 May 1955.

Railwaymen and women of all three railway trade unions had been negotiating for a pay rise since early in 1946. One request was that the War Bonus supplement – money paid to keep up with inflation of prices – should now become absorbed into the normal wage. In July 1946 that and other increases were granted. Train fares and freight rates, meanwhile, were still held down by government decree to one third of the rate of inflation as they had been since 1939 – this was done as a subsidy to manufacturing industry and the general public.

In spite of the freezing cold and a shortage of engines, coal, carriages and men, the holiday and parcels traffic for Christmas 1946 was carried almost as if the war had not happened. No-one outside the railway thought this was exceptional service – that was what the nation expected of the railway. Between 20 and 29 December 1946, 473 long-distance trains were run from Paddington. On 24 December 41,160 long-distance passengers left Paddington in sixty-seven trains and over the whole GWR network, eighty-three extra trains were conjured up from somewhere to transport 53,700 military personnel who were on leave.

Mr Victor Collins, MP for Taunton, and from 1958 ennobled as Lord Stonham, appears to have been going around with his eyes shut in December 1946, and as a result felt his ego bruised at Paddington during the Christmas period. On 29 January he asked the Minister of Transport: 'If he is aware that unnecessary hardship was caused to large numbers of Christmas period passengers by the inadequate arrangements at Paddington Station; and if he will make an investigation with the object of avoiding chaotic conditions during the periods of heavy passenger traffic.'

The Minister replied, perhaps a little wearily: 'I regret that shortage of rolling stock and staff made it impracticable for the railway company to deal promptly with the heavy passenger traffic at Paddington during the Christmas period. The situation was aggravated by adverse weather conditions and may be regarded as having been exceptional.'[4]

During the first two weeks of January 1947 the income from passenger travel was 8.24 per cent down on the same period in 1946. Goods revenue was down 17.3 per cent but coal haulage revenue was up by 23.5 per cent. On 6 January 1947 the GWR was short of motive power for hauling coal and vital supplies of food from the docks and so seven long-distance expresses were cancelled for the time being:

> 12 noon Paddington–Kingswear
> 12 noon Torquay–Paddington
> 7.50 a.m. Birmingham–Bristol
> 2.15 p.m. Bristol–Birmingham
> 11.10 a.m. Wolverhampton–Weymouth
> 10.30 a.m. Weymouth–Wolverhampton
> 11.00 a.m. Plymouth–Penzance

On 9 January the government forbade the running of passenger trains for any special events in order to keep engines available for the haulage of coal and other vital traffic. A lot of coal was normally conveyed by sea from South Wales to the London power stations but severe gales in the Bristol and English Channels between 30 November 1946 and 9 January 1947 prevented sailings, and in that time of bitter cold and fierce winds the GWR worked an extra thirty-one coal trains – each a full load[5] for a '28xx' class engine – to the London Power Company at Battersea. Heavy streams of traffic were passing to and from the GWR and LMS to the Southern Railway over the GWR/LMS joint 'West London line'. This route was a congested 'bottleneck' and an idea of the severity of the situation can be gained in that some north–south GWR freight trains which normally got onto the Southern Railway via West London were diverted to the fiercely graded, but double-track, Didcot, Newbury & Southampton route. Some LMS to Southern trains had to be diverted via the Birmingham–Cheltenham line so as to get onto the Southern Railway via Cheltenham Lansdown Junction, Andoversford Junction, up over the Cotswolds, Wiltshire Downs and Salisbury Plain to Andover and Southampton. This was a sure sign of desperation, as this was a single-track, steeply graded route which seriously restricted the tonnage engines could haul over it.

As from 27 January the 7.40 a.m. Penzance–Manchester train was temporarily terminated at Bristol Temple Meads, the 1 p.m. Cardiff to Brighton, and the 11 a.m. Brighton–Cardiff trains, both of which ran via Dr Days and North Somerset Junctions, Bath, Westbury and Salisbury, became temporarily 'Saturdays Only', to release motive power for coal trains.

Great Western engines before the war ran on fine Welsh steam coal but, from July 1945, the newly elected government decreed that this coal was reserved for export only. The GWR then had to find whatever coal they could get from dozens of collieries located in all the mining districts of England as well as South Wales. While a lot of it was good coal in general terms, on GWR engines the men would say 'it burns like paper'. Some of it was only a little better than dust. Prices varied according to the amount purchased and the quality. Some 780 tons of 'Glamorganshire Washed Nuts' was to be supplied over a period of twelve months at £2 5s 8d a ton; 1,680 tons of 'Opencast Small Coal' from Monmouthshire cost £1 15s 0d a ton; 4,672 tons of 'Washed Small Coal' from Staffordshire cost £1 15s 11d; 2,999 tons of 'Washed Small Coal from Glamorganshire' was £2 1s 0d a ton. Other collieries from which the GWR bought coal included Donisthorpe Colliery, Ashby de la Zouch: 3,824 tons at 15s per ton, and 1,864 tons from Bolsover Colliery, Derbyshire, at £1 17s 0d a ton. In the four weeks ending 11 January, GWR locomotives burned 47,790 tons of coal.[6]

The GWR Chief Mechanical Engineer, Mr Hawksworth, and the Locomotive Committee directors realised that using what was, for their engines, inferior coals was a serious problem to be tackled at once. Their answer was oil firing. This was a well-known technique in North and South America. Fuel oil contains a greater amount of energy per pound weight than the best coal and its quality never varies, whereas being forced to buy unsuitable coal from non specific collieries was buying the unknown. In October 1945, 2-8-0 No 2872 (then renumbered 4800) was the first GWR locomotive to be converted to burn oil. No 2854 (4801) followed in November.[7]

This was a pilot scheme so some rough-and-ready means of fuelling the two engines would have been adopted. The oil that was used was a thick, viscous type that did not flow easily. It had to be warmed by heating elements within the tender. This was achieved by placing tubes heated by boiler steam in the engine's tenders. The oil would also have to be kept warm in its storage tank before being transferred to the 1,800-gallon tank on the engine's tender. An electric pump was used for the transfer. The Minutes of the GWR Directors' Locomotive Committee show that the expenditure on permanent oil-fuelling facilities at Severn Tunnel Junction and Llanelly sheds was authorised on 28 March 1946.

The oil-burning engines were enabled to generate steam at a greater rate than ever before. And of course there was no great pile of cinders, ash and clinker to be removed and carted off to be dumped. The higher calorific content of oil over coal is well illustrated by an eyewitness account. When 2-6-0 No 6320 had an oil burner installed, in March 1947, my friend Ernie Nutty, who was a senior figure in the Drawing Office, rode on its footplate when it was used on an express passenger train from Gloucester to Swindon. He told me that 6320 was the equivalent of a 'Castle' class when climbing Sapperton bank. I do wonder what that treatment would do to the firebox over time. Five 'Castle' and eight 'Hall' class trains were converted during 1946 and 1947.

With the trials of the two engines working well, the Minister of Transport requested, in September 1946, that the other three companies should start converting their locomotives to oil burning. The government told the GWR that it would increase its imports of fuel oil from 280,000 tons to 920,000 tons by June 1948. And so, in September 1946, the GWR invited contractors to tender for the construction of oil-fuelling installations at fifteen major engine sheds around the GWR territory. Expenditure on oil-fuelling facilities for Westbury (Wiltshire) was authorised on 15 January 1947. Installation took several months owing to a shortage of contractors and materials. By the end of June 1947 the GWR had completed the installation of oil-fuelling points at the fifteen designated locomotive depots and had converted thirty-four locomotives.

On 15 July 1947 the Prime Minister, Mr Attlee, was obliged to lift the wartime prohibition on the convertibility of sterling into any currency. The reason for this was that the US government had agreed to loan Britain $3.5 billion – but only on condition that the pound sterling be freely convertible into US dollars. This resulted in all foreign governments, banks and individuals that were holding shaky British pounds using them to buy the almighty dollar. The fuel oil required by the GWR had to be purchased with the American dollar, and within days of lifting the wartime controls on sterling, the dollar was in very short supply in Britain – and dollars were required for other important imports such as food for the population and steel for the car industry.

On 20 August Attlee was forced – by the free market in currency draining Britain's gold reserves – to revoke convertibility. The GWR had just then completed the conversion of three more locomotives to oil burning and these were the last. The process of re-converting to coal burning began in September and the last oil-burning locomotives on the GWR were re-converted in April 1950. The cost of constructing the oil-fuelling installations at the engine sheds totalled £127,938 but – wonderfully – all that cost was paid by the Ministry of Transport.

The GWR were not just short of locomotive power – at Paddington they were short of flesh-and-blood horse power. There were 216 horses stabled at 'The Mint' mews at Paddington and by mid-January 134 were off sick with influenza. The company's vet was treating them and meanwhile motor lorries from other stations were brought in to continue Collection & Delivery (C&D) services.

At their January meeting the directors authorised expenditure of £578,100. This was for ninety new steam locomotives, comprising ten 'Castle' class for £106,700, ten 'Hall' class for £91,300, ten 'Manor' class for £88,300 and sixty small tank engines for £291,800.

The Company did not have the materials to start on this building programme in its entirety – the expenditure was authorised so that when they could get hold of some metals – which were expected to be acquired by 1948 – the work could go ahead at once. Also planned for 1948 was the construction of £244,000-worth of goods, wagons and 200 21-ton, locomotive coal-carrying wagons. Completion of a re-signalling scheme at Blaengwynfi was authorised at a cost of £138, and this improvement enabled the Blaengwynfi West signal box to be abolished. Other projects included the partial reconstruction of the rail-over-road bridges at Oxford and Reading stations, and £69,250 was allocated to repair the Landore and Chepstow viaducts, the latter costing £68,000. A house was purchased for renting to a station master, and electric lighting was installed at various places. The list of improvements is very long.

On the commercial side, the GWR continued to support the growth of industry within their territory. In January Viscount Portal opened the Welsh Industry Fair. Eighty-three firms attended and were visited by 39,000 people, resulting in £5 million-worth of orders being placed. The company leased their lands beside the railway for new industries in South Wales and around London. One hundred and fifty-seven sites had been sold during 1946, of which 118 were in South Wales. Factories built there were for producing tools, castings, glass bottles, tiles and concrete units. From Cowley, Oxford, Morris Motors sent away by rail 1,328 cars for export and 967 from the Austin works at Longbridge. The Gloucester Railway Carriage & Wagon Company sent off 135 tons of carriage underframes for the Sao Paulo Railway of Brazil. The Birmingham Railway Carriage & Wagons works at Handsworth sent away by rail thirty-three railway vans to Dover for Poland and Czechoslovakia. This was part of an order for 500, and they also sent 36 tons of steel tube.

The company *prospected* for traffic. The Mexican El Oro mining company set up a subsidiary called British Lignite which bought land around Bovey Tracey and Heathfield to quarry the brown semi-coal fuel, and the GWR were in great hopes of doing business there. The government was constructing, on the old RAF airbase at Harwell, the Atomic Energy Research Establishment and 8,000 tons of steel was on rail to Didcot for the building work. Local hauliers who had been acting as collection and delivery (C&D) agents for the GWR were bought-out regularly as indeed they had been for years before the war when the company set up their 'Zonal' road distribution network. In January Mrs Lewis, the GWR C&D Agent in Cardigan, sold her two lorries to the GWR for £624. Throughout 1947, with nationalisation getting closer by the day, the GWR developed their Zonal delivery system.

The Great Western's gross income for the last three weeks of January was £2,374,000 which was £286,000 – 10.5 per cent – down on January 1946. Passenger traffic earned £187,000, down 15.34 per cent, general merchandise was down £141,000 (13 per cent), but coal haulage earned £42,000 more than in January 1946.[8]

I have the complete record for freight trains that 'broke apart' (partings or breakaways) for January. Sixty-two partings took place in the thirty-one days of the month. The frequency of these incidents must be due to years of poor maintenance of wagons and, especially, privately owned wagons. In the fifteen years I worked with trains on BR(WR), 1960–75, I only once experienced a coupling breaking: I actually saw it snap. A friend who worked on the Southern Region as a goods guard in the days of chain-link coupled wagons never experienced a coupling or draw hook breaking. Seventeen GWR wagons broke a coupling: eight were three-link couplings, one covered van had a stripped thread on a screw coupling, three had a broken drawbar hook (one of these was on a brake van) and five GWR brake vans had their 'Instanter' coupling break.

Twelve LMS wagons broke away: nine three-link couplings and three drawbar hooks broke. Six LNER wagons, working on the GWR, broke away, four due to a link

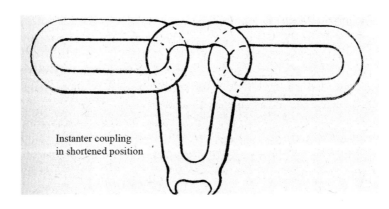

Drawing of an 'Instanter' coupling copied from GWR *General Appendix to the Rule Book 1936*.

Instanter coupling in shortened position

breaking, and two due to a stripped thread. Twenty-six privately owned wagons broke couplings, had a hook break or a drawbar pulled out of the frame. One train parted because the link 'jumped off the hook'. The owner of the wagon was not recorded.

During the month there were the usual incidents of derailments due to passing a signal at danger, or misunderstanding a hand signal, or the signalman moving a set of points prematurely for a variety of reasons. These included pure mental aberration, or, because he could not see them and was waiting to move them, he misread the signs: a signalman in some circumstances had to listen and watch as best he could and interpret what he *could* see and hear, and then act accordingly. Sometimes he got it wrong.

At Honeybourne South Junction on 1 January the 3.30 Worcester–Paddington goods train was starting the climb of Honeybourne bank. There were seventy wagons hauled by engine 0-6-0 No 2884, with Driver Brown and Fireman Knibbs of Worcester, assisted in the rear by the Honeybourne banker, 0-6-0 No 2274 with Driver Brown, also of Worcester. A GWR 'Fruit' van from Evesham to Paddington, fitted with the vacuum brake and with the vacuum pipe connected to the engine, was coupled behind 2884. The pull of the engine and the weight of at least half the train behind – depending on how well the bank engine was doing its job on the gradient – proved to be too much for the worn thread. The nut was dragged off the thread and the driver was alerted to the breakaway by the very sudden acceleration of hard-working 2884, followed by a sudden stop as the vacuum pipes between engine and 'Fruit' van were pulled apart. The bank engine driver would have had a nasty shock as the whole weight of seventy wagons bore down onto his little engine. But breakaways were common enough between Honeybourne and Moreton-in-Marsh. The men were practised. When the train was stationary they used the tender's coupling to re-couple to the 'Fruit' van and off they went – with just 12 minutes' delay.

At 12.45 a.m. on 2 January the 10.25 p.m. (1.1.47) goods train, travelling from Worcester to Pontypool Road, was comprised of forty-six wagons hauled by LMS 2-8-0 No 8449. Driver Sale and Fireman Morris of Worcester were travelling on the Down Main, coming down the 1 in 90 descent from Colwall tunnel towards Ledbury. Approaching Cummings Crossing, the gradient changes to a short stretch of 1 in 124 uphill – but this was long enough to cause a tug which broke the drawbar on an ICI-owned wagon twenty-second from the engine. The guard realised at once and screwed down the brake on his 20-ton van, bringing the twenty-four rearmost wagons to a stand within the protection of Cummings Crossing's signals. The signalman there sent seven bells – meaning 'Stop & Examine' – to Ledbury North, where the driver was informed that he had lost half his train.

The signalmen at Ledbury North End and Cumming's Crossing 'conferred' and agreed how to clear the line. There was nowhere at Cummings to leave the defective wagon; it could not be pushed through to Ledbury because of the risk of another breakaway on the downgrade, and it could not be hauled to Ledbury because it had no drawbar.

The banking engine for the climb from Ledbury to Colwall was standing at Cummings and this was used to draw the rear portion through the crossover to the Up Main. The Ledbury signalman then set his crossover for the Up Main. He wrote out a Wrong Line Order 'D' permitting the driver of the front part of the divided train to return to Ledbury down the Up Main. The driver then 'set back' through the crossover, onto the Up Main, propelling his portion of the train uphill, through the tunnel, back to Cummings to meet against the rear part.

The bank engine could push the train up the 1 in 124 and on the 1 in 80 downgrade the train engine would hold the train under control. In this way, a very tricky, skilful, piece of driving, carried out in darkness, was accomplished. The wagon was put away in a siding at Ledbury by the bank engine and the train was re-coupled and went on its way.

On 2 January at 8.15 p.m. the shunters at Yeovil Pen Mill were working with the heavily delayed 8.40 a.m. Bristol East Depot–Weymouth goods train, hauled by No 5351. The train passed southwards through the station on the Down Main, stopped south of the Sherborne road bridge and whistled-up. The signalman pulled over point lever 31 and signal lever 32, and the buffers clashed and rang as the engine reversed its train into the goods yard.

The signalman was standing by, waiting to turn the points to shunt the train into the yard. He was in his box, which was at the north end of the station. It was dark, the island platform canopy prevented him from seeing what was happening, and there were no track circuit lights in his track diagram to show him the position of the train. He heard a whistle, took that to be his signal, and reversed the points, and derailed 5351, engine and tender. The whistle had come from another engine working at the north end of the station.

The signalman sent 'Obstruction Danger' – six bells – in both directions at 8.18 p.m. and then informed the Station Master. He set about organising single-line working over the Up line and the signalman called on Yeovil engine shed for the crane. Steam had to be raised in the crane which left the shed at 12.18 a.m. and arrived alongside the derailment at 12.23 a.m.

The breakdown gang had to separate the engine from the tender and then lift each back onto the rails. They worked all night and got the tender re-railed and struggled with the engine but it was well and truly 'on Olde England'. A second crane was essential. The Bristol Bath Road crane was ordered at 9.50 a.m. on 3 January. Steam was raised and a hauling loco had to be found from scarce resources. The crane and tool vans left Bristol at 11.55 a.m. for the lengthy run to Yeovil arriving at 2.55 p.m. The engine and its tender were re-railed at 7.30 p.m.

On 3 January the 12.45 p.m. Bodmin Road–Wadebridge passenger train left for Bodmin at 12.50 p.m. Signalman Blake at Bodmin accepted the train at 'Line Clear to the buffer stops' although there was a horse box standing against the stops. The train consisted of two coaches hauled by No 5531, driven by Engineman Drew. Signalman Blake lowered all his signals when the train left Bodmin Road and 5531 had an uninterrupted run into Bodmin station. If Mr Blake, knowing that the line was not clear to the buffers, had brought the train nearly to a stand at his Home signal before lowering it, he would have corrected his earlier error.

The train ran in smartly and stopped in the platform, the coaches were uncoupled from the engine and the engine ran forward towards the buffers so as to get clear of the run-round points. The engine had to be at the other end of the train to continue the journey to Wadebridge. The fireman on the engine did not see the horse box standing a few yards ahead of his engine and neither did Driver Drew because he was looking backwards to see when the engine was clear of the points, and so he hit the wagon with a mighty thump. Signalman Blake had to take all the blame because he had made two signalling errors. He was 'spoken to'.

On 26 January at 7.58 p.m. the 12 noon Oxley–Stoke Gifford goods train, consisting of forty-one, equal to fifty, wagons, hauled by No 6961, arrived in the lengthy Up Goods Loop just behind Honeybourne Station North Box. The engine had to be detached to go and pick up wagons for Stoke Gifford – these were standing in the Up Sidings adjacent to the Up Loop. The guard screwed down the handbrake in his van and pinned down the wagon brakes on the three wagons next to his van. The engine was uncoupled and went away. The weight of the train then overpowered the brakes (which had been applied) and started to run backwards due to the falling gradient. The signalman ran out of his box, aiming to pin down some more brakes but was unable to do so, because the wagons were moving too fast. He dashed back to his signal box and up the stairs, panicking and not thinking properly. The wagons would soon reach the end of the Loop where the lie of the points would bring them into a dead end where the rails were covered in sand in order to slow down and stop wagons for just this kind of eventuality. But he pulled lever 42, which changed the lie of the points to make a route into the Sheenhill military stores depot. The 20-ton brake van, wheels locked but driven by forty-one wagons and gravity, crashed through the closed iron gates and smashed into a line of twenty-three loaded wagons, resulting in the derailment and destruction of four, with five more damaged. When the brakes on the runaway train were examined they were all found to be screwed down, or pinned down – hard. This just goes to show what the force of gravity, namely the weight of forty-one wagons, can do.

At midday on Wednesday 29 January, what had been the coldest winter for years exploded into a blizzard of legendary proportions. The heaviest snow and the lowest temperatures since 1891 commenced in areas of the eastern counties of London and moved westwards, with increasing severity. The London Division was the least affected according to the report Mr Matthews sent to Sir James Milne on 3 February. Matthews noted that the water troughs at Aldermaston were solid ice and water columns at Newbury were frozen. Not even the Didcot–Newbury line, which must surely have been snowed under, got a mention.

In some hilly places railwaymen crawled on all fours up steep pavements to reach their workplace. In country areas they struggled through snow up to their waists to get to work. Signalmen, trying to follow their usual route, found they were walking on snow at hedge-top height – I am not exaggerating. Long piles of coal were lit between rows of engines standing outside sheds to keep the frost away. The hose between the engine and the tender, carrying water to the injector, froze as the engine moved along the track, lineside water columns froze, water troughs were either emptied or turned to solid ice, signal wires were frozen to their pulleys, and even where the point blades were kept free of snow their driving rodding was apt to become encased in ice.

Coal was the bedrock of the British industry and domestic wellbeing. Even before the blizzard began barely enough coal was being delivered to the power stations. There was a serious shortage of coal miners. Snow over South Wales began on 21 January, frequently preventing miners from getting to work on time. Not all miners could travel to work by train. They had to queue for buses and even their vital work did not guarantee them a seat. The buses had difficulty on the hills. Miners were walking home across snowy hillsides. Then the blizzard of Wednesday 29 January burst over southern and western England and Wales. In South Wales 200 collieries were blocked in and thousands of loaded coal wagons were buried under tons of snow on the colliery sidings of the Welsh valleys. From Wiltshire westwards through Dorset to Devon the railway was badly affected but the railway passenger service continued to operate longer than public service road vehicles. At 4 p.m. on the 29th, the part GWR-owned Devon General bus company had to suspend its service but at that time the railway was still operating. The blizzard condition continued until 7 p.m. that evening, when it eased to the condition of 'very heavy snow' and continued to fall heavily until 3.15 p.m. the next day. The Moretonhampstead, Brixham and Kingsbridge branch trains continued running until the end of services on the 29th.

The main-line trains were kept running by calling out every permanent-way man on the main lines and branches to keep points clear of snow. Men struggled from their homes to their stations through the pitch dark and the blinding snow, and then worked all through the night of the 29th until 4 a.m. keeping the points and signal wires free. Engines with steam lances were also used.[9] The Plymouth Laira and the Newton Abbot snowploughs were used to clear the main line and then attended to the branches. The Brixham line was reopened at 8 a.m. on the 31st and the Moretonhampstead reopened at 10.10 a.m. that day.

At 3.15 p.m. on 31 January, the engine of the 3.25 Brixham to Churston was derailed by deep snow covering the coaling siding. The Newton Abbot breakdown crane was ordered at 3.35 p.m., arriving at 4.15 p.m., and the engine was ready for action at 5.30 p.m. – and all that time the snow was reported to be 'falling heavily'. Three return trips from Brixham to Churston were cancelled and the roads were impassable for buses. The last two round trips of the day were run, 20 minutes late each.

Notes

1   See Appendix I.
2   National Archives *Rail 250/63*.
3   *Rail 250/482*.
4   House of Commons, *Hansard, vol. 432* cols. 228–9, 29 Jan. 1947.
5   A 'full load', unassisted, from Severn Tunnel Junction station to Patchway, for a '28xx' class 2-8-0, was '40 Class 1' – 400 tons. GWR Working Time Table.
6   *Rail 250/672*.
7   See Appendix III.
8   *Rail 250/469*.
9   A steam lance is a long, small-gauge pipe, with a wooden carrying handle, attached by armoured hose to a tap on the front of the locomotive smoke box. When the tap was opened boiler pressure steam was ejected from the pipe to blow away soot and cinders from inside the boiler tubes of the locomotive – or ice and snow from the track.

GREAT WESTERN RAILWAY
MAGAZINE

FEBRUARY · 1947

VOL. 59 · NO. 2

Pride in the Job—I
(See Page 36)

PRICE ONE PENNY

FEBRUARY

The snow stopped on 3 February only to start falling again on 7 February and for two days after that. The deep frosts deepened to minus 15 and even minus 21°F. The General Manager reported to the directors thus:

> The severe weather conditions experienced towards the end of January and during the present month have seriously affected the movement of passenger and freight traffic throughout the system. The freezing of engines, points, signals, and water troughs caused widespread delays to passenger trains from the week commencing 27th January and the severe snowfalls made matters much worse. In the West of England and South Wales conditions were the worst for many years. On the night of January 29th/30th deep snowdrifts were wide spread and snowploughs had to be used on the Princetown, Launceston, Kingsbridge, Moretonhampstead and Brixham lines all of which were closed until the drifts could be cleared. On the morning of 3rd February a landslide occurred on the Teign Valley line between Alphington Halt and Ide, blocking the line. An omnibus service was instituted for the conveyance of passengers between Exeter and Christow.
>
> The dislocation to freight traffic necessitated the imposition on January 30th of an almost complete stop on forwardings to Taunton and stations west thereof which remained in force until February 3rd. Less severe restrictions were placed on traffic to the London and Northern areas.
>
> Further snow from February 7th to 9th caused difficulties in many areas, particularly in South Wales where train services were interrupted between Colbren Junction and Devynock, Dowlais Top and Fochriw, Abertillery and Bryn Mawr, Cwnbargoed and Bedlinog, Rhymney and Rhymney Bridge.

On 6 February the Prime Minister, Mr Attlee: 'expressed his warm appreciation for the splendid efforts of railwaymen, dock workers and others to maintain essential services in the face of their great difficulties and hardships brought about by the exceptionally severe weather'.

On 10 February, during a debate on railways in the House of Commons, Sir Ralph Glyn, MP for Abingdon from 1924 to 1953, asked the Minister of Transport, Alfred Barnes: 'When were you first aware of the serious position of the main line railways in regard to shortages of locomotives, carriages, wagons, coal supplies, and track sleepers, arising from causes beyond the control of the railway companies?'

Mr Barnes replied:

The deterioration of railway rolling stock and reductions of railway stocks of track sleepers are the result of enforced deferment of maintenance and replacements during the heavy wartime traffic and since. The accumulation of these arrears was known at the time I took office and was beginning to show its effects in varying degrees. During the winter of 1945-46 the condition of the wagon stock gave me particular cause for anxiety. Special steps were taken, and have been sustained, to expedite repairs and large orders for new wagons of standard type were placed by my Department. Deterioration of the locomotive stock became marked at a later date. Stocks of sleepers, already much below normal, fell sharply, during last years owing to the failure of supplies.[1] Stocks of railway coal have been reduced, in common with stocks of all other users, owing to the inability of production to keep pace with consumption.[2]

The total number of locomotives 'on the books' hardly changed throughout the year. In the four weeks ending 22 February the GWR had in stock 3,859 of their own engines, plus sixty-nine on loan from the LMS and nineteen from the War Department, making a total of 3,947. In the four weeks ending 9 August there were 3,937, and during same period ending on 4 October the number was 3,929. The fluctuations were due to borrowing in or lending out engines. Of the February total there were 2,994 available for work, 76 per cent of the total fleet and, actually in use, on average, during that four-week period, 2,912 – 97.26 per cent of those available. In the twenty-eight days ending on 9 August there were only 2,659 locomotives in use, 88.5 per cent of those available. In the four weeks ending 4 October, 3,084 engines were available for use, 78.4 per cent of the total fleet, while in daily use there were 2,979: 75.8 per cent of those available for use.[3]

In order to release more engines to haul coal and general merchandise, as from 3 February, the 8.15 a.m. Newcastle on Tyne–Bournemouth and the 10.30 a.m. Bournemouth–Newcastle were suspended. On 13 February thirteen express trains to and from Paddington, Cheltenham, South Wales and Penzance were either suspended or curtailed to shorter distances. The suspended services were the 1.45 p.m. Paddington–Hereford, the 7.10 p.m. Paddington–Wolverhampton, the 7.55 p.m. Paddington–Swansea, the 11.42 p.m. Plymouth–Paddington, the 9.10 a.m. Worcester–Paddington and the 9.5 p.m.* Swansea–Paddington. The 2.15 Paddington–Cheltenham started from Swindon, and the 7.20 a.m. Plymouth–Paddington ran on Mondays only. The 4.30 p.m. Paddington–Plymouth ran on Fridays only. The 6.30 a.m. Birkenhead–Paddington terminated at Wolverhampton. The 5.30 a.m. Paddington–Penzance terminated at Plymouth. The London suburban inner and outer distance trains – Uxbridge, Slough, Henley and Reading services – lost twenty-eight trains. Twenty-one local trains on the Minehead–Taunton, Cardiff–Swansea, Hereford–Worcester and other routes were also suspended or ran only on a Friday or a Monday.

---

* This is authentic 1947 GWR notation meaning 9.05 p.m. and this style has been kept throughout the book to maintain authenticity.

The snowstorms continued all week, requiring the incredibly tough men of the permanent-way (p-way) gangs to be out in the freezing blizzards night after night. They were there to place an exploding 'fog signal' on the rail at the Distant signal when that was showing 'Caution'; their job was also to brush points free of snow and to serve as a back-up to the signalman for the sighting of the tail lamp of each train: the p-way man would stand out on the track to watch for the red lamp in case the signalman up in the box missed it. In heavy snow and freezing temperatures, the exhaust steam from the locomotive billowed in thick clouds and persisted to hang there heavily, at low level. There might also have been a leak from the train steam-heating pipe on the rear coach, which would obscure the lamp to all but a close observer.

Superintendent of the Line, Mr Matthews, reported that the ex-M&SW line was under snow with some drifts 4ft deep across the high Cotswolds and the Marlborough Downs. The line remained closed from Wednesday 29 January until the afternoon of Sunday 2 February, while the Swindon snowplough was busy on the main lines. The Swindon plough was sent up to Swindon Old Town and the southern M&SW section at 11 a.m. on 2 February and cleared the line through to Ludgershall at 2.40 p.m.

In the bitter cold darkness of that Sunday night, the driver of the 7.25 p.m. Paddington train noticed a lurch as he approached Knighton Crossing's Down Distant signal, and he stopped to report it at the signal box at 9.25 p.m. The Uffington Ganger was called out of his bed – by whom is not reported, but the line of communication would have been tortuous by modern standards – and told to examine the Down Line eastwards from Knighton's Down Distant. He found that the embankment had slipped a little and placed a 5mph restriction of speed on it. The signalmen at Uffington and Knighton stopped each train and informed the driver of the circumstances and then allowed him to continue. Meanwhile the Ganger had cycled around the villages to call out his gang and 'the necessary attention was given and normal working was resumed at 12.45 a.m. on 3 February'.

On 8 February Lengthman Frank Hatherall booked on duty at 10 p.m. at Asbury Crossing, near Shrivenham, after nine-and-a-half hours' rest. At 4 a.m. on 9 February he and sub-Ganger Basson were in Shrivenham signal box and were asked by the signalman to clear snow from the Down Relief to Down Main points. They went out into a blizzard and pitch darkness and cleared those points and then, because of the heavy snow, decided to clear the Up Main to Up Relief points main. Frank Hatherall was walking five yards in front of Basson. Both men were half-blinded by the driving snow and the darkness; the lighted hand lamp they had brought with them had been blown out by the gale. Basson saw the lamps of an Up train approaching and called out a warning to Hatherall.

Hatherall made an acknowledgement and both men continued to walk towards the Up Main points. Basson lost sight of his mate in the snow and as Basson reached the points, still on the ballast, the train passed at about 30mph. After it had gone by he called out for Frank Hatherall but there was no reply. He had walked into the track right in front of the train. His body was found in the 'four-foot way', 100yd up the line. He was aged forty-eight and left a wife and seven children aged between 5 months and 19 years. Mrs Hatherall received a lump sum of £707 10s from the GWR in full compensation for her loss.[4]

The Southern Railway route from Exeter to Plymouth, high up over the bare moor through Okehampton and Tawton, was absolutely blocked. The 6 p.m. Waterloo–Plymouth, which started from London on Saturday 1 February, had to turn back from Okehampton and return to Exeter St David's. The Southern passengers were put into the 9.50 p.m. Paddington–Penzance around 4 or 5 a.m. on the 2nd.

Even with every available engine hauling coal, this fuel continued in short supply at power stations, offices and homes, owing to a shortage of miners and the difficulty the miners encountered travelling to work. Snow blocked the tracks to the collieries and coal froze solid in the wagons while waiting to be hauled away. The locomotives were vulnerable to the icy cold because water froze solid in the hose from the tender, or in the copper pipe from the tank to the injector. The water lying within an injector that was not in use could freeze. Any of these eventualities prevented water being injected into the boiler, and if desperate remedies did not result in a thawing, the engine had to

GREAT WESTERN RAILWAY

MAGAZINE

March & April · 1947   Vol. 59 · No. 3

Beating the Blizzard
HOW THE MAIN LINE RAILWAYS BROUGHT THE COAL TRAINS THROUGH

WINTER has dealt hardly with us all since the last issue of the *Magazine* appeared. The fearful blizzard which swept the country, freezing transport and agriculture, well-nigh paralysing industry generally, and causing incalculable national hardship, gave such a setback to our entire programme of national recovery as will take a long time to overhaul.

In this serious national predicament the main line railways had a dual burden to bear. Coping with their own unprecedented troubles in order to restore communications was only the first part of their task; the second stage was to give the rest of the country the means of starting up again—by carrying the coal for lack of which the nation's industrial and domestic life was perilously near a standstill. Coal trains were the factor essential to every other phase of recovery—and yet the coal train routes were snowbound. It was thus that the greatest peacetime transport battle of all time began—the main line railways and King Coal in league against King Winter.

The fuel and power crisis has interfered with the publishing arrangements of many periodicals, and it has been found necessary to combine the March and April issues of the Magazine into this single number. Each prepaid subscription affected will be extended for a month at the close of its currency, to make up the full number of issues covered by the sum paid.

No better illustration can be given of the formidable problem which the railways faced than the situation in South Wales at dawn on Tuesday, March 4. In that area the worst blizzard within living memory had already severed rail communications with two hundred collieries normally producing about half a million tons of coal a week—and the storm was still raging. In some places the tracks were buried under snowdrifts fifteen and more feet deep; where the railway passed through cuttings there was often nothing to distinguish the site of the line from the surrounding expanse of snowbound fields.

Every available snowplough was brought into action, but even these, though propelled by several engines, could not always force a way through the heaviest drifts; some became so firmly embedded that they had to be abandoned. Steam lances (to play jets of steam from engines on to the snow) were also used, but the greatest factor in the struggle was, as always, man-power. When the ranks of the shovel brigade had been packed with every available permanent way man, the force was still totally inadequate, so reinforcements were brought up—men from practically every department of the railway, including clerical and technical staffs; a thousand more recruited through the labour exchanges, plus British troops, Polish troops and German prisoners of war. In one Welsh valley an appeal for men was broadcast over the rediffusion service; in one town the station master armed himself with a handbell and tramped the streets like a town crier to summon more

A BLEAK PICTURE OF THE NEWLY CLEARED TRACK, AT CWMBARGOED, NEAR DOWLAIS (CAE HARRIS).

be declared a failure and the fire thrown out. It is remarkable, given the exceptionally cold weather, that any steam engine worked at all. And of course if diesel locomotives had been in use they would have been immobilised by the fuel oil 'waxing'.

A national plan of electricity cuts was brought in on 10 February; the GWR had their power cut in major stations and at their docks. At large places there were diesel generators to maintain supplies but oil was in short supply too and cranes and lifts were at risk of being put out of action. The company made 'urgent representations' to the Minister of Transport as to the additional difficulties these cuts placed upon the railways, which had been charged with keeping the country moving. The Ministry responded with assurances that the railway would be exempted from power cuts at major places in order that essential services could be maintained, but asked that all stations reduced their use of electricity as much as possible.

The Plymouth Division was the worst affected of the GWR's English divisions. Freight trains approaching the West Country were terminated at Taunton – or at any place further to the north and east where they could be got in out of the way. Coal supplies to the west, which had been sparse and uncertain up until then, were now completely stopped.

The engine for the 8.45 a.m. Plymouth–Paddington on Saturday 1 February battled through snow varying from 2ft to 3ft in depth from Laira shed to Plymouth North Road station and started for London at 10.10 a.m. It actually got up Hemerdon bank but only to stop at the top, by the signal box, at 10.35 a.m., unable to get any further. Snow on the line had filled the cutting. Deep snowdrifts blocked the main line at many places between Plymouth and Newton Abbot. The most spectacular was between Cornwood and Ivybridge, leading off from the east side of Blatchford viaduct, where the snow was 6ft deep for 1 mile.

Laira shed staff had to search for the snowplough stabled on a siding at Tavistock Junction because it, along with all the other wagons, was completely buried under a smooth blanket of snow. Everywhere the deep snow made operating possible only by the most extreme physical efforts of gangs of stalwart men. These were not just GWR permanent-way men but soldiers – British and Polish – Royal Navy ratings and even German prisoners of war.

After the snowplough had cleared the Kingsbridge branch on 31 January it was sent to clear the Princetown line. The snow-clearing train consisted of a tank engine – its number not recorded – pushing a snowplough and pulling a 20-ton brake van. The train crew consisted of Laira shed Foreman Harold Luscombe, Mechanical Foreman C. Davies, Fitter Leslie Hancock, Enginemen J. Watson and W. Norman, Fireman Len Hooper and Goods Guard George Jefferies. In the van would have been a gang of GWR permanent-way men.

The train left Yelverton at 4.12 p.m. on 31 January. The line rose continuously at 1 in 40, making the engine's task more difficult and it was 6.5 p.m. by the time the line was cleared as far as Lowry Road Crossing, 3¾ miles from Yelverton. It was pitch dark and there were 'vast drifts' ahead. Nothing more could be done until the following day so the train returned to Plymouth. Overnight the Divisional Engineer obtained thirty naval ratings from Devonport barracks to assist his men. The plough left Dousland, 1½ miles from Yelverton, at 10.55 a.m. on 1 February and reached King Tor, 6 miles away, at

Mrs Mead and her children at King Tor halt. They lived at Hill Cottage on the moor, near Princetown. Note the branding 'Oxford' on the brake van.

DELIVERING BREAD ON THE PRINCETOWN BRANCH.

3.40 p.m., where the engine 'failed on account of water shortage'. The fire was thrown out and the engine was then 'dead'.

One of the crew had to walk back to Dousland signal box carrying the Electric Train Staff for the Dousland–Princetown section and, from Dousland, telephone Laira shed for a fresh engine. This arrived quickly – all things considered – and, with the man who had the Train Staff on board, entered the section to rescue the stranded engine and men. Again, the report does not give a number but surely a tender engine would have been sent? The men were sheltering from the cold in the goods brake van when the assistant engine arrived. It was hooked on and hauled the train back to Dousland, arriving at 5.45 p.m. Here the naval ratings left the train and returned to Devonport by naval transport while the train went on down to Yelverton. The report states that: 'the assistant engine took water at Yelverton and re-entered the section at 6.42 p.m. with the snowplough and van.'

The snowplough crew set out surrounded by an intense frost under a clear, starry sky and a quarter moon to clear the line from King Tor to Princetown. They had been at work in the icy cold all day. For respite they were able to warm up in the guard's van, where there was plenty of coal for the stove, and they had some food and a kettle to boil water for tea. The engine charged the drifts, many of them 14ft deep, moved some snow, got embedded in the drift, and the men dug it out using spades. So the courageous gang hammered their way uphill – with the line rising continuously on gradients varying from 1 in 40 to 1 in 42 – finally breaking through to Princetown, 10½ miles from Yelverton, at 8.40 p.m. Here they had some supper – probably at the Railway Inn just outside the station.

The train with all the gang set off from Princetown for Plymouth at 9.35 p.m. but the wind had filled a cutting meanwhile and in the darkness the engine ran into a massive snowdrift. They were stuck. A man was needed to walk to Dousland signal box and ask for assistance, but in such dark and awful conditions it was decided that five would make the walk. Struggling through the snow the five men got to Dousland at 12.15 a.m. on 2 February. Those men, now thoroughly exhausted, were eventually conveyed back to Plymouth but by what means was not reported.

Eight men were left high up on the moor in the brake van but it was known that they had coal for the stove, hot drinks and food, so their safety was assured. Princetown station was advised of their position and at dawn the Princetown station staff set out to take flasks of hot drinks, more sandwiches and coal to the stranded men. At about the same time another snowplough was obtained, which left Yelverton at 11.39 a.m. The plough which had remained on the branch during the night was dug out in the early morning and made its way to Princetown, arriving there at 12.35 p.m. The second plough reached Princetown at 5.25 p.m. on 2 February. The passenger service was reinstated by the train which left Princetown at 1.13 p.m. on 3 February.

Sir James Milne wrote a terse 'thank you' to the Commander-in-Chief, Royal Naval Barracks, Devonport, thanking him for the loan of thirty sailors:

Royal Navy sailors clearing snow from Peek Hill cutting above Burrator reservoir.

3rd February 1947.

Dear Sir,

I should like to take the opportunity to express my appreciation of the valuable assistance which you were good enough to afford the Company by arranging for thirty naval ratings to assist in clearing the line to Princetown on the 31st ultimo and shall be glad if you will convey my thanks to the personnel concerned.

Yours very truly,

J. Milne

While labouring under arctic temperatures and deep snow the company were looking forward to the work they would get from the new industries that were opening along the South Wales coast. The government's policy to get out of debt was to expand engineering industries of all kinds – to make items for sale at home and abroad. The GWR played their full part and made land available by the railway lines for five factories to be built manufacturing light castings, bicycle components, wire mattresses and enamelware.

I have the complete record of freight train partings for February. Sixty-one took place: sixteen GWR; ten LMS; two SR; seven LNER, and twenty-six privately owned. Most were breaks in three-link couplings.

The 'slip portion' on four carriages was to be detached at Bath. In accelerating out of Paddington the pull of the hinged hook of the slip coupling was so strong – or the wedge which held the hook in place was so worn – that the hook swung down on its hinge and the parting took place.

The Slip Guard stopped his portion and the signalman at Westbourne Bridge stopped the main train. This was shortly allowed to continue and the four coaches were drawn back into Paddington station. The Passenger Pilot had been requisitioned to take over the 9.15 a.m. departure because the engine on that train had failed. Passengers and luggage from the four-coach slip section were transferred to the 9.15 a.m., which left at 9.56 a.m. It called at the main stations to Bristol and was semi-fast, thereafter to terminate at Taunton.

On 14 February, the National Union of Railwaymen (NUR) and the Railway Clerks Association (RCA) put in a modified 'pay and hours' claim. This was for a £1-a-week pay rise and a 40-hour week for wages staff. The NUR also wanted their members to be paid double-time from 4 p.m. on Saturday to midnight on Sunday/Monday mornings. The RCA wanted a £52 p.a. rise for clerks and supervisory grades with a 35-hour week. The Associated Society of Locomotive Engineers & Firemen (ASLEF) claimed pay rises of various amounts for cleaners, firemen and drivers, with the highest single rise being £1 9s 6d an hour for the most senior drivers, and a 44-hour week. The cost of living was rising, the staff had to eat but the government was holding down increases in railway fares and freight charges because these charges affected the entire British economy, domestic and industrial. The railway companies were, as usual, subsidising the rest of the country. The GWR tried to get the government involved in the pay claims and the General Manager wrote to the Minister of Transport to ask 'whether, as these applications raise questions of national importance, he wishes to express any views as to the course the Company should adopt'. No reply was forthcoming.

As a result of the 1944 Education Act, the school-leaving age would rise to 15 in April. The Directors' Minutes comment was:

> It is expected that some difficulty will be experienced in future in maintaining an adequate junior staff and this may result in the employment of a greater number of adults. In anticipation of the raising of the school leaving age arrangements were made some time ago for boys leaving school at 14 to be recruited into the service to the greatest extent possible before April 1947.

The Ministry of Works asked the company to find large buildings, all or part of which could be used as factories for the construction of the components for the prefabricated housing ('prefabs') which had been designed as an emergency, rapid response to the housing shortage, because large areas of the great cities had been destroyed. The GWR gave the Ministry details of likely premises in Newport, Cardiff and Shrewsbury. As a result, in February, part of the International Alloy factory at Cardiff was taken over to accommodate a plant making wood-wool thermal insulation that was to be sandwiched between the double-skin walls of these new 'prefabs'.

Sir James Milne reported the great news that a new electricity generating station was to be built by Newport Corporation, at the mouth of the River Usk. Milne wrote:

> During construction the railway would be required to carry to the site – to level it – 60,000 tons of colliery spoil, 50,000 tons of steel and large quantities of bricks and cement. A section of it will come into use in 1951 when the boilers would require 590,000 tons of coal a year and when the whole plant is complete one million tons a year will be required.

Another nice windfall came to the company in February. As far back as October 1932 the GWR provided land, sidings and trains to carry 'anthracite duff' to be dumped. This was coal dust the Amalgamated Anthracite Collieries (AAC) did not want, and they were glad to have somewhere to put it. The GWR became the owner of the duff once it had been tipped on their land. In February 1947 the AAC asked to *buy back* 22,500 tons of this anthracite dust and pay the GWR £10,000 for it, plus transport costs.

At 5.30 a.m. on 18 February there was a head-on collision on the single-track branch line 1½ miles from Hallen Marsh Junction going towards Pilning Low Level. The night was very dark, clear and frosty, with 3in of snow on the ground. Signalman J. Wheeler was on duty. He was aged twenty-two, and had been a signalman for three and a half years, having spent the last six months at Hallen Marsh Junction. At 3.41 a.m. that morning he had the 1.45 a.m. Cardiff–Avonmouth goods train standing at the Home signal on the branch, while a banking engine ran across the junction, on the Up Main towards Henbury.

With the engine clear, Wheeler pushed lever 14 into the frame, setting the points for the branch, and reversed 16, which closed the catch point in the branch line, and reversed No 51 lever so as to turn the crossover from Up to Down Main. He pulled signal lever 40 and the train set off for Avonmouth. When it had gone

Wheeler replaced lever 51, setting the crossover points for ordinary – Up and Down – running but did not re-set 14 or 16. The route remained set for 'Up Main to Up Branch'.

At 4.37 a.m. he accepted under the 'Warning Arrangement' from Pilning Low Level, the 8.45 p.m. Cardiff–Avonmouth goods train, and at 5.10 a.m. that train passed Pilning Low Level. The train was 2½ miles away. At 5.18 a.m. Wheeler accepted at 'Line Clear' the 9.20 p.m. Avonmouth–Salisbury goods train. He got 'Line Clear' from Henbury and lowered his Advanced Starting signal, lever 63, which was the Henbury side of the junction, but when he tried to pull lever 64, his Up Main to Henbury line Starting signal, he was unable to do so because the route was set for the branch. The signal directing to the branch was 62. When the 9.20 p.m. train from Avonmouth came to a stand at signals 62/64 Wheeler told the driver that the lock had failed on the operating lever for the main-line route but all was in order – he could pass the signal at danger and proceed towards Henbury.

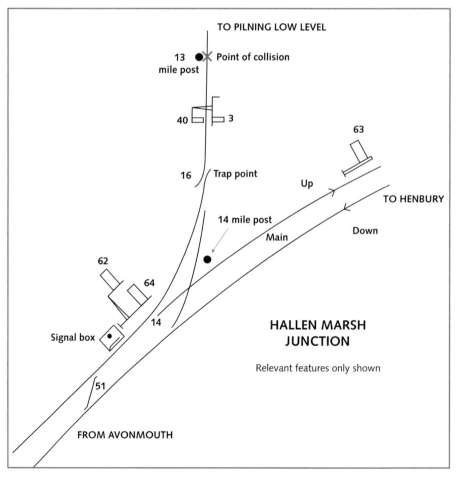

Hallen Marsh.

The driver set off, Wheeler sent 'Train entering Section', two beats on the bell, to Henbury and then went to his Train Register to enter-up times. He had his back to the train. When he looked up he saw that the train was going along the branch line and had passed the branch Advanced Starting signal – 61 – at Danger and showed no sign of stopping. The driver must have thought there was a reason for him being sent the very long way round to get to Filton Junction and was working his '68xx' class 4-6-0 engine hard to accelerate his 600-ton train. Signalman J. Wheeler was now faced with the terrifying knowledge that a head-on collision was inevitable, and when he heard the awful thumping, crunching, sounds 1½ miles away he telephoned Bristol Control with the news.

The 8.45 p.m. Cardiff train, hauled by a 'Dukedog' '90xx' class 4-4-0 engine pulling 350 tons was travelling slowly because the driver had been 'Warned' to be ready to stop at Hallen Marsh Junction. The closing speed was estimated at 37mph. The view ahead from the Cardiff train was so restricted that the driver had no time to apply his brakes or blow his whistle. Both engines and their tenders were derailed, and all six men of the two trains were injured. Twenty-six wagons were derailed, some of which were petrol tankers, and other wagons were smashed to bits. Clearing the line was delayed by having to clear away so many wagons before they could get a crane to the derailed engines. The collision happened at 5.30 a.m. on the Tuesday. The line was clear and fit for normal running at 6 p.m. on the Thursday.

The Inspector of Accidents for His Majesty's Railway Inspectorate was Brigadier Langley. At the end of his report he wrote:

> I have no recommendations in connection with this accident. There is no justification for the provision of safety equipment. It required successive mistakes by two men to cause the accident. The young signalman jumped to a wrong conclusion and an experienced driver passed a signal at danger without authority and did not notice he was on the wrong route.

Notes

1 In November 1939 the GWR sold 39,000 new sleepers and 31,900cu ft of sleeper timber to the government at replacement price – except of course it would be hard to replace the stores during a war. In January 1940 the government requested 3,640 tons of used steel rail to be cut into 12ft lengths and sold to the Ministry at scrap price. On 23 May 1941 the Admiralty purchased from the GWR 5,752yd of blue serge at replacement price.

2 House of Commons, *Hansard, vol. 433* cols. 30–32.

3 See Appendix III.

4 Relative to the retail price indexes of 1947 and 2011, £707 10s in 1947 is roughly equivalent to £22,500 in 2011. (HMRC Inflation 3,192 per cent 1947–2011).

GREAT WESTERN RAILWAY
MAGAZINE

MARCH & APRIL · 1947

VOLUME 59 · NO. 3

Pride in the Job—2
(See Page 58)

PRICE ONE PENNY

MARCH

Business and Money Matters

On 6 March 1947, the Annual General Meeting (AGM) of Great Western Railway shareholders took place. The Right Honourable Viscount Portal PC, DSO, MVO, GCMG presided. There is a small curiosity here because in the minutes of the meetings of the Board of Directors dated 29 March the first states that Viscount Portal was elected Chairman of the Company and the Early of Dudley as his Deputy as from that date. But it is commonly stated that Portal was Chairman from 1945.

Viscount Portal spoke of the period 1946–47 and it is clear that far from merely 'marking time' and waiting for the inevitable dissolution of the GWR at the end of the year, the Great Western directors were working to rebuild their railway as if there was no such thing as nationalisation. Viscount Portal said:

> ... In addition to the fixed annual payment made to us under the Railway Control Agreement we have brought in this year a credit of £297,466 in respect of balances which have become available and to which I shall refer later. Interest and dividends from our excluded properties amount to £499,321, an increase of £266,339 over last year (1945). Of this increase £130,800 is a special dividend received from the Birmingham & Midland Motor Omnibus Company.
>
> Including the balance of £269,305 brought forward from last year and the profit of £245,074 secured this year on realization of investments, the amount available for appropriation amounts to £7,981,769 against £7,405,560 last year (when £150,000 was transferred from the contingency fund) an increase of £576,209.
>
> In considering the dividend to be paid on the Consolidated Ordinary stock we had regard to clause 22 and 23 of the Transport Bill. These clauses provide that – for the final period before the proposed date of transfer, consisting of the two years to December 1947 – payment of interest and dividends by a controlled railway company shall be restricted to the aggregate for the period of the fixed annual sum payable to the Company under the Railway Control Agreement and the revenue from the Company's interest in certain subsidiary undertakings excluded from that agreement after meeting any liability which may arise in respect of agreements disclaimed by the Commission and compensation for loss of office.

The effect of these provisions would be to prevent the distribution of any free reserves built up from previous years' profits and thus nullify the advantage which stockholders would have derived from the prudent course followed by the Company in past years. They also prevent any account being taken of other undistributed profits and sources of revenue which would otherwise have been available for appropriation.

Examples of such items are the amounts of £297,466 shown in the accounts in respect of the period prior to January 1, 1941 and the profit of £245,074 realised on investments during 1946.

Taking all the circumstances into consideration, however, we feel we can safely recommend a dividend of 3% for the half year ended 31 December making 5% for the whole year with a carry forward of £845,514 as against £269,305 last year, the increase of £576,209 mainly representing the special items to which I have just referred.

The position regarding war damage is yet to be finally determined but the effect on net revenue is not likely to be appreciable.

Net revenue has been charged with a standard allowance for maintenance equivalent to the average amount charged in the years 1935/6/7 for the repair of assets of every description adjusted for variation in assets and increased costs. The amount of these charges from August 31 1939 to December 1941 which remains unspent is £18 million. In addition, the four main line companies have made representations to the Ministry of Transport that their assets have suffered abnormal wear and tear and in the case of this Company this amounts to approximately £7 million to the end of last year.

When on 1 July 1946 the Government decided to raise our charges to 33½% above pre-war level for passenger train traffic (other than season and workmen's tickets) and by 25% for freight traffic it also announced its intention to refer to the Railway Charges Consultative Committee the question of determining the level of charges necessary to produce in 1947 the amount payable by the Government under the Railway Control Agreement. A public inquiry was held and the Company was invited to assist the Committee in its task. Financial evidence was given on behalf of all the companies by this Company's Chief Accountant, Mr. C.R. Dashwood and by Mr. F.A. Pope, vice-President of the LM&S.

The main recommendations resulting are that the rates on passenger traffic be raised by 36% over pre-war and that rates on goods train traffic should be raised to 35% and that dock dues should be increased from 40 to 60% over pre-war. The Minister of Transport announced that he did not propose to take any immediate action but would review the situation at the end of March. I would like to point out that even if he allows the full measure of these increases the level of our charges will still be much less than the increase in our expenses and the general rise in prices since 1939. We carried in 1946 21 million passengers which is 23% more than the total for 1938. But the fares charged were 36% lower than the costs of 1946/7 demanded.

We intend to convert approximately 1,200 locomotives to oil burning in order to save coal. The scheme involves the conversion of 184 of our engines and the provision of sixteen oil storage installations. It was hoped that the conversion of these engines would be completed by 1 January 1947 but unfortunately we were unable to obtain the equipment and materials required for the storage installations and so far only 17 oil-burning locomotives have been brought into traffic.

The government was urging the railway to save coal but would not release steel to effect the saving. We are continuing to experiment with new materials for coaches and have completed designs for a prototype coach with an aluminium alloy underframe and a body incorporating light alloys where a reduction in weight can thereby be effected. We are also experimenting with light alloys and plastic for coach panelling and interior fittings.

During last year the Company's steamships St. Julien, St. Helier, and St. Andrew were released from government service. The St. Julien and St. Helier have been reconditioned and are now in service on the Fishguard–Waterford and Weymouth–Channel Islands routes respectively. The reconditioning of the St. Andrew will probably be completed this month and the opportunity has been taken to modernize and improve the accommodation.

A Proud Ship

LAUNCH OF THE GREAT WESTERN'S NEW "ST. DAVID" AT BIRKENHEAD

SCENE ON THE LAUNCHING PLATFORM AT BIRKENHEAD.

"I NAME this ship St. David. May God bless her and all those who sail in her". The Countess of Dudley spoke the simple words that vested Vessel No. 1182 with a personality; the bottle of christening champagne swung and smashed against the bows, and the handsome great hull, a still body until now, came to life. Amid cheers from a throng of well-wishers—the Company's chief officers and guests on the dais and shipyard workers perched at every possible vantage point—the new St. David glided down the slipway to meet and kiss the Mersey.

Inevitably the thoughts of the watchers on that February morning flashed back to January, 1944, when that other St. David, serving as a hospital ship off Anzio beachhead, was bombed and sunk with the loss of her master, Captain E. W. Owens, and fifty-seven other lives. This new St. David has good cause to be proud of her name. So will he sister ship, St. Patrick, shortly to be launched at the same yard to replace the previous St. Patrick which was bombed and sunk in the Irish Sea in June, 1941—in wartime, but while engaged on a normal passenger voyage.

Paddle Steamer to Channel Queen

At the luncheon after the launch, Sir Robert Johnson, Chairman and Managing Director of Messrs. Cammell Laird and Company, toasted the new ship and the lady who launched her, and reminded the gathering that his firm had built fourteen ships for the Great Western Railway—the first of these a paddle steamer.

Responding to the toast, the Countess of Dudley said she had always longed to launch a ship. The carriage of goods and passengers had for centuries proved Britain's lifeblood, and during the war the shipyards of the United Kingdom had maintained a glorious record. As she had walked around the engine rooms and the docks that morning, she had found it impossible to feel depressed about Britain's

Photos.: Stewart Bale Ltd.

THE NEW "ST. DAVID" GLIDES PROUDLY DOWN THE SLIPWAY

future. Proposing a toast to "The Builders", the Earl of Dudley, Deputy Chairman of the Great Western Railway, said the Company had always realised the necessity of employing the best shipbuilders. The firm of Cammell Laird and Company had always given the greatest possible satisfaction. Sir William Reardon Smith, a Director of the Great Western Railway, seconded the toast.

65

The Countess of Dudley, centre right, launched the SS *St David* in a blizzard.

St David going into the water, the coat of arms of the great company proudly on the bows.

Last year we placed orders for two new passenger steamships to replace the vessels lost during the war. The first of these, the St. David[1] was launched last month and the St. Patrick will be launched in April and completed towards the end of this summer.

Agreement was reached in December 1946 providing for the consolidation of the special war wage into the basic pay of all wages and salaried staff. This amounted to £73 per annum for salaried staff and 28 shillings a week for wages grades. The National Union of Railwaymen are pressing their claim for a 40-hour week and have submitted a claim for a wage rise of £1 a week. The Railway Clerks are pressing for a 35-hour week and a rise in pay of £52 per annum. The Associated Society of Locomotive Engineers and Firemen are claiming revised scale of pay for engine drivers, firemen and cleaners involving a similar increase in pay but instead of their previous claim for a 40-hour week they are now asking for a 44-hour week. At the last census, taken in March 1946, the average earnings of adult, male, railway staff was £6 1s 6d a week compared with £5 14s 1d for the average weekly earnings of adult males in the principal industries of this country.

Commenting on that, in his report to the Board, the General Manager pointed out that in the engineering industry outside the railway workshops, working hours had been reduced from forty-seven to forty-four a week as from 6 January. He then wrote:

It will be difficult to withstand a request for a similar reduction for our workshop staff and that reduction in working hours cannot be limited to the workshops. If the standard working week for all railway staff was to become 44 hours additional staff to the extent of 33,500 would have to be employed in the wages grades and 2,700 in the salaried grades at an estimated cost of £9¼ millions. The matter is being reported to the Minister of Transport and his attention has been drawn to the Unions' claim for an all-round increase of £1 a week and reduced hours which would cost an additional £70 million a year. In view of the statement made in the Economic Survey for 1947 that 'the Nation cannot afford shorter hours of work unless this can be shown to increase output per man' the Minister is being asked for some guidance as to the course he would like the Companies to pursue.

Portal's speech continued:

... Approximately 14,600 members of staff were serving with the armed forces on 'VE' Day and of those 10,000 had resumed duty by the end of 1946. In addition the Company has recruited approximately 9,200 new entrants from demobilised members of the armed forces. The Essential Work Order ceased to apply to railways on 31 August 1946 and 6,600 members of staff resigned from the Company's service. This loss has to some extent been made up by recruitment but we are still short of 1,800 staff. The total number of full time staff employed on the Great Western, to date, is 113,601, a decrease on the same time last year of 1,369.

We are still in the transition stage from war to peace and staff problems continue to present themselves but the well-earned reputation of our employees, both men and women, for loyal and devoted service have been fully maintained and on the shareholders behalf I should like to express your warm appreciation of their efforts.

Viscount Portal then spoke of how 'The Transport Bill' would affect the shareholders and the nation. Among his observations were:

The railway companies and other inland transport undertakings oppose the Bill and will continue to do so not only to protect the interest of the stockholders and the staff but also because there is nothing in the Bill to indicate the means by which a more efficient and economical transport service is to be provided. Although it has long been recognized that the main transport problem is to be solved by a greater measure of co-ordination between the various forms of transport the Bill contains no constructive plan for dealing with this problem. It merely lays down that it will be the duty of the British Transport Commission to work out a scheme.

A very vexed question was that of paying the owners of the railway for their property. The government intended to give railway stockholders government bonds in exchange for their railway shares. There were a large number of categories of railway shares. The government's supposition of the value of each type of railway share would be its average selling price on the Stock Exchange during six days in November 1946. These government bonds to be given in exchange carried a lesser rate of interest than any of the GWR shares. GWR stockholders would lose income depending on the type of GWR share they held – the loss would vary between 4½ per cent and 2½ per cent.

The government decided that the value of the assets of the GWR were equal to the price of GWR shares. This was not the real value of the railway – and the Council of the London Stock Exchange protested that this was not a proper valuation. Share values on the Exchange were the result of a transaction between a willing buyer and a willing seller – the basis of any financial transaction – but the stockholders of the GWR's shares were not willing sellers. The government was seizing the physical assets of the railway: the land, stations, hotels, ships, docks, engines and rolling stock – not the paper shares. Viscount Portal concluded his speech:

> ... The total market valuation of our undertaking – based on the compensation terms set out in the Bill only amounts to about £163 million. While it is not possible to give any accurate figures of the value of the physical assets which the government will acquire, it is safe to say that they are worth more than the proposed compensation. Our rolling stock which stands on our Capital Account at £22 million is estimated to be worth double that, even after making full allowance for the expired life of the stock and accumulated arrears of repairs. The strength of our financial position is demonstrated by our balance sheet. In addition to our physical assets our liquid reserves amount to £49 million. Moreover, a conservative estimate of the market value of our investments in associated road undertakings would be £7 million compared with £3 million shown in the Capital Account.

The National Insurance Act of 1946 was one of the legal foundations of the 'Welfare State'. For the first time ever, employers, employees and the government were to make compulsory contributions to an insurance scheme which would provide a pension for those reaching 65 years of age plus all medical services free, and other benefits. Employees were obliged to have 4s 11d a week deducted from their wages and all employers had to pay a contribution equal to a percentage of each man's or woman's wages. The cost of this to the Great Western was large and as a result the company began deducting money from retired employees' *ex-gratia* pensions. Such pensions were granted by the company when the latter had *no obligation* to do so but no money was deducted from company pensions to which the employee had contributed wages:

Persons retiring between	Deduction per week
1 October and 31 March 1947	6s
1 April and 30 September 1947	7s
1 October and 31 December 1947	8s

Supplemental pensions to members of the Pension Society and Enginemen and Firemen's Mutual Assurance, Sick & Superannuation Society

1 April and 30 September 1947	2s
1 October and 31 December 1947	3s

The General Manager's Report on Labour Matters made dismal reading for the directors. On 17 March the Directors' Labour Matters Committee met the railways workshops staff representatives and heard their claim for £1 a week pay rise and a reduction of hours from 47 to 44. Because these alterations had already been made in outside engineering works, the Committee felt that they could not withstand the claim. The General Manager, Sir James Milne, believed that the pay rise and shorter hours would have to be given to the whole GWR wages and salaried staff. He calculated that a 44-hour week for all railway wages grade staff would require an additional 32,500 men and 2,700 extra salaried staff which would cost an extra £9¼ million a year – otherwise the existing staff would continue their old hours and be paid overtime for the additional 3 hours.

Milne wrote:

> With regards to the manpower position in the country it would be necessary for the present to adopt the latter course and that would be even more expensive. The matter is being reported to the Minister of Transport and his attention drawn to the fact that the Unions' claim for an all-round increase of £1 per week and a reduction in hours would, if conceded, involve an additional cost of over £70 millions p.a. In view of the statement made in the Economic Survey for 1947 that 'the Nation cannot afford shorter hours of work unless these can be shown to increase output per man-year' and the difficulties likely to arise if any reduction in hours were limited to cases where output per man-year could be increased to make up for time lost, the Minister is being asked by the General Managers (of all four railways) for some guidance as to the course he would like the companies to pursue.

At this meeting the NUR asked that the membership of a trade union be made obligatory for all railway employees. Milne wrote: 'The Board will be aware that the railways have hitherto consistently adhered to a policy of impartiality towards the question of trade union membership but in the light of present circumstances it is suggested that the Companies should decline to make trade union membership compulsory.'

Milne's report did not mention whether the Minister of Transport had replied to his letter of February asking for the Minister's view on the course of action to be adopted in the face of the pay claims.

The estimated receipts for the GWR for the six weeks ended 16 March amounted to £4,259,000, a 21.3 per cent decrease compared with the same period in 1946. Without a doubt the appalling weather had everything to do with that. The revenue for the full year 16 March 1946 to 16 March 1947 was down 18.2 per cent for passenger and 14.2 per cent for freight.

The foul weather continued and this, together with a growing shortage of motive power, caused the government to order even more cuts in passenger train services so as to release locomotives for coal haulage for industrial and domestic use. The 'abnormally high number of locomotives and wagons awaiting repair' was because of 'a shortage of steel and timber', according to Sir James Milne's report to the GWR directors. The government was in a bind because the UK could not produce enough steel and timber for its needs and had to import from the undamaged industries of the USA and Sweden but did not have the currency to pay for all that was needed. The building materials that were available were allocated to the motor car industry, so that British cars could be exported to the USA to earn dollars.

As a result of 'repeated representations' by the railway companies regarding their inability to carry out repairs Mr Attlee issued, in March, the following directive to the Ministry of Supply: 'Railway freight locomotives and wagons intended for the transport of fuel to receive for their repair the full allocation of steel and timber.'

The Chief Signal & Telegraph Engineer, Mr F.H.D. Page, OBE, retired on 14 March. The directors noted this in a Minute:

> Mr. F.H.D. Page retired on the 14th of this month having been Chief Signal & Telegraph Engineer since February 1936. In that time he has made many improvements to the Company's signal and telegraph arrangements. The Directors desire to place on record their appreciation of the skill and ability with which Mr. Page has carried out his duties and of the devotion to the Company's interests which he has at all times displayed and particularly during the war when his responsibilities were exceptionally heavy.

Frederick Page was from the Bedwardine district of the City of Worcester. He had commenced his life in engineering, aged 16, on 1 March 1898, when his father paid £250 for his apprenticeship with the signalling contractors McKenzie & Holland of Worcester, makers of interlocking machines and the levers to operate them, plus every type of signal, electric signalling instruments and repeaters. He served five years with

The entrance and some buildings of the GWR Signal & Telegraph Works on the Caversham Road, Reading, immediately north of the railway overbridge. (Author's Collection)

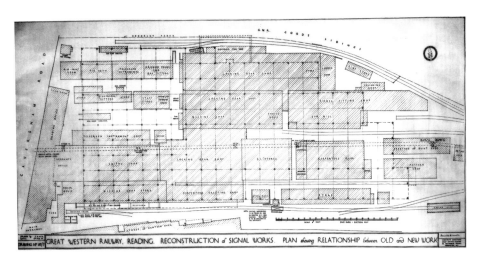

Plan dated 2nd February 1947. (Author's Collection)

McKenzie & Holland, during which time he learned practical engineering skills and attended evening classes at Worcester Technical College. At the end of his time he went to work for the Taff Vale Railway but came to the Reading signal works of the GWR, as a draughtsman, on three months' probation, on 31 December 1906. In July 1912 he was appointed a Surveyor of Interlocking, in which capacity he remained until May 1921 when he was appointed an 'Assistant' and in January 1926 he became Divisional Signal Engineer, Cardiff. Two years later he was brought back to Reading headquarters to be an Assistant to the Chief Signal Engineer, Mr A.T. Blackall, and there he remained, working next to his Chief, until the latter retired on 3 February 1936, leaving Page to move into the Chief's position.[2]

During the war Mr Page had directed the reorganising of Reading signal works to provide for the re-signalling of the Didcot-Newbury-Southampton route as a double-track railway. The Andoversford–Andover route remained a single track, but required some signalling improvements, as well as the signalling needed for the large new marshalling yards, established around the GWR. New signal boxes and locking frames were required, in addition to signals, signalling instruments, track circuits and instruments. There was also the problem of repairing bomb-damaged signalling equipment, and in between the work there were frequent royal trains on the GWR, all of which had to be accompanied by the Chief Signal Engineer, Mr Page. He was awarded an OBE in 1943 for his services to the public through his work for the GWR. In 1946–47 he was involved with the construction and electrification of the new Central Line of the London Passenger Transport Board, from North Acton to West Ruislip.

Nowhere in the Minutes is there any reference to his being paid a bonus for shouldering extraordinary responsibilities during six years of war. The Company did, however, buy him a house in the country, near Reading, after he had retired. There is no Board Minute for this expenditure, so it must have been a private gesture on the part of the directors.

Extraordinary Weather Conditions, New Industries

The very abnormal weather of February and into March dislocated the train service over much of the GWR. A severe blizzard blew continuously at 70 to 80mph over most of Great Western territory from 4 March until 6 March. The deepest drifts in South Wales were from Colbren Junction to Sennybridge, Dowlais Top to Fochriw, Abertillery and Brynmawr, Cwn Bargoed and Bedlinog and between Rhymney and Rhymney Bridge.

Sixty-eight collieries in South Wales were completely cut off by rail and miners struggled on foot across snow-blanketed hillsides to and from work. The 3.4 a.m. Brecon–Merthyr train of 5 March became snowbound between Torpantau and Pentir Rhiw. The snowplough could get nowhere near it and 100 soldiers were brought in as close as possible by special train, to carry blankets, food and hot drink for the passengers, and then to dig the train out of the drift. Other Welsh trains were snowbound in the Crumlin Valley, at Dowlais, Tonfanu, Lampeter, Pantydwr and St Harmons. The 5.50 p.m. Highworth–Swindon train became snowbound 5 minutes after leaving Highworth and was released at 4.05 p.m. next day, but the line remained closed until 5.30 p.m. on 7 March.

So much snow accumulated on the tracks between Dowlais and Brecon that they began to look like a glacier. The various semi-glaciers had to be removed, and the train service anxiously awaited a thaw. Early in March the scale of the problem suggested to someone within the GWR that aircraft jet engines might be useful. The Ministry of Supply was asked to loan a couple of Rolls-Royce 'Derwent' engines and these were produced. Two of these were very securely mounted, spaced 4ft 6in apart, on a flat-bed wagon.

The tubes to direct the hot gases from the engines were fitted at an angle of 15 degrees below horizontal. Behind this assembly was a second railway flat wagon carrying an RAF fuel tanker holding 325 gallons of aircraft fuel. The train was positioned at the site of a long, thick sheet of ice and snow around Dowlais Top. Engineers from Rolls-Royce, the National Gas Turbine Establishment, the RAF and

Desperate measures at bleak Dowlais Top on the Bargoed–Brecon line on 27 February.

the GWR were present. The jet engines were fired up: in the official photograph one man at least looks extremely worried, biting his fingertips. The blast from the depressed tubes ripped away yards of compacted ice and clouds of snow. Great chunks of ice were flung hundreds of yards and a huge cloud of powdered snow blotted out the scene as the screaming noise of the jets blotted out everything else. Everyone agreed that it had been a very interesting day and much ice had been removed but, on balance, picks and shovels, although slower, proved to be the safest way forward. One by one the colliery sidings were made accessible and precious coal was dragged out and worked away to the power stations.

The March reductions in the passenger train service took out another thirty-eight through trains and ninety local trains representing a reduction of weekly passenger train mileage of 31,000. The seriousness of the motive power shortage is shown by the suspension of the 10.30 a.m. Paddington–Penzance train, the 'Cornish Riviera Express'. The Minister of Transport also ordered that the summer timetable should not be introduced until 16 June, at least two weeks later than usual, and that, when this timetable was brought into use, there would be 10 per cent fewer trains than in 1946.

Oil firing continued to expand. On 10 February contracts were signed for constructing fuelling points at Laira, and similar constructions agreed for fuelling points at Old Oak Common on 21 February, and at Banbury on 25 February. In March contractors for building these were appointed for Cardiff Canton on 13 March, Reading on 21 March and Bristol St Philip's Marsh on 28 March.

The suspension of some merchandise and passenger train services and the diversion of those locomotives to hauling coal seriously reduced the company's freight earnings. Simultaneously factories old and new were being opened or reopened. The Great Western had made fifteen sites available for new factories between 1 January and 27 March. Twelve of them were in South Wales. The Tredegar Industrial Estate was expanded by some of these developments, all rail connected. These were to

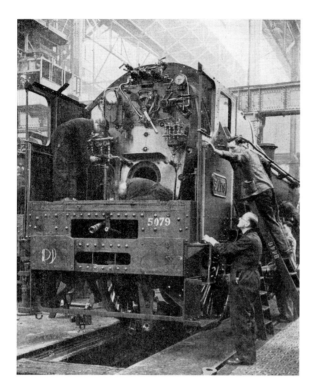

'Castle' class No 5079 *Lysander* in Swindon 'A' shop being fitted up for oil burning. The craftsman bending over on the left is dealing with the oil flow controls.

make radios and gramophones, machine tools, water softeners, domestic electric appliances and agricultural machinery. On the outskirts of London, at Slough and Hayes, new factories were being built and old ones restarted. Output from these new industries would be carried away 'by the GWR in 1948' – as the General Manager's report put it.

In the period 12 to 26 March the GWR hauled away to various ports 1,226 cars from Morris Motors in Cowley, Oxford, and 148 cars from the Austin factory at Longbridge, Birmingham, making a total of 3,669 from both factories since 1 January. The GWR also had the problem of finding engines, crews and wagons to haul 25,000 tons of barbed wire from the Ordnance sidings at Taplow to the Port of London for shipment to Canada. By 27 March the company had managed to move 2,000 tons in 676 wagons. Dismantled wooden huts, 730 tons of them, were hauled in two special trains of fifty-eight wagons each from Long Marston Ordnance depot to Manchester docks for shipment to the Persian Gulf. Exports of 65 tons of firebricks were moved from Cradley Heath to Holland, as were thirty-four new railway wagons from Birmingham Railway Carriage & Wagon Works at Handsworth, part of an order of 500 for Poland and Czechoslovakia.

On 26 July 1946 the GWR directors had placed an order with the Swiss firm Brown-Boveri for the design, construction and delivery of a 2,500hp gas turbine-electric locomotive capable of hauling a ten-coach train at 90mph. The GWR would share half the costs of design, construction and trials. Those costs could not be known but the directors were willing to take the risk. In March 1947 they placed an order –

The tender
of No 4855
(old 3813)
standing by
the oil-fuelling
point in
Swindon shed
yard on 4 July
1947. (H.C.
Casserley)

Filling up with
oil.

under the same conditions as agreed with Brown-Boveri – with Metropolitan-Vickers for a 3,000hp gas turbine-electric. Both locomotives arrived on the railway after nationalisation and were numbered 18000 and 18100 respectively.

And so it went on, with the Great Western trying to serve everyone in spite of shortages – and the weather – and the threat of annihilation.

Every month the directors authorised the expenditure of thousands of pounds to restore the railway and improve it. £1,000 was allocated for the rebuilding of a 50ft 'Siphon' – an eight-wheeled milk van. This had been converted into an ambulance train ward car in 1940, and in March 1947 the steel chassis and wheels were returned to Swindon – the body having been destroyed by fire 'on the Continent'. 'Ocean' saloons 9004 and 9005 were refurbished throughout, not only to include the passenger accommodation but also to give improved steam heating and the installation of new brake gear for £740.

The sleeping car services were to be reinstated. The Locomotive Committee Minute records:

> Consideration has been given to the modernisation of the 1st class and composite sleeping cars and as the work cannot be carried out at Swindon owing to the shortage of labour, arrangements have been made with Messrs Hampton & Sons to modernise one car as an experiment. This vehicle, 1st class Sleeping Car No 9066, has been dealt with, and is in traffic and the alterations and re-furnishing is regarded as very satisfactory.

Consequently the directors placed an order with Hampton & Sons to refurbish fourteen more sleeping cars at a total cost, including the prototype, of £75,542. In addition, Metropolitan-Cammell Carriage & Wagon Co. was given an order for 100 corridor brake, third-class carriages, costing £580,400. These were to be matched with the 100 third-class corridor coaches ordered from the Gloucester Carriage & Wagon Co. in 1946. The Birmingham Railway Carriage & Wagon Co. took on an order for twenty non-corridor third-class carriages for £121,480. The carriages were produced slowly due, as usual at this period, to labour and materials shortages consequent to the priorities dictated by the Ministry of Supply.

While such large subjects were in view, the directors did not neglect small things which were important to their staff. They voted £480 for electric lighting along the path from Banbury station to the engine shed, and £480 for a motor-cycle park at St Philip's Marsh shed. A large house at 171 King's Road, Reading, was purchased from Mr A. Skelt for £2,500, to be converted for use as a staff hostel.

On 4 March the 'B2' trip left Elliot Colliery for Bassaleg marshalling yard at 11.50 a.m. The engine was an ex-Brecon & Merthyr 'D' class 0-6-2 tank, No 698, running bunker-first. Behind the engine were eight 20-ton wagons and seven 10-ton wagons loaded with coal and equal in weight to twenty-two 10 tonners. This was a light load compared to the usual fifty loaded 10-ton wagons, and thus one to be easily held in check by the engine on the steep descent of Maypole bank. The driver was Henry Vaughan, the fireman Brian Curtis, both of Newport Dock Street shed, and Guard John Russell of Bassaleg. The day was very cold with a light snow falling.

The gradient was falling at 1 in 290 and this carried the train along at 20–25mph through Church Road station. The Maypole incline Stop Board was 1 mile further on. Trains were required to stop there so that the handbrakes on the wagons could be pinned down tight by the guard. Passing Church Road, Vaughan said he told Curtis to screw on the engine's handbrake to commence stopping for Maypole. Speed continued to increase. The guard noticed this and screwed down his handbrake but that locked the wheels so that they were skidding. He released the brake, opened his rail sanders and screwed down again. The sand came out in dribbles and the wheels started to skid again. Meanwhile on the engine, they had opened their sanders and applied the brake. The sand did not run at all and the engine's steam brake locked the driving wheels. Driver Vaughan released the brake, put the engine into reverse, and put on steam. With the deep note of the brake whistle sounding, the train accelerated past the Stop Board and commenced the 1½ miles of 1 in 82 descent to Bassaleg Junction. The engine's wheels locked. Driver Vaughan put it into forward gear and tried to brake. The wheels locked again. He went on down the bank, desperately reversing the engine and braking, then into forward gear and braking. Rhiwderin's signals were at 'Danger' but they went through at about 30mph. Vaughan, understandably panicking somewhat, yelled out to the signalman, 'We're running away!' Rhiwderin sent bell signal 4-5-5, meaning 'Train running away on Right Line' to Bassaleg North box about three-quarters of a mile further on. The signalman set the route for the runaway to enter the sorting sidings. The Bassaleg signalman had no control over the way the points were set inside the sorting sidings – they were all hand operated. He telephoned Yard Inspector Wilkinson to tell him that a runaway was about to enter the sidings and to get the Pilot out of the way, but the speed of the train was such that it was not possible for Wilkinson to get to the shunting engine to warn the crew.

Just before reaching the points into the sidings Vaughan and Curtis jumped from the engine – which was running at 40mph in their estimation. They were severely injured but survived. The runaway train took the 15mph points at speed without derailing and all the wagons followed. The whole train ran in clear of the Down Main complete with tail lamp and continued along the siding from which all other sidings branched off. As the runaway came in over the points from the Down Main and passed the signal box, the Pilot engine, 0-6-0 pannier tank No 1890, came along the main siding, and stopped at the shunters' cabin.

The fireman, Ben Williams of Newport Dock Street, got off the engine and had started to walk to the cabin when he saw the runaway approaching at what he estimated to be 'about 50mph'. He shouted to his driver, Thomas Hughes. Hughes' engine was chimney-facing No 698. Hughes instantly heaved the reversing lever into reverse and opened the regulator wide and got his engine moving when No 698, with 220 tons behind, struck.

Hughes was not hurt in that collision and, still with tremendous presence of mind, shut his regulator and applied the brake before jumping off his now fast-moving engine. He hurt his hands, legs and feet, but not enough to keep him from work the next day.

The runaway pushed No 1890 – wheels skidding over the rails – 350yd, rammed it through the buffer stops and continued to run for another 30yd, demolishing a Permanent-way department store hut and a Traffic Department oil hut before scattering wagons onto the platform at Bassaleg station. Both engines remained upright all the while. Driver Vaughan was judged to have been careless in his approach to the Maypole Bank Stop Board and he was cited as the cause of the incident.

Three passenger trains, and three 'parcels' or 'milk' trains parted in March. To put those figures in context, mileage of engines hauling passenger trains in March was 2,665,422.

Passenger and 'passenger stock' vehicles on the GWR were usually coupled with a shackle fitted with a screw thread so that the vehicles could be coupled with their buffers firmly together. Some GWR passenger carriages were coupled with the American

'Automatic coupler' but that device never features in the reports of breakaways. The two 'U'-shaped shackles were attached one on each side of a strong nut running on the screw thread. Once a shackle was slung over a draw hook the screw could be turned to keep the buffers of the opposing vehicles touching. On passenger and parcels stock the breakaways were most often caused by the nut being ripped off the screw thread, but the coupling hook would break, or the whole drawbar could – rarely – be pulled out of the frames.

The brakes on the train were more powerful that those on the engine and so when a driver applied the brake all the vehicles pulled back against the engine. Thus a pull of several tons was exerted on the nut on the screw thread.

Various mishaps occurred and these included:

1. Highbridge. The 4.10 p.m. Plymouth–Paddington parcels train, at 8.55 p.m. The engine was No 4042 *Prince Albert*, with eleven vehicles, with personnel Driver Oram and Fireman Tiley of Bristol. It parted in stopping at Highbridge. There was a broken coupling hook on LNER brake van No 4164, fourth from the engine. Vacuum pipes were destroyed. The vehicle was re-coupled with shackle on the third vehicle. The train proceeded with three vacuum-braked vehicles. The LNER van was detached at Weston-super-Mare.

2. Chippenham. The 7.30 p.m. Paddington–Weston-super-Mare, at 11.10 p.m. Engine was No 5901 *Hazel Hall*, with fifteen coaches, 420 tons tare and Driver Drake of Bristol. As the train stopped at Chippenham the thread of the shackle screw was stripped at the tenth vehicle: brake third, No 4607. The vacuum pipes were undamaged. The shackle of the adjoining vehicle was used to re-couple.

3. Newton Abbot. The 3.25 p.m. Bristol–Plymouth North Road 'parcels' train with eleven vehicles, weighing 186 tons. The engine was No 21C.113 *Okehampton*, and the driver was Colman of Plymouth Friary. It occurred at 8.38 p.m. While stopping, a coupling broke on LNER brake van No 2117, sixth from the engine, and an emergency screw coupling was used to re-join the unit.

4. Reading East Main. The 10.15 p.m. Paddington–Plymouth parcels train, with nineteen vehicles, weighing 313 tons. The engine was No 6961 *Stedham Hall*, with Driver Smith of Old Oak Common. The train stopped at Reading East Main Down Main Inner Home signal for 16 minutes. A coupling broke on restarting on GWR milk tank No 2548, ninth from the engine, running empty from Bow to Lostwithiel. The train set back and was re-coupled and then drew into Reading station. A new vacuum pipe was fitted and the train left after 15 minutes.

5. Machen. The 1.5 p.m. Newport (Mon.) to New Tredegar. The engine was No 3700, with 'B' sets 6778 and 6779 and Workman's third 1316, with Driver Francis of Ebbw Junction. The train was reversing into No 2 siding to pick up another 'B' set and Workman's coach as per schedule when the engine's coupling slipped off the hook of Set 6778, severing vacuum and steam pipes. The engine stopped at once and the train stopped after 6ft. The coaches were drawn out and put into No 1 siding and the engine coupled to the Set in No 2 siding to continue its journey, resulting in 10 minutes' delay. The damaged pipes on Set 6778 were replaced and these coaches were taken forward by the 5.10 p.m. Newport–New Tredegar train.

6. Penpergwn–Nantyderry. The 10 a.m. Crewe–Newport (Mon.) train, with seventeen vehicles. The engine was No 4953 *Pitchford Hall,* weighing 265 tons, with Driver Innes of Hereford. The train parted while slowing for a signal. The thread was stripped on the shackle of an LNER brake van. The two parts of the train stopped 4ft apart. The train set back and was re-coupled and the defective brake van was detached at Pontypool Road, resulting in 10 minutes' delay.

During March sixty freight trains broke away. Freight trains ran 1,503,689 miles in March. Goods wagons were coupled by a three-link chain or by a screw shackle. Breakaways were caused by a fierce tug, or 'snatch', on the coupling. Such a tug could happen when the train was starting, stopping or just running along, when going downhill, or going uphill and even going uphill with a banker pushing behind the guard's van. These incidents were dealt with through the initiative of the train crew and the watchful signalmen. The Rule Book and Signalling Regulations covered all eventualities and the railwaymen simply carried out their instructions without recourse to any 'higher authority'.

Fifteen coupling problems occurred with GWR, sixteen with LMS trains, eight happened with LNER trains and twenty-one breakaways occurred on privately owned trains. Of the GWR partings, one was the screw thread stripping on the locomotive's shackle. The engine was No 4998 *Eyton Hall*, climbing the 1 in 100 eastbound in the Severn Tunnel. She hauled fifty-three loaded coal wagons, equal to seventy-two ordinary merchandise wagons, assisted in the rear by No 3184.

Seven such accidents were caused by the guard's brake van coupling snapping, one was a hook breaking, and two were instigated by drawbars breaking. Most GWR brake vans that suffered a broken coupling were those fitted with the patent 'Instanter' coupling. This was a three-link chain which could be made shorter by turning the link vertically with the hook of the shunting pole.

Four LMS wagons had broken drawbars, as did one LNER wagon. Seventeen of the private owner wagons had a three-link coupling break, plus one hook break and three drawbars pulling apart.

On 4 March and the following day there was one final, Russian-style blizzard coming in from the west that swept over Wales and on across England into Scotland. Railwaymen, with the great loyalty they had to their patch of railway, battled with the snow, trying to keep the trains moving. There was not the remotest branch line that did not have its devoted defenders – including the single track out of Bala Junction, a single-track thread of railway climbing and contouring through the bleak and inhospitable moors to Blaenau Festinog. The snowplough with its brake van, guard, footplate crew, Chester Locomotive Inspector and gang of shovellers, accompanied by the Corwen District Inspector E. Thorne, were out on that branch, working as hard to keep it open for traffic as if it was the London main line. The fact that the all-day and night operation was successful was due to the two *temporary* signalmen at Arenig: W.R.E. Jones and E.D. Roberts.

In the sub-zero temperatures, these two men, each on their turn of duty – and indeed, beyond their booked times – kept the locomotive water supply tank and column at Arenig free of ice. Working in a blizzard at Arenig would have been something akin to working in Siberia. Arenig became the only source of supply on the 25½ miles of the branch beyond Bala Junction. The efforts of the two temporary signalmen, working in atrocious cold, were noticed by everyone on the snowplough gang. The Locomotive Inspectors, who did their shifts over the two days, praised the efforts of Jones and Roberts to the Divisional Locomotive Superintendent at Chester. He asked the Divisional Traffic Superintendent, N.H. Briant, to make inquiries and he wrote to Inspector Thorne at Corwen asking for his opinion. Thorne replied:

> I am pleased to say that I can endorse the remarks of both the Locomotive Inspectors of the efforts made by the Arenig signalmen to maintain a water supply there. They were all the more appreciated as there was no water at Trawsfynydd and none at Tan-y-Manod or Blaenau Festiniog. I understand that the tank had to be cleared of ice several times and I shall be very pleased if you can consider some form of recognition for exceptional services rendered under the most trying conditions.

The various letters went with a recommendation from the Superintendent of the Line to Sir James Milne, dated 6 May:

> Mr. Briant advises me that the Divisional Locomotive has directed attention to the valuable assistance rendered by the above named signalmen in connection with the working of the snow plough in the Bala area during the recent severe weather. The efforts of the two men enabled a constant supply of water to be maintained at Arenig when all other supplies on the area were frozen.
>
> The actions of the two men were well commented upon by the Locomotive Inspectors in charge of the snow plough. Their remarks being endorsed by the Traffic Department District Inspector.
>
> The water supply was maintained under the most trying conditions. The men worked well beyond their booked hours of duty, cleared the water storage tank of ice on several occasions and attended to the fire at the water column.
>
> As an appreciation of the interest and the efforts displayed, a recommendation has been made for the granting of a gratuity of two guineas to each man and that they should be paid for the voluntary overtime they worked. I shall be obliged if it is possible for the way to be seen to agree to the proposal which has my support.
>
> Yours truly
>
> Gilbert Matthews

The payments were made.

On 8 March a thaw began which caused dense fog, severe gales and heavy rain. Over the next several days very serious flooding and landslides occurred at various places on the GWR. Water was over the rails between Hinksey South and Kennington as the Thames broke its banks but steam engines can cope with quite deep water and they passed through at 'Caution' but the Marlow branch was actually shut because of the depth of water over the rails.

At 1.45 p.m. on 10 March a landslip in the cutting leading to Marlborough tunnel blocked the route to Andover and Savernake Low Level. The line to Savernake Low Level was cleared at 2.20 p.m. the same day and the Andover line was cleared at 4.45 p.m. on 12 March. On 13 March the cutting slipped again and all services were suspended until 19 March.

At Midgham on Sunday 16 March the Down platform moved forward to within ½in of the loading gauge. The ganger spotted this small but potentially disastrous defect and informed the signalman. He stopped each Down train and warned the driver to pass through at 2mph.

Early that Sunday morning a strong wind sprang up which developed into a Force 9 gale by the evening. Didcot station lost part of its roof. The roof of Windsor station moved on its walls. Signal posts were blown over at Henley-in-Arden and Trowbridge and shortly after the latter went down a landslide occurred nearby. Three RAF gliders were blown through the airfield fence and across the track at Brize Norton and others were arrested by the fence, but each of these had a wing reaching out over the line.

There was severe flooding in Worcester City on 18 March and the company put on a special shuttle service with a diesel rail car between Henwick station and Worcester Shrub Hill in an effort to assist travel across the city. On 19 March the railway became submerged at Holme Lacy between Hereford and Ross-on-Wye, as the Wye broke its banks. A 10mph speed limit was imposed. The following day the land slipped and the line was closed until 4 p.m. on 24 March. An emergency bus service was instituted.

The Gloucester to Ross-on-Wye and Hereford single line crossed the River Wye three times north of Ross and ran within yards of it at other places. The heavy snowfalls and all-out blizzards of January and February continued into the first eight days of March. Each successive layer of snow was preserved by sub-zero temperatures. The

FLOOD DAMAGE IN THE WYE VALLEY, MARCH, 1947. DROPPED SPANS OF STRANGFORD VIADUCT, NEAR FAWLEY.

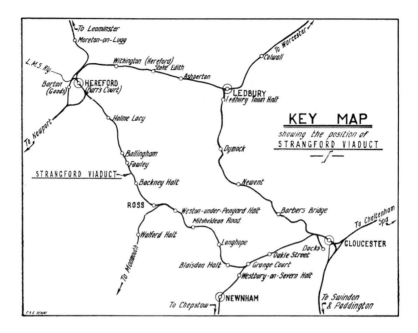

thaw began on 10 March, and with it came torrential rain. The River Wye rising on the snow-piled mountains of central Wales was soon flooding through the towns along its valley.

About 1½ miles north of Ross-on-Wye station the railway crossed the river for the second time on the Strangford viaduct, 276ft long, built in 1853–54 and brought into use on 1 June 1855. The viaduct was formed of deep, wrought-iron plate girders supported by six piers built of local stone. The bed of the river was solid rock, the piers were cemented to that and the bonding protected by rocks and gravel. At the end of March the Wye in that area was 17ft 6in above the usual winter flood level, and the rapid flow was washing away the underwater protection of the mid-stream pier of the Strangford viaduct. At about 11 p.m. a goods train passed over it and about 10 minutes later the pier was toppled over by the undermining force of the water.

About 700yd across the meadows, north-west of the viaduct, was the lane from King's Caple to the Fawley road. Walking home at around 11 p.m. from the 'British Lion' pub at Fawley station were two young men, J. Alford and E. Davies. They heard the grinding crash of the pier and the girders falling and immediately realised the need to warn the railway. The nearest signal box was at Fawley station about three-quarters of a mile back the way they had come. They set off at the double. As they approached the station they met Signalman Bowett, walking home after completion of his tour of duty – he had switched the box out of circuit. Mr Bowett went back to the station, and hurried three-quarters of the way along the track to check the young men's story. Once the danger was confirmed he came back to the station and woke Station Master Ingham. They discussed and agreed that the signal box should be brought back into circuit in order to send the vital 'Obstruction Danger' signal to Ross

North box. Signalman Bowett had come on duty at 2 p.m. on 28 March and stayed on duty until 2.30 a.m. on the following day, when he was relieved.

A bus service replaced the local trains between Ross and Fawley station until the viaduct was repaired. The Superintendent of the Line, Gilbert Matthews, wrote to the General Manager that he and the Chief Engineer of the railway 'considered that the actions of the two youths, J. Alford and E. Davies and also Signalman Bowett were most commendable and it is recommended that they each be awarded a gratuity of five guineas (£5 5s.) I shall be obliged if you will kindly say whether you agree.'

Milne wrote 'Spoken to SoL. Agreed. £5 5s' at the foot of Matthews' letter and the awards were paid.

Notes

1   The good ship *St David*, 3,352 tons, was launched from Cammell Laird's yard on the Mersey at Birkenhead by the Countess of Dudley in February 1947. There was a blizzard blowing at the time. The ship took up its duties on the Fishguard–Waterford route in July.

2   I am indebted to Mr F.H.D. Page's grandson, Michael – who became Divisional Signal & Telecommunications Engineer, Cardiff – for biographical details of his grandfather which are not to be found in official records.

GREAT WESTERN RAILWAY
MAGAZINE

MARCH & APRIL · 1947

VOLUME 59 · NO. 3

Pride in the Job—2
(See Page 58)

PRICE ONE PENNY

Note that the magazine produced only one issue for March and April 1947.

APRIL

Talented People and Expanding Opportunities

Fifteen directors met at Paddington on 25 April, with Viscount Portal in the Chair. The Minutes of their eight sub-committees were read and approved. It was reported that the government – in the form of the nationalised British European Airways – had taken possession of the 'Channel Islands Airways' company, jointly owned by the GWR and the Southern Railway. The Ministry of Aviation was offering the companies compensation of £250,000. This was declined and the matter had been put into arbitration. The Chairman of the Boards of Channel Islands Airways, Great Western and Southern Airlines Ltd, the Railway Air Services, British and Foreign Aviation Ltd and other railway-owned airline companies was Keith Grand.

Grand was indeed a grand railwayman. He started on the GWR, aged 19, in 1919, in the goods shed at Park Royal and three years later he was working at Paddington in the General Manager's office. He moved rapidly upwards until he became Principal Assistant to the General Manager in 1939, by which time he was also chairing the Boards of these railway airlines. The directors put in the Minutes their 'appreciation of the valuable services rendered in the air line business by Mr K.W.C. Grand'. They then went on to sanction expenditure on improvements to the railway:

> Clearing snow, defrosting and repairing track resulting from recent snowstorms and floods (£290,000) ... repairing damage to signals and telegraphs caused by gales and floods (£11,000) ... provision of modified automatic train control equipment on locomotives (£25,000) ... general overhaul and improvements in the crew accommodation of the S.S. *Sambur* by the Penarth Pontoon & Ship Repairing Co. (£6,977), of which £1,344 is recoverable from the Ministry of Transport.

The *Sambur* was a GWR cargo vessel launched in 1925 and commandeered for the Royal Navy in 1939. She was used in the evacuation of the British Expeditionary Force from France in May 1940, and was damaged by Nazi fire, when Royal Naval and GWR crew members were killed.

Other expenditure authorised at this meeting included the purchase of No 3 Oxford Villas, Trelawny Road, Plympton (£2,500) 'for a member of the staff and the purchase of 35 Cotham Park, Bristol (£4,250) for use as a staff hostel'. Total expenditure of about £431,000 was sanctioned. That was the easy part – the great problem was finding the materials and labour to carry out the work.

From sanctioning expenditure the directors moved on, in the usual, stately sequence of business, to grant pay rises to thirteen higher ranking officers. The salary of Mr L.W. Conibear, Commercial Assistant to the Superintendent of the Line, went from £973 p.a. to £1,175. J.F.M. Taylor, Divisional Superintendent, Worcester, earned £973 p a but was now promoted to superintend the Swansea Division and his pay was raised to £1,250 p.a. David Blee, Chief Goods Manager, had his annual pay raised from £3,000 to £4,000. Mr A. Lane, Chief of GWR Police, saw his salary increase from £1,273 to £1,500 p.a. Mr Christian Barman was appointed as from 28 April as an Assistant to the Chief Officer of Public Relations, at £2,000, which would seem to indicate the great importance the directors attached to public relations.

The Directors' Minutes recorded that in April they had received from Mr B.R. Hunt of Johannesburg, South Africa, a 7¼in gauge working model of No 6000 *King George V*, together with a model of composite class carriage No 6484. As a comparison, Mr Hunt also built a working model of George Stephenson's *Locomotion No 1*[1] and the first, enclosed, railway carriage *Experiment*. The directors stated: 'The models are of extremely fine workmanship. They have taken Mr Hunt over 12 years to complete and are contained in a show case 26 feet long.' The show case and contents were placed on 'The Lawn' at Paddington on the opposite side to the buffers, where they were continuously regarded with great admiration.

The report of the Directors' sub-Committee on Labour Matters was brief. Negotiations over pay were still under discussion with the unions. Meanwhile the railway unions had approached the Minister of Transport with suggestions 'for securing the closer co-operation of railway staff during the present difficulties'. The GWR directors agreed to have such discussions and that meetings would be held between the company's Divisional and District Officers and the elected representatives of the staff – at Local Departmental and Sectional Council levels. These meetings were not about wages and hours but to see what management and workers could think of to ease the difficulties under which the railway was operating.

There were 1,050 people over the age of 65 still working for the company and '2,150 women are employed in wages grades work normally performed by men'. The company was short of 3,826 men, who were serving with the armed forces. They were also short of materials.

In April the GWR had 3,861 steam engines and thirty-seven diesel rail cars on their books plus forty-six 2-8-0 engines on loan from the LMS and fifty 2-8-0 engines from the War Department. The total was 3,949, of which 2,962 – 75.01 per cent – were, on average, available for work each day of the month. Of that total 2,900 – 97.91 per cent – were actually used. The number of hours, per day, that each engine in use worked was 12.28 and the average number of miles run in that time was 95.07. The average miles run per engine hour was, for passenger trains, 12.65, and, for goods trains, 8.19. All these figures were less than for April 1946.

The General Manager reported that the estimated receipts for the four weeks ended 13 April amounted to £3,385,000, a decrease of £388,000, or 10.28 per cent, compared with the same period in 1946. Passenger receipts were down £43,000, which was 2.47 per cent. Considering the awful weather and the cancellation of so many passenger trains this was better than might have been expected. General merchandise was down £392,000 (25.45 per cent) as the company concentrated their motive power getting coal to power stations and domestic users. The money earned from coal haulage increased by £47,000, up 9.5 per cent on 1946.

The Minister of Transport had ordered the continuation of the extreme efforts to haul coal. More wagons, normally used for general merchandise traffic, were to be requisitioned for coal haulage and the existing restrictions on passenger train services were to be continued. The Minister also ordered that the demurrage charge – paid by consignees on coal wagons not unloaded quickly enough – was to be raised to penal levels in an effort to ensure a steady flow of empties back to the collieries.

The Easter holiday came early in 1947, Easter Sunday being 6 April. There was a restricted service on the GWR – compared to 1946 – and in total 143,940 passengers were taken from Paddington between Maunday Thursday and the following Tuesday. The peak days were Thursday, when 45,000 people were transported in sixty-three main-line trains – 714 per train, and Tuesday, when 33,300 passengers departed in fifty-eight main-line trains – 574 per train.

The coal shortage was such that the GWR were forbidden by government decree to run special trains to carry football fans to any of the Cup Finals played in April. These were the Scottish F.A. Cup on 3 April, the International match on 12 April, and the F.A. Cup Final at Wembley on 26 April. However, the Minister relented on this in so far as the GWR could run unadvertised 'Relief trains' where publicly scheduled trains were going to be overcrowded and obliged to leave large crowds of disappointed – and perhaps angry – fans on the platforms.

The introduction of the summer timetable would be delayed by a month, until Monday 16 June, and would run until 5 October. The timetable was already drawn up. Every detail of the complexities of running trains over a far-flung network had been considered. These factors included the availability of engines and crews, the booking-on/off times of crews, their rest periods, the 'double-home' workings of some men, in addition to engine changing at distant points in the journey, and the opening of little 'break section' signal boxes at the right places to avoid delays to trains running close behind each other. Additional sailings of GWR boats to the Channel Islands and Ireland were co-ordinated with the trains. And doubtless the many GWR hotels had made their own arrangements to meet the summer demands.

In order to provide for the anticipated heavy summer-holiday traffic at weekends, it was necessary to curtail the service of local trains running on Mondays and Fridays. The usual 'Saturdays Only' trains had been seriously reduced and on Sundays there would be no services on the Clevedon, Minehead and Devil's Bridge lines. Western National buses would provide the passenger services between St Austell and Newquay and from St Erth to St Ives. The 'Cornish Riviera Express' – 10.30 a.m. Paddington and 10 a.m. Penzance – and the 11 a.m. Paddington 'Torbay Express' were reinstated for the summer timetable. Additional cross-country services were planned to and from Liverpool, Manchester and the West Country, including the 'Devonian' but the inter-Company cross-country trains such as Newcastle–Bournemouth and that very remarkable through train from Newcastle to Swansea which, before the war, ran via Banbury, King's Sutton Junction and Stow-on-the-Wold, were to remain in suspension.

The summer service would have a daily mileage of 89,050 by locomotive-hauled trains, which was 9,213 miles less than in 1946. With fewer summer passenger trains allowed to run, seat reservations were to be suspended on most long-distance trains for the summer.

The efforts of GWR staff to serve the public were great and none more so than among the shed maintenance staff: fire droppers, fire lighters, locomotive fitters and coaling plant men. They put in weary hours to carry out filthy jobs in the freezing cold and rain – and often worked in the dark without the benefit of an electric torch, unless they supplied it themselves. The company issued what were inaccurately called 'flare lamps'. One of these looked – at first glance – like an oil can with a thick wick protruding from the spout. It was the sort of thing the ancient Egyptian labourers might have used when working inside the chambers of a pyramid.

But the macho men kept the wheels moving and in April the Ministry of Food sent a message of:

> High appreciation of the assistance given by the Company in connection with the delivery of meat to South Wales and Monmouthshire. The untiring efforts of the Company's Officers and staff enabled the weekly meat ration to be maintained throughout the area during the recent snow blizzards, gales, heavy winds and floods.

The General Manager noted in particular that during April three more rail-connected building sites in South Wales were sold or leased for factories to make piano keyboard actions, steel radiators and wireless sets. Morris Motors had sent away by rail 925 cars in the previous fortnight and Austin had railed away 503 from Longbridge. Explosive ammonium nitrate, 2,270 tons of it, had been sent from the Pembrey ammunition factory to Cardiff, Bristol and Middlesbrough docks. Reading exported 81 tons of electric cable to Belgium, firebrick from Brettell Lane and 20 tons of nickel plate from Port Talbot to Switzerland via Dover; 895 tons of French onions were shipped into Weymouth and 117 tons of Dutch onions were unloaded at Brentford docks. And all of this was taken forward by GWR special trains. Britain was still able to import fuel oil at this stage: 16,070 tons of it was unloaded at Avonmouth in March and taken away by the GWR.

On 11 April a dinner was held in honour of the retiring Chief Signal & Telegraph Engineer of the GWR, Mr Page. The venue was, of course, the Great Western Royal Hotel. The Chairman of the occasion was the Assistant General Manager of the railway, Mr Keith Grand. No members of the GWR Board attended as it was a Chief Officers' tribute to Mr Page. In attendance were the Superintendent of the Line, Gilbert Matthews, the Chief Civil Engineer, Mr Quartermaine, CBE, Chief Goods Manager, David Blee, Chief Accountant, C.B. Dashwood, OBE, and the Company Secretary, Mr F.R.E. Davis, along with six other 'Chiefs' of Departments. Sir James Milne was not there, but he was likely to have had a very good reason for his absence.

At 6.30 p.m. on 13 April a schoolboy, one Norman Plested, was walking along the railway line near Wheatley when he came across a gap in the crown of the rail. A 4¾in-long section of the top of the rail had fallen out. He raced back to the village, to the house of his next-door neighbour Mr Smith, who was a lengthman for that stretch of line. Mr Smith immediately went outside, got on his bike, and pedalled hard to the signal box and warned the signalman, before cycling more steadily back into the village to fetch his Ganger. Back to the station they went, collected a length of rail, put it on their four-wheeled trolley and, with the key token for the single track, went out to replace the rail.

A report was sent to the Chief Engineer of the GWR, A.S. Quartermaine. He sent a memo to the General Manager, suggesting that 'although Master Plested was in fact trespassing, in view of the serious consequence for the next train had he not been there, I think that two guineas would be a suitable gratuity'. Milne halved that – Norman received one guinea. The Ganger and lengthman each received the same and were paid at overtime rate for the hours they put in repairing the track.

The General Manager published a 'thank you' message to all GWR employees in the March/April combined edition of the *Great Western Railway Magazine*:

A Message to the Staff from
Sir James Milne, K.C.V.O., C.S.I., General Manager

We of the Great Western will not easily forget the trials of those recent weeks – the blizzard itself, the existing scarcities it aggravated, the new privations and disruption it caused and the long, hard battle to restore vital communications and services.

I wish to thank everybody and most sincerely, Great Western staff of every rank and grade for the virile and resourceful way in which they won back their track, length by length, so that the nation could resume its business and, above all, so that top priority traffic – coal trains by the hundred – could be kept moving.

Breakaway trains

Forty-four goods trains broke apart in April. Nine of them were GWR wagons, including three goods brake vans whose massive 'Instanter' links gave way. Two were due to draw hooks breaking and one was a drawbar parting. Sixteen were LMS wagons, their faults including one broken hook and three drawbars breaking – one was pulled out through the wooden headstock. Five of these mishaps were on LNER wagons: one of them was caused by a broken draw hook, and three SR couplings broke. Eleven Private Owner couplings failed, the causes including four draw hooks and two drawbars. Mileage run by goods trains in April was 1,670,847.

The train crews and signalmen dealt with all the incidents routinely but there are a couple of incidents worth describing. At 9.50 a.m. on 24 April the 4.40 a.m. Avonmouth–Severn Tunnel Junction entered the east end of the tunnel. The train of fifty-four wagons was hauled by two engines: GWR 2-6-2 tank engine No 3182, with

Driver Baker and Fireman Jones of Severn Tunnel shed and, as Pilot, No 3181, a Newton Abbot engine driven by O. Dodd of Severn Tunnel shed. The guard of the train was H. Rathbone of Severn Tunnel station.

Working a loose-coupled, un-braked goods train through the 7,668yd of the Severn Tunnel was a matter of great skill. From the east end the tracks fall at 1 in 100 for exactly 2 miles – 3,520yd – the track is then a dead level for 12 chains – 264yd – and then rises at 1 in 90 for 2.2 miles – 3,884yd. A quarter of a mile before the start of the level track there was a white light fixed to the wall of the tunnel about 3ft 6in above rail level, and 40yd before the end of the level section there were two white lights, one above the other.

I have travelled through the Severn Tunnel on the footplate of a '28xx' hauling seventy loose-coupled, empty 16-ton coal wagons, un-braked. I made a tape recording of the transit. We rolled out of the goods loop at the east end by gravity and entered the tunnel freewheeling with the guard's handbrake applied with the intention of keeping the wagons' coupling chains drawn taut. After a mile, judged by the driver in total darkness, he put on steam and began to draw the engine away from the train and thus make it a certainty that the couplings were drawn out. When the engine was pulling hard the guard got the benefit of the exhaust fumes from the engine's chimney. This is why GWR guards' vans were built with only one entrance. The other end was a solid wooden wall, with a window, the theory being that, on trains going through any tunnel, the blank end of the van was facing the smoke. It was a nice idea but of course it could not always work.

By the time the engine passed the first white light the train was going quite fast. I cannot say how fast, but the rapid clanking of the crosshead on the slide bars – and anything else in the axle boxes or side rods that was slack – echoing off the tunnel wall, sounded like being inside a belfry when the bells were being rung by lunatics; and to judge speed was difficult. If the rear part of a long train still had the wagons running with couplings slack then the train started to go uphill, those wagons would run back the length allowed by the slack coupling and there would be a heavy tug from the forward moving front part. This could break a link or a hook. A train of un-braked, loose-coupled wagons was an unruly assembly that always needed very careful handling wherever it was running.

The 4.40 a.m. Avonmouth passed the Intermediate Block Home signal, 1 mile inside the tunnel, at 9.52 a.m.

Guard Rathbone was in his van in total darkness – unless one counts the little light of the burning wick of his railway-issue hand lamp. He could hear – and feel – the steady click-click-click of the wheels of his van over the rail joints, the rumble of the train and the resounding bark from two engines' chimneys. The thick clouds of fumes from the two engines were rolling back over him. Freight guards through the tunnel – or any long tunnel for that matter – needed to keep calm and not worry about suffocating, and had to keep their wits about them, and use all their instincts and experience to guard the train.

Rathbone realised that his end of the train had broken away when the rhythmic click of the wheels began to slow down while the double gunfire sound of the engines grew fainter. He screwed down his handbrake as tight as he could and when he was certain that he had come to a stand he got down, carrying his hand lamp, and walked across the Up Main to locate and break the tell-tale wire.[2] With the tell-tale bells ringing in the East and West boxes no train would be allowed into the tunnel until the situation within the tunnel was known. That was at 10.08 a.m.

Next Rathbone went back into the 'six-foot' – the space between the two tracks, in order to assess the situation. How many wagons had he in front of his van? Were they all standing correctly on the rails and was the opposite track clear or was it obstructed? He walked forwards counting, until he reached the further end of the line of wagons. From there he stepped across the Down Main, into a footpath set against the wall of the tunnel, until he reached the next telephone.

There were eight telephones in man-sized recesses on the Downside through the tunnel. He found telephone No 5 and rang in at 10.19 a.m. He was 2 miles from the western end of the tunnel – the breakaway had taken place as the wagon passed off the level and started up the gradient. The signalman in West box answered the phone and Rathbone reported: 'Guard of 4.40 Avonmouth. I'm stationary at phone number 5. I've seven wagons and my van. All wagons on the rails. Up line clear.'

At 10.31 a.m. the two engines with forty-seven wagons in tow passed Severn Tunnel West box. The signalman shouted to the men as they passed that they had left eight wagons behind. The train was diverted into the yard at Severn Tunnel station.

The Pilning Junction Inspector, riding on a light engine which had been standing at Pilning, entered the east end of the tunnel under the provisions of Regulation 14A, at 10.35 a.m. The men on the engine knew the rear part of the train was in advance of the double white lights so they could go on for 2 miles at a reasonable pace and then they would be looking out for the triple red lights facing them from the rear of the guard's van. The engine buffered up and propelled the eight wagons uphill, passing Tunnel West signal box at 11.11a.m. Tunnel West sent, 'Train out of Section at 11.11 a.m.' to Tunnel East box and the tunnel was then ready for business as usual.

During April one passenger train, one milk train, and one parcels train had breakaway problems. On 5 April the 8.48 Fishguard–Paddington parcels train was brought to a stand by signals at Standish Junction. The engine was an LMS 'Black 5' No 5442 with eighteen vehicles for 499 tons behind the tender. The driver was Boyle of Gloucester shed. On starting the coupling broke between an LMS parcel van and a GWR 'Fruit C' van. The latter also lost its vacuum pipe. The wagons were re-coupled using the other vehicle's shackle and the train went on to Stroud with the vacuum brake working on the first fourteen vehicles. At Stroud the parcels van and the fruit van were put off and the 'Black 5' blasted away towards Sapperton bank and Swindon, causing 23 minutes' delay.

The one passenger train that broke away in April was the 10.15 a.m. Swansea–Sheffield. On 27 April a GWR engine brought the train – five coaches – into Swindon and then uncoupled and went to the shed. An LNER 'B1' class engine, No 1088, was standing on the Engine Line alongside No 8 Platform with a restaurant car attached. The driver was Aston from Sheffield, an LNER man with a large knowledge of routes. The 'B1' was used to carry out the shunting moves in order to fit the restaurant car into the train, second from the engine. The LNER coaches were all fitted with the automatic 'buckeye' couplings but the gravity pin did not drop down into position to support the massive casting forming the coupler. When the train started, the couplers parted and the vacuum pipes of both coaches were ripped apart. Two new ones were fitted and the train left, 14 minutes late.

On 30 April the 6.20 p.m. Penzance–Paddington milk train was turned off the main line at Hanwell to go up to the Birmingham–Paddington line at Greenford. The load was eighteen wagons, made up of vans and tankers, a gross tonnage of 501 hauled by an 0-6-0 pannier tank No 3727, driven by Harper of Southall shed. The train was brought to a stand at Greenford South Loop Junction, awaiting 'Line Clear' from East Loop box and on restarting the coupling broke between the sixteenth and seventeenth wagon. The train being fitted with the automatic vacuum brakes throughout, it stopped immediately. The vehicles were re-coupled and proceeded to Paddington with the last tanker and the eight-wheeled guard's van at the rear. The incident had been dealt with in 19 minutes.

Cup Final Day in 1947 was 26 April. Burnley were playing Charlton Athletic. The 7.25 a.m. Shrewsbury–Paddington express was going to be packed leaving Shrewsbury – with passengers from Chester and Birkenhead joining the Shrewsbury crowds – and then there was the stop at Wellington before Wolverhampton. The crowd was getting larger on Birmingham Snow Hill platform. A Relief train was therefore arranged – at a moment's notice – from Snow Hill at 8.50 a.m. and to run 'Right Away' to Paddington. The signalmen would fit it into the scheduled train service. The train came 'empty coaches' from Cannock Road sidings – thirteen coaches for 364 tons tare, hauled by No 4945 *Milligan Hall*. In charge of the train was Guard R. Stirzaker, aged 61, for thirty-seven years a passenger train guard on the Great Western Railway.[3] The driver was Harold Turvey, stationed at Wolverhampton (Stafford Road), while the fireman's name is not given.

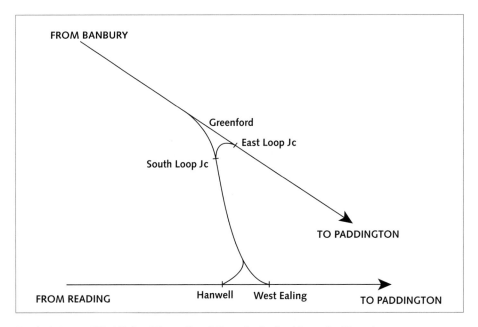

Tracks between West Ealing/Hanwell and Greenford – the 'Greenford Loop'.

They set off on time and were booked to pass Leamington at 9.19 a.m. – 29 minutes for 23¼ miles. A large crowd of football supporters was on the platform at Leamington. They had bought tickets – expecting, as a matter of course, that the GWR would be running a train for them, and were now anxiously expecting a train to magically appear. The Station Master got permission from Control to stop the 8.50 Relief. The train stopped at 9.22 a.m., by Guard Stirzaker's log, and the waiting throng swarmed aboard. Stirzaker reckoned he had 400 passengers on board when they left Leamington at 9.25 a.m. The weight behind the engine was about 400 tons as they set out on the 12-mile uphill slog to the summit beyond Fenny Compton. The load limit for a 'Hall' on this section – set before the war when engines were in better condition – was 420 tons.

Fosse Road signal box was about 3¾ miles out of Leamington, roughly in the middle of a 1 in 187 rising gradient. In charge was a 'temporary signalman', 23-year-old Roger Griffin. He had been a signalman for three months. As the train passed, he was looking towards the engine and saw 'that the third coach from the engine appeared to be bumping and that small splinters of wood were flying off what I thought was the footboard'. He sent the 'Stop & Examine' signal, seven bells, at 9.32 a.m. to Southam Road & Harbury signal box. The 'bumping' was because the trailing wheel-set of the rear bogie of that coach had become derailed as he watched. The wheel-set re-railed when it encountered the points trailing into the Up Main from Fosse Road Up Goods Loop: they had been derailed for 37yd.

Griffin had informed Southam Road signalman why he had sent the seven bells signal, and the Station Master there was informed. When the train arrived the latter went onto the track to the rear bogie of the third coach – No 1461, a GWR third-class corridor carriage. Guard Stirzaker got down to join him and a Birmingham signalman, 29-year-old Hughie Leonard, working as a Ticket Collector for the day, had also come to look.

Here is Guard Stirzaker's statement:

When I reached the third vehicle from the engine – corridor 3rd No 1461 – the damaged wheel had already been discovered. I was able to observe that the wooden wheel centre near the axle was flaking but it was not broken through and the wheels were on the rail. I had by then been told that the wheels had been off the road at Fosse Road. I decided that the vehicle would be detached and placed in the Up Refuge siding. The signalman set the road and the setting back movement commenced. As soon as the defective wheel reached the barrow crossing, the wheel collapsed and the bogie derailed.

The Up Main was blocked at 9.50 a.m. Ten coaches were north of the barrow crossing and three, with the crippled coach at the rear, were on the south side. The procedures for opening single-line working (SLW) were set in motion and the Banbury 36-ton steam crane and breakdown vans were called up at 9.55 a.m. Signalman/Temporary Ticket Collector Leonard was appointed pilotman. He walked south to Greaves Siding signal box, three-quarters of a mile further south, towards Banbury, where the 7.5 a.m. Paddington train was being held. Leonard issued the Greaves Siding signalman with an

Coach 1456, built in 1937, one of the same batch to which No 1461 belonged.

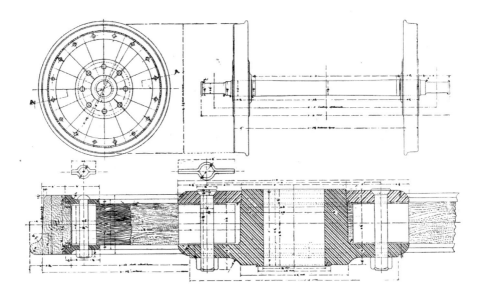

Showing how segments of teak formed the central web of the wheel.

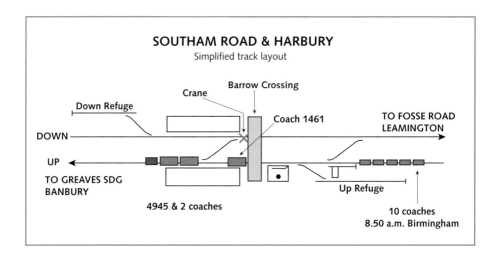

SOUTHAM ROAD & HARBURY
Simplified track layout

Barrow Crossing

Crane

Down Refuge

Coach 1461

TO FOSSE ROAD
LEAMINGTON

DOWN

UP

TO GREAVES SDG
BANBURY

Up Refuge

4945 & 2 coaches

10 coaches
8.50 a.m. Birmingham

SLW form. From then until the form was cancelled, no Down train could leave Greaves unless the pilotman was present in the signal box to permit it. Leonard set off 'right road' for Fosse Road on the locomotive of the 7.5 a.m. Paddington train at 10.20 a.m. At Southam he issued the Station Master and signalman with an SLW certificate and again at Fosse Road he issued Griffin with his certificate to establish SLW. Now Up trains could travel over the Down line to Greaves *provided* that the pilotman was at Fosse Road to permit the movement.

The 7.25 a.m. Shrewsbury–Paddington had followed the 8.50 a.m. Birmingham train from Birmingham, and had been standing at Fosse Road for 95 minutes when Hughie Leonard boarded the locomotive of that train to conduct it over the Down Main to rejoin the Up Main at Greaves Siding crossover.

On the 8.50 Birmingham train Stirzaker was well aware of the rising panic of the football crowd on his train: would they get to Wembley in time? He suggested to Station Master Jones that the 7.25 be stopped at Southam to take on board as many as possible of the very anxious crowd. About 400 were crammed into the 7.25 Shrewsbury train which set off at 11 a.m., leaving ninety on the 8.50 Birmingham train, of whom forty-five were football fans. Stirzaker calmed them somewhat by telling them that he would arrange for the train to stop at South Ruislip, where they could get the Underground to Wembley and the stadium. Driver Turvey was informed as well as Station Master Jones. The latter got in touch with London Control and informed them of what had been decided.

But until coach 1461 could be moved into the Refuge siding the 8.50 Birmingham train could not go anywhere. The coach, built in 1937 weighed 32 tons, but 10 tons of that was made up by the two bogies.[4] The trailing wheel-set of the trailing bogie was of Mansell's design dating from the 1880–90s. There were still approximately 2,000 of these in use on the GWR in 1947 according to the GWR report into this incident. This old wheel-set was in good order and would have been put on while the standard wheel-set was originally sent away for re-profiling of the tyre.

The Banbury-based 36-ton steam crane and breakdown vans, ordered at 9.55 a.m., arrived at 11.24. They were accompanied by the pilotman, who would have had to stay at the station while it occupied the Down Main line. It had taken 90 minutes for the crew to gather, to find an engine and travel 13½ miles to Southam. The train was 'Breakdown vans going to clear the line' and was signalled as an express train – four bells – with a 'box to box' message giving the emergency purpose and destination. The breakdown van crew – as always – were experienced locomotive mechanics with a Foreman mechanic in charge of the operation. At the scene of an incident his word was law above all other ranks.

What followed was a splendid piece of practical railway work rapidly carried out, although not as fast as is stated in the official report. I have to make educated guesses of timings because the times given in the report do not make sense. At just about 11.30 a.m. the crane came alongside the crippled coach on the Down Main and the foreman, having looked at the job, formed his plan.

The rear end of the coach was lifted by the crane high enough to disengage the pivot from the bearing at the centre of the bogie frame. To attach the lifting gear below the buffers and make the hoist, and to move the carriage clear of the bogie using the crane, took until about 11.40. A platelayer's trolley was placed on the track underneath the coach with slabs of timber on the bed of the trolley to raise the height and the coach body was lowered onto the trolley. The time was now about 11.50 a.m.

The GWR report states that the bogie was not clear of the Up Main until 1.50 p.m. Guard Stirzaker had stated that his train left at 11.54 and the Station Master stated that it left at 12 noon. Until the bogie was removed from the Up Main the crippled coach could not be reversed off the Up Main into the siding, nor could the 8.50 Birmingham train leave.

Stirzaker states that the train arrived at South Ruislip at 1.29. So taking 1.29 p.m. as a correct time, I guess that once the coach was resting on the trolley, the bogie was lifted by the crane onto the grass bank on the Upside by 12 noon. The report states that the engine and two coaches now dropped back down onto the cripple and all three coaches were moved with extreme care into the Up Refuge. The passengers had gone away earlier on the 7.25 Shrewsbury train. The crane meanwhile was placed inside the Down Refuge. Engine 4945 dropped onto its train coupled to the leading coach, which was uncoupled from the rest, drew forward and placed it in the Up Refuge. The nine-coach train was then drawn forwards, clear of the crossover, reversed onto the Down Main and, with the pilotman on the footplate, departed for Greaves Sidings and London. I suggest departure time was 12.15 p.m.

At Greaves Siding, three-quarters of a mile away, the train stopped to let the pilotman off. At 12.20 the train crossed to the Up Main and away to London, stopping at South Ruislip at 1.29 as stated by Stirzaker. According to my more realistic timings No 4945 covered 71 miles in 69 minutes, giving an average of 61.7mph. It was an exciting dash to get forty fans to Wembley for the Cup Final kick-off.

Delays were:

Up Trains

8.50	Birmingham–Paddington	160 minutes
7.25	Shrewsbury–Paddington	95 minutes
8.42	Wolverhampton–Oxford	82 minutes
9.30	Shrewsbury–Paddington	48 minutes
9.55	Leamington–Banbury	155 minutes

Down Trains

7.5	Paddington	30 minutes
8.10	Paddington	40 minutes
9.10	Paddington	35 minutes
9.45	Paddington	20 minutes
11.10	Paddington	25 minutes

And Charlton Athletic beat Burnley one goal to nil.

On Monday 28 April the 2.20 p.m. Talyllyn–Moat Lane goods train was derailed at Llanidloes station at 8.5 p.m. The train consisted of the twenty-six wagons, four loaded, including the Bristol–Welshpool 'Station Truck' coupled next to the tender of 'Dean Goods' 0-6-0 tender engine No 2382. Station Trucks carried perishable or easily damaged items, for instance delicate groceries, cakes or wines, from a large centre to rural stations. The train crew were Driver A. Evans and Fireman A.G. Humphreys and Guard W.A. Freeman, all stationed at Moat Lane. Driver Evans was 47 years old with 31 years' service, 9 years as a driver. Fireman Humphreys was aged 25, with 9 years' service, 6½ of those years as a fireman. The guard was 49 years old, with 32 years' railway service including 4 years as a Goods Guard. Evans and Freeman were both ex-Cambrian Railway employees.

Evans and Humphreys had booked on at Moat Lane at 1 p.m. and worked the 2.40 Moat Lane passenger train, calling at all stations to Brecon, as far as Rhayader: nine stops and 21½ miles from Moat Lane. That included climbing Pantydwr bank – 7¼ miles of 1 in 60 and 1 in 80 on a serpentine road. They got to Rhayader at 3.35 p.m., handed over their engine and train to Brecon men and took their ease until the 2.20 p.m. Talyllyn Junction–Moat Lane goods train arrived at around 5.30 p.m. It seems likely to me that they would have strolled to some favourite place of refreshment during this interval.

Guard Freeman had booked on at 2.15 p.m. and, after working some other train, took charge of the 6 p.m. Moat Lane–Brecon goods train arriving at Rhayader at 7 p.m. The 2.20 p.m. Talyllyn goods train was waiting for him, all shunting completed. He had a look around his train. There was no wagon to be put off at Llanidloes so he hoped there was no wagon to pick up at that place and that they could look forward to a non-stop run home to Moat Lane. Then he opened the Station Truck and saw that there was one package for Llanidloes – a bale of paper, 20in x 15in x 8in, and weighing 91lb.

This weighty – and disappointing – package constituted a considerable nuisance in the eyes of Mr Freeman and the footplatemen too. The problem was that the train had to stop at Pantydwr Stop Board, 7 miles beyond Rhayader, at the top of the 1 in 80 and 1 in 60 hill, which was continuous to Llanidloes station platform. Brakes would be pinned down at the Stop Board and in order to unpin them it was necessary for the train to draw past Llanidloes platform so that the guard could lay his hand on the wagons' handbrakes. They would have to run through beyond the platform so that Freeman would have space to release the handbrake levers. But then the train would have to reverse back to the platform so that the 91lb bale could be easily lifted out onto a two-wheeled trolley.

This would mean more delay. The less delay at Llanidloes, the better chance they would have of getting through to Moat Lane before the 8.10 p.m. Moat Lane–Llanidloes passenger train wanted the single line. If they could only be quick they would get finished at Moat Lane early. It did not occur to Mr Freeman that he could use the 'off-side' handbrake levers to pin down the wagon brakes. If he had done so the train could then have stopped at the platform and he would have space in the 'six-foot' to unpin the brakes.

Surely the best thing to do would be for Fireman Humphreys to take the package on the engine and hand it off to the porter (whose name was Jack) at Llanidloes, since they went through at walking speed.

The 2.20 Talyllyn Junction goods train ran past Llanidloes platform at 4mph. Porter Jack was waiting on the platform to receive the package. Fireman Humphreys struggled with it, positioning it in the gap between the engine and the tender. He squatted, grabbed hold with both arms around it and stood up. But there was no way that he could hold out a weight of 91lb so that Jack could take it. He half threw it, half let it go. The package bounced against the platform edge and fell onto the track. There was a lurching and bumping. The Station Truck and the empty cattle truck behind were dragged over it and derailed. 'Whoa!' shouted Humphreys. Driver Evans brought the train gently to a stand 90yd further on. It was 8.4 p.m.

The breakdown vans were called at 8.40 p.m. when it became clear that the locals could not get the wagons back on. The vans arrived from Oswestry at 11.21 p.m. and the wagons were re-railed at 2 a.m. Evans and Humphreys had then to work the train home.

On 29 August the 12.40 a.m. Park Royal–Worcester via Thame goods train with forty-six wagons, including the 20-ton GWR brake van No 68624, was stopped at Saunderton's Down Home signal at 'Danger' at 3 a.m. The engine was No 4991 *Cobham Hall*, with Driver Harris of Oxford shed. The guard was R.J. Andrews of Acton.

Why was the train stopped *outside* the protection of the Home signal? When a signalman does not 'have the road ahead' for a train, the safe and usual course is to 'bring it inside the Home signal'. That is, to stop it at the Starting with the Home at 'Danger', thus protecting the rear of the train. Thinking as an ex-signalman, it is very likely that the signalman was asleep – and the 3 a.m. time is very significant in that respect. He had given 'Line Clear' to West Wycombe for the train to approach, taken the 'Train entering Section' bell and went to sleep immediately afterwards. It is not an unknown occurrence. The effect was that Driver Harris would blow the engine's whistle for the signal without effect and would then send his fireman to the signal box to remind the signalman that they are standing there (Rule 55), and thus the signalman is woken.

The fireman then walks back and reports to his driver, in a few choice words, and he, feeling indignant, starts his train a bit sharply. This is merely an educated guess.

To return to facts. The starting 'tug' broke the brake van's 'Instanter' coupling. Driver Andrews went on his way with forty-five wagons without looking back to see if he had all his train – signified by a white light waved at him from the brake van, which was now standing forty-six wagons' lengths plus the length of the engine and tender outside the protection of the Home signal.

The Saunderton signalman saw that the brake van was missing and, knowing that there was a falling gradient towards West Wycombe, he sent 2-5-5 'Train Running away in Wrong Direction' to West Wycombe and seven bells – 'Stop & Examine' – to Princes Risborough South, 3 miles further on.

Guard Andrews now walked back to protect his van, which was an obstruction on the Down Main. He carried his hand lamp with the red shade over the flame and five detonators – exploding 'Danger' signals – in his pocket (railwaymen called these signals 'shots'). After a quarter of a mile he put down one on the crown of the rail, securing it by wrapping the two lead straps around the head of the rail. He walked on another quarter of a mile and put down another shot. At three-quarters of a mile he put down three shots, 10yd apart. According to the report he walked on to West Wycombe box, 2¾ miles, to see if an engine could be sent from High Wycombe to clear his brake van from the Down Main. That seems an odd thing to do, when Saunderton box was much closer.

At about the time he was putting down the three shots, his train was turning into the Platform Loop at Princes Risborough South box. The obvious course of action was then taken. The engine crossed to the Up line and ran back to West Wycombe, expecting to collect the guard and the three shots on the way. The engine and the walking guard arrived at West Wycombe together. The engine crossed to the Down line and, with Guard Andrews on the footplate, went into the section and propelled the van through to the rear of its train at Princes Risborough. The section was clear and ready for traffic at 4.40 a.m.

Notes

1   As a matter of historic fact, the model of so-called 'Stephenson's *Locomotion No 1*' shows the engine after it had been rebuilt by Timothy Hackworth. The George Stephenson original engine suffered a boiler explosion, wrecking the entire engine. Hackworth rebuilt it and incorporated his inventions of the coupling rod between driving wheels, which were also Hackworth's design, and also a properly designed blast pipe to draw up the fire which the original had not possessed.

2   Throughout the length of the tunnel there was a wire carrying an electric current – the 'tell-tale'. It was carried along the brick wall, 5ft above the floor. In the event of a train stopping in the tunnel, the guard of the train would locate this with his hand lamp light and break it with his hand, and this would at once start a warning bell ringing in the signal boxes at each end of the tunnel.

3   See 'October' chapter, the 7.10 a.m. Wolverhampton.

4   Pictorial Record *Great Western Coaches*, p. 225.

GREAT WESTERN RAILWAY
MAGAZINE

MAY & JUNE · 1947

VOLUME 59 · NO. 4

Pride in the Job—3
(See Page 81)

PRICE ONE PENNY

MAY

GWR Clubs and Societies and Getting New Business

Thirteen directors were present with Lord Portal in the Chair for the meeting on 23 May. Their first resolution (Minute No 3) was to approve the expenditure of £540 as the company's contribution to £1,040 for the restoration of the GWR Staff sports fields, athletic ground and tennis courts at Castle Bar, West Ealing. The Club was founded in 1900 by the GWR directors at a cost of £1,000 for a grand pavilion – beside the acres of green sward accommodating the cricket and football pitches and tennis courts. In 1912 a house was built there for the groundsman and his family. It was all placed on GWR land, latterly used for the convalescence of sick GWR cart horses. There was more ground than the horses needed and seventeen acres was turned over to the sports ground. Four silver cups were donated by the then General Manager, Mr Wilkinson, for boating, swimming, cricket and football. In 1929 the new pavilion had a bar, a lounge, a restaurant, badminton court and table-tennis room and a large hall for dancing, amateur dramatics, choral evenings, symphony concerts and concerts by silver bands, catering for all the very civilised and intellectual pursuits which GWR employees of all grades provided for their colleagues. GWR Castle Bar was probably the finest works recreation centre in the London area.

During the Second World War the ground was cratered by a land mine. Now the directors agreed to 're-plan and refurbish the ground, providing a six-rink bowling green, ten tennis courts, a croquet green, two cricket pitches, three hockey pitches, two soccer pitches and a rugby pitch'.

The annual London cart horse parade took place in Regent's Park on 26 May. All seven of the GWR horse teams entered were awarded the first prize in their respective classes.

In May the Assistant General Manager of the Great Western, Keith Grand, was summoned to the Embassy of the United States of America, and there was presented with President Roosevelt's 'Medal of Freedom with Bronze Palm' by the American Ambassador, His Excellency Mr Lewis Douglas.

The Great Western employed around 113,000 men and women in the vast triangle of its territory from Paddington to Birkenhead, Afon Wen, Weymouth and Penzance. Forty thousand employees had enrolled in the Great Western Railway Staff Association (GWRSA), which was an 'umbrella' organisation for canteens at depots, GWR football teams, rugby and cricket teams, as well as operatic societies, amateur dramatics, tennis, darts and the GWR Golfing Society. GWRSA branches had monthly

Mr K.W.C. Grand receives the Medal of Freedom with Bronze Palm.

GWR rugby.

THE first meeting of the Newport division women's section since the war resulted in the election of the following officers:—Mrs. A. Collier, Hirwaun, chairman; Mrs. R. C. Dyer, Newport, secretary, and Mrs. Netherton, Aberdare, treasurer. Delegates later took tea, served by Mrs. Holman and Mrs. Sims, of Newport women's committee.

SLOUGH retired section met in strength to wish Godspeed to Mr. G. R. Ellis, a former section chairman, who is sailing to Australia. Mr. Sellers, chairman, handed him a case of pipes, and Mr. G. Triscott, M.B.E., presented a wallet and a purse on behalf of the London divisional council. Formerly a foreman in the locomotive department at Slough, Mr. Ellis retired in 1942, and was a

(*Above*) ALL-LINE RUGBY FINAL BETWEEN ABERBEEG AND GLOUCESTER. (*Right*) ABERBEEG WINS THE CUP. (*Below*) THE TWO TEAMS IN THE MEMORABLE FINAL.

meetings for socialising and Grand Annual Dinners. Retired members of staff retained their membership of the GWRSA. The Cardiff branch had a Retired Members' Choir.

Footplatemen took a profound interest in their work. Most engine sheds had a 'Mutual Improvement Class' where experienced drivers gave weekly lessons to any member of the loco staff on the technicalities of driving, firing, and how the locomotive and its brakes worked. Sometimes the classroom was a grounded coach body, and sometimes the lessons were given at a driver's home. The 'MIC' was entirely a voluntary activity, and for some instructing was their hobby. The GWR had no official part in the proceedings which were supported by the time and money of the men. Some engine sheds had a model engineering society: drivers, firemen and boiler smiths made miniature coal-fired locomotives which they ran on miniature tracks in municipal parks and/or the grounds of stately mansions.

With 113,000 employees the company employed an army of intelligent, ingenious and variously talented people. Mr C.R. Pearce, Chief Docks Supervisor at Plymouth, built and played pedal-pumped organs from scratch. He had a three-manual thirty-nine stops instrument at his home and built a large electrically blown and electrically operated keyboard action for a church in London. In between making these he built 500ft of model railway with all points and signals electrically operated from a miniature lever frame.[1]

The Great Western ran through South Wales and up into the Valleys where music, song and poetry were as natural as breathing. All over Great Western territory there

The GWR organ builder and musician.

What is Your Hobby?

GREAT WESTERN MODELLIST, ALDERMAN AND ORGAN BUILDER TELL THEIRS

READERS have quickly responded to our query last month: "What is your hobby?" We print below the accounts of three contrasted pursuits. This new feature in the *Magazine* is specially meant for readers' own contributions. What about YOURS? Even if your hobby is not quite so ambitious as those recounted here, we are still interested, and so may your fellow readers be. Glance through last month's article again, and see what you can do about it.

• • •

MANY men specialise in a single branch of model making, but MR. R. E. WICKS, a checker in Paddington goods, who won the premier award at the Arts & Crafts Exhibition this year, prefers to range a wide field. He makes many types of models with equal skill, and on occasion has moved out of the miniature class to build furniture for use in his own home.

At Hayes, Middlesex, this genial 18-stone railwayman pursues his hobby in a workshop he also built himself. His fine selection of tools includes a home-made metal cutting jigsaw. While working, Mr. Wicks entertains his faithful audience—neighbours' children who squeeze into the workshop to appraise the models taking shape before their fascinated gaze. And the questions they ask—!

Youth at the Helm

On his sixth birthday young Master Wicks made his first model—a ship. Since then he has built 39 galleons. The latest, the *Lion*, a full-rigged colourful beauty of 1747, was fashioned from blitzed roof timbers, and exhibited at the Arts & Crafts Exhibition, with his model of No. 1005, *County of Devon* locomotive, emerging from a tunnel.

During the war Mr. Wicks gave much of his output to charitable causes. A galleon, *Prince*, raised £90 for H.M.S. *Suffolk* Comforts Fund. When he presented a model aeroplane to the R.A.F. Spitfire Benevolent Fund, the earflaps of the pilot's helmet were two grains of rice, varnished and joined by a thread.

Modellists are severely handicapped to-day by scarcity of materials; plywood, glass beads, perspex and whipcord are particularly difficult to obtain. Fortunately, Mr. Wicks brings a philosophic attitude to this problem. A friend's remark that Mr. Wicks' hobby must require extraordinary patience prompted the reply from the modellist: "I think it takes much more patience to sit still and do nothing!"

IN September ALDERMAN W. H. VAUGHAN announced his retirement from the Port Talbot Council after 20 years' unbroken service. "Labour Party colleagues and opposition members," said the *Port Talbot Guardian*, "all praised his services and expressed regret in his decision".

Mr. Vaughan is a goods guard at Duffryn Yard, who began his railway career in 1908. He has devoted much time and energy to public service.

Elected an Alderman in 1939, he was Mayor of Port Talbot in 1941-42; as chairman of the local electricity committee he is largely responsible for the electrical development scheme which is now being considered by the Commissioners.

In political life Mr. Vaughan numbers Cabinet Ministers among his personal friends. An active member of the executive of the Aberavon Divisional Labour Party since 1926, he has been agent to Mr. W. G. Cove, M.P., since 1934. He has worked tirelessly in the promotion of Agriculture in South Wales, and was awarded the gold medal of the National Union of Agricultural Workers. A member of several county committees, Mr. Vaughan was appointed as one of the three Welsh representatives on the Forestry Commission. During the war he was on the Court of Referees and Employment Committees, and head A.R.P. warden.

MR. W. H. VAUGHAN.

One night in 1936 Mr. Vaughan found a severely injured man lying on the track, having been run down by a train. Single handed he improvised dressings and apparatus and treated the patient until he could be taken to hospital. As a result of his skilled handling of the emergency Mr. Vaughan was awarded the First Aid Gold Medal.

Pipe Organ Installed in a Bungalow

MR. C. R. PEARCE, chief docks supervisor, Plymouth Docks, a church organist since the age of 13, writes:—

Being very keen on the actual working and construction of organs, I started in 1929 to build a 3-manual and pedal organ in my home (then at St. Germans). It consisted of 39 stops, and the idea was always to build an electric action different from orthodox practice. The console (keyboards) was in the sitting room and the organ and accessories, electric relays and electric blowing in a cellar underneath the dining room; the sound rose through a grille in the floor and through swell shutters in the door to the cellar.

In 1940, when appointed organist at Saltash Wesley Church, I removed my home, and as it seemed impossible to accommodate the organ in a bungalow I sold all the organ except the console. The remote relay boards, containing about 200 magnets and 2,000 contacts, were subsequently used in a church organ somewhere in or near London. The console remained at Saltash for a time, while I built an extensive 4 mm. scale model railway with about 500 feet of track, 40 sets of points, and electrically operated, including the points and signals.

Now the organ has started to come into being again, in 2-manual and pedal form (28 stops) built on the extension principle, with the console in the sitting room and the organ in the loft with a grille in the ceiling.

Owing to the lack of certain material, the old slogan, "necessity is the mother of invention," has proved its truth. All magnets, relay switches, contact frames, etc.,

Oxford drivers and firemen, all members of the Mutual Improvement Class, at the presentation of a shield to Driver Albert King in 1948. He, and the large man standing next to him, Driver Algy Hunt, were instrumental in forming the National Federation of Mutual Improvement Classes. The man on the left, wearing a trilby, is Reg Brown, Shed Foreman on that shift. Albert retired at this point to take a teaching position at Ruskin College, Oxford.

Viscount Portal sits next to the Lady Mayoress of Reading. Edric Cundell sits on her left. Sir Edward Cadogan, a GWR Director, sits on the left of the picture.

were employees who formed theatre groups, choirs, orchestras, silver and brass bands, and there were virtuoso solo singers, players of instruments, poets and artists.

The GWR Paddington Silver Band regularly played their music on 'The Lawn' at Paddington. On any other railway the space behind the buffers at a great terminal station was a 'Circulating area' or maybe 'The Concourse' but on the Gentlemen's Railway, the area at the bottom of the steps leading up into the Great Western Royal Hotel was – 'The Lawn'. And behind the music of the band, the buffer stops and the hiss of steam, the echoing sound of a whistle, or, from the far end of the platform, the gunshot exhaust of a locomotive starting, a heavy train blended in as the perfect accompaniment.

There was so much musical and other talent that, starting in 1927, an annual festival was organised. From 1932 it was held annually in Reading town hall. No festival had

" The Rebel Maid "

FIRST POST-WAR PRODUCTION BY THE G.W.R. (LONDON) OPERATIC SOCIETY

A SCENE DURING THE FIRST ACT OF " THE REBEL MAID " AT THE SCALA THEATRE, LONDON.

The Rebel Maid was a favourite play for keen amateur thespians. GWR productions had a great many in the chorus because there were so many who wanted to take part!

Driver Alex Kerley, playing the euphonium virtuoso piece *La Belle Americaine* at the Alexandra Palace studios.

by courtesy of the BBC.

MR. ALEXANDER KERLEY GOES ON THE AIR.

been held from 1939 to 1946 – but through the last week in March 1947 the Great Western Railway Festival of Music and Drama took place again – the seventeenth and the last.

The venue was the town hall in Reading. The Festival was opened by the Lady Mayor, Phoebe Cusden, supported by the directors and chief officers of the company.[2] The competitive events, and performances of choirs, orchestras and soloists, went on

Mr Edric Cundell, Principal of the Guildhall School of Music and Honorary Director of Music for the GWR Staff Association.

for six days from a 10 a.m. start until late into the evening. Different chief officers presided over the morning, afternoon and evening sessions. The adjudicator for the choral, vocal and instrumental classes was a well-known musician, composer and teacher, Principal of the Guildhall School of Music, Edric Cundell.[3] Mr Cundell was Honorary Director of Music to the GWR Staff Association. Mrs Page, wife of the Chief Signal & Telegraph Engineer, had donated a silver cup for best solo piano; Cyril Lloyd, a director, donated a trophy for the best drama.

There were many people to compete for many classes of performance and each day was full of 'heats', working towards the finals of the Friday. In the class of 'drama' there was the Carmarthen Locomotive Department Drama Society. Shrewsbury District Goods Manager's Office Staff put on a play written by one of their number. Cardiff (General) Dramatic Society performed the heartbreaking 'Riders to the Sea' by J.M. Synge. The festival was attended on Saturday by Viscount Portal PC, DSO, MVO and his wife and Sir Edward Cadogan, a director of the GWR and President of the Staff Association.

A very lengthy list of prize-winners was published in the *GWR Staff Magazine*. Driver Alex Kerley of Swindon was the winner in the 'Brass or Woodwind solo' class. He played 'La Belle Americaine' on his euphonium with such brilliance that the BBC invited him to play to the nation. And so, at 9.25 p.m. on 2 April he appeared on thousands of 9-inch and 12-inch television screens and played his winning piece – in his engine driver's cap and overalls.

The May/June edition of the *GWR Staff Magazine* reported that letters of thanks were pouring in for the Herculean efforts of GWR staff during the first three months of 1947. Two were published:

I have been requested to convey the thanks and appreciation of the Abertillery Chamber of Trade to the officials and men of the Great Western Railway who, despite the worst weather conditions in living memory, maintained by devotion to duty, regular goods and passenger services to and from this area. The story of your effort is worthy of the greatest traditions of the British railways.
C. Lewis, Hon. Secretary.

From the Northern Aluminium Company.

On behalf of the General Production Committee, which consists of representatives of both employer and employees, we have been asked to express our appreciation of the very fine and successful efforts made by your staff in transporting our personnel to and from Rogerstone during the severe weather conditions. This splendid achievement has resulted in very little lost time and the production at the factory has on that account been little affected by the appalling conditions.

The least I can do after the successful efforts of your hauliers and prompt attention of your staff at the Goods Department during the strenuous weeks of storm and flood is to ask you to accept my little offering of thanks and appreciation. The courtesy and skill of the members concerned with the deliveries of foodstuffs has been most commendable and I ask you to convey to all under your charge my sincere thanks.

D.T Benbow, Depot Supervisor, R. Silcock & Sons Ltd., Liverpool.

A meeting took place on 9 May between the Minister of Transport, Alfred Barnes, the General Managers of all four railway companies, Lord Ashfield – one of the greatest of British public administrators, creator of London Underground – and representatives of all the different railway trade unions, to discuss the unions' claims for more money and a shorter working week at a time of national emergency. Barnes refused to take part in the negotiations but asked both sides to bear in mind the steadily declining income of the railway companies and the effect that increased wages and shorter hours would have on freight rates and fares – and thus the national economy. But railwaymen and

MEMBERS OF THE GENERAL MANAGERS' CONFERENCE (FOUR MAIN LINE BRITISH RAILWAYS) WITH MR. PERCY A. CLEWS ON HIS RETIREMENT FROM THE CANADIAN NATIONAL RAILWAYS AT THE GREAT WESTERN ROYAL HOTEL, PADDINGTON, ON FEBRUARY 3, 1947. *From left: Sir James Milne (G.W.R.); Sir Charles Newton (L.N.E.R.); Sir Eustace Missenden (S.R.); Mr. Clews; Sir William Wood (L.M.S.R.)*

women had to have some increase in wages given the rate of inflation in prices, and the claims were referred to arbitration.

Meanwhile the directors continued to spend money on restoring the railway to its pre-war condition. Apart from that the directors continued to run their railway as if it was their responsibility forever. These people consulted with industry on how best the GWR could serve their needs. Spare land was 'made available' to develop industry, provide much needed employment, and to create an income for the company. In May, Richard Thomas & Baldwins began the building of their Margam Abbey steelworks on what had been GWR land.

Fairford engine shed, at the terminus of the branch line from Oxford, had a 45ft turntable which was worn out. In May the directors approved of its replacement with a new 55ft table, so that the branch trains could be hauled by the relatively new '2251' class of 0-6-0 tender engines. The cost was estimated at £5,850.

For £4,100 they purchased 29 Woodfield Road, Ealing 'for a member of staff' and also No 81 Radford Road, Leamington as a staff hostel at a cost of £3,650. The motor vessel *Empire Seasilver* was chartered at the rate of £1,700 a month to carry Channel Islands tomatoes to a Cornish railhead or Weymouth. £3,100 was to be spent on repairing damage to signals and telegraphs after the gales of April and £20,000 was paid to Holloway Brothers for the repair of the Strangford viaduct over the Wye. Sixteen 'Sundstrand' Accounting and Payroll machines were installed in the twelve Divisional Locomotive Superintendents' offices by Underwood Elliott Fisher Ltd for £12,288.

At the Sea Wall pumping station, on the English side of the River Severn, Lancashire boilers Nos 27 and 52, which were 60 and 46 years old respectively, were in a bad condition and had to be replaced. The thrifty housekeeping of the GWR had a couple of these boilers set aside for the time they would be needed and these were to be refurbished and installed, while No 27 was to be converted into a storage tank for water, incidentally condensed from steam traps and condensers. The condensate, being free of lime and mud, would then be fed into the working boilers. The whole refurbishment would cost £3,100. The GWR hotel 'Tregenna Castle' had all its drives and pathways refurbished. The list contains thirty-two approvals for expenditure. What seems to have been the last contract for oil-fuelling points was signed on 14 May – for Bristol Bath Road.

The directors approved the promotion of Mr K.J. Cook, Swindon Locomotive Works Manager, to Chief Assistant to the Chief Mechanical Engineer, Mr Hawksworth. Mr Cook's salary rose from £1,750 to £2,000 p.a. This produced a shuffling along in the queue for top jobs in the Works. Mr H. Randle, Carriage & Wagon Works Manager, replaced Mr Cook. Randle had earned £1,223 and now he rose to £1,500 p.a. – which was £250 a year less than Cook got. C.T. Roberts, Randle's Assistant, who had been getting £723 p.a., took Randle's place but only at £1,000 p.a.

The company's income continued to decline. The estimated receipts for the four weeks ended 11 May amounted to £3,473,000, a decrease of £273,000 (7.29 per cent) compared with that period in 1946. Receipts from passenger traffic went down by £412,000 (21.14 per cent). The Easter holiday did not produce as great a flood of passengers as expected – and indeed, was hoped for. Income from the carrying of general merchandise went down by £31,000 (2.3 per cent), but coal traffic – which was receiving the attention reserved for a National Emergency – increased by £170,000 (37.95 per cent). From 11 May to the end of the month the revenue from general merchandise traffic was estimated by the General Manager to be 11.4 per cent less than for the same period in 1946, but passenger traffic was up by £102,000 (7.8 per cent) and income from coal traffic was increased by £29,000 (7.23 per cent) on May 1946. The total estimated income for the last three weeks of May was £2,775,000, an increase of 0.36 per cent over May 1946.

The agricultural show season got underway in May. The company ran special trains to take horses, sheep and cattle to the Oxfordshire show at Banbury on 13 May and to the Shropshire & West Midland Show on 21 May and on the following day. Besides that, 190 wagon-loads of unspecified material went by goods train, and 290 consignments of poultry, bees and honey went to these shows in the guard's compartment of passenger trains. Nothing was too much trouble for the railway.

The Whitsun holiday, 23–27 May, did not produce large numbers of passengers for the long-distance trains. Maybe Sir James Milne's article in the *News of the World* had had the desired effect. The number of people carried out of Paddington – over Whitsun – on the long-distance expresses totalled 132,368, a decrease of 41,175 compared to the numbers carried during Whitsun 1946. The peak days were Friday 23 May, when 38,000 people left Paddington on sixty-two long-distance trains, and Tuesday 27 May, with 39,500 passengers on fifty-eight main-line trains. Special trains for military personnel going on leave were permitted by the government, and the GWR put on thirty-seven trains to carry 26,000 men and women.

At this time the company was complying with the Minister of Transport's request to complete the construction and electrification of the London Passenger Transport Board (LPTB) Central Line between North Acton and West Ruislip as a matter of urgency, with a target of opening the electrified route through to Greenford on 30 June 1947 and to West Ruislip in June the following year. This was work the GWR had undertaken in 1935 on behalf of the LPTB's New Works programme which envisaged major extensions of the 'tube' network. The works were funded in part by government grants and guarantees on interest and the raising of £42,286,000 of share capital – worth £2.13 billion today. Between 1935 and 1940 the GWR had laid an extra pair of electrified tracks alongside the main line to Birmingham. The war had, of course, prevented completion. The Great Western completed the track-laying to Greenford and to West Ruislip on time.

The widespread introduction of the five-day working week made difficulties for the railway because wagons that would have been ready to take away empty on a Saturday were locked away behind the factory siding gate – conversely wagons could not be delivered to private sidings. The railway companies made a survey of 18,000 companies and found that only 2,300 were able to take in loads or let out empty wagons on Saturdays. This was reducing the number of empty wagons available for reloading, and that reduced the wagons available for carrying coal. The problem was referred to the Minister of Transport who asked the Board of Trade to 'exert pressure' on companies to provide staff for the reception, unloading and release of wagons on Saturdays 'or else severe demurrage charges may have to be imposed'.

The GWR always tried hard to obtain as much heavy goods traffic as possible and had incentive agreements with shipping companies and dock authorities to persuade them to put traffic on rail. C. Shaw Lovell & Sons, a company still in existence, were agents for the GWR. In 1942 the incentive agreement between the GWR and Lovell was suspended in favour of a fixed annual payment of £1,500. In May 1947 a new arrangement – backdated to 1 January – was agreed. The GWR would pay Lovell 6d for every ton of imported steel and iron, destined for places in the West Midlands, which Lovell put onto the GWR at the dock of import. Other traffic would be paid for at 10 per cent of the GWR's revenue from carrying it. Export traffic routed through GWR Docks would pay 3d a ton – and here the GWR seems to be prepared to carry at a loss: 'no commission will be paid on traffic giving a rail revenue to the company of less that 3s 4d per ton'. The arrangement was subject to Lovell & Son forwarding not less than 10,000 a year over the GWR.

The Commercial Department of the GWR had concluded arrangements for four more sites on GWR land for the erection of new industries which included manufacturing of plastic sleeving for electric wire and self-locking units for aircraft and motor cars. These four brought the total number of sites provided by the GWR since the start of 1947 to twenty-two, seventeen of them in South Wales. Meanwhile the Board of Trade had forty-two factories under construction in South Wales and Monmouthshire.

And the good news of budding industry, which would put its products on rail, continued. A large 'continuous hot strip steel mill' was to be constructed at Margam near Port Talbot at a cost of £50,000,000: 'Coke ovens, blast furnaces, steel melting shops and ancillary plant would be required and of course the building materials, raw materials and finished products would have to come in and out by rail.'

There was also a very welcome windfall for one of the remotest stations on a remote branch line in the GWR empire: Llanrhaiadr-Mochnant, high in the Montgomeryshire hills, far down the single-track Tanat Valley line from Blodwell Junction: 'Work has commenced on the construction of the fourth pipeline in connection with Liverpool Corporation's waterworks extension at Hirnant near Lake Vyrnwy. Special arrangements have been made by the Company for the delivery over the next fifteen months of approximately 5,100 tons of pipes from the railhead at Llanrhaiadr-Mochnant.'

Hirnant was 5 miles away and 17 tons were to be delivered each working day, for which lorries would be needed, along with lodgings for the drivers, a crane and its operator. The station had limited siding space which required extension – but to the GWR all traffic was good.

Between 7 May and 21 May 1,381 cars were carried away from the Morris Motors plant at Cowley and 713 vehicles moved from Austin at Longbridge. Two-hundred-and-fifty drums of electric cable, weighing 410 tons and wanted urgently in Russia, was forwarded in a single train of forty-two wagons from Woolwich to Swansea Docks on behalf of Siemens Bros, who were so pleased with the same-day delivery to the dockside that a letter of appreciation was sent to Milne. Milne also mentions 3,500 tons of 'zinc residue' to be taken from Sutton Coldfield to London docks for Paris, 25 tons of photographic paper from Wooburn Green on the High Wycombe–Maidenhead line, 20 tons of steel tubes from Tyseley – and an oil painting valued at £15,000 carried from Paignton to Paris. Two hundred tons of French broccoli arriving from Roscoff was rapidly conveyed from Weymouth to Covent Garden.

The company was continuously expanding its organisation of Country Lorry services and with each report came news of a new scheme. In May the lorry stations at Taunton, Bridgwater, Langport, Watchet and Minehead began road delivery around the outlying villages of their respective areas, comprising small consignments of goods traffic. This was part of the specific policy of rail/road co-ordination which also extended to passenger transport with the existence of the part railway-owned bus companies.

In May the locomotive situation showed a very slight improvement on the previous four months. There were twenty-eight more engines 'available for use' in May but the 'total in use' was only seven more than had been in use in April. The average miles per day of each engine in use was the same as in April, and the average hours each engine in use worked was the same as in April but the miles-per-engine hour in May was 12.8 for passenger trains, as against 12.65 in April, and was 8.3 for goods as against 8.19 for goods in April. Coal consumption was increased.[4]

A 20-year-old fireman from Swindon, G.W. Bennet, was posted to Old Oak Common in May 1947. Subsequent events do not reflect well on the conduct of his superiors. He was allocated Compartment T1 in sleeping coach No 1130. This was a converted passenger coach, built in 1901. It was 58ft long, with a leaking clerestory roof. Its steam-heated radiators were supplied with steam from a stationary boiler but the radiator control did not always admit steam to the heater. A leak in the roof over Compartment T3 was reported on 21 February 1947, which was not repaired for ten days. On 5 March the roof was leaking over the corridor but was mended that day. On 20 May Fireman Bennet reported that the roof in his compartment was letting in rain. The hole was sealed four days later.

The wooden coach was damp. Bennet's bunk was damp. Around 25 May he contracted influenza and lay in his damp bed. On 30 May he was feeling much worse and wanted to go to his parents' home in Swindon. He went to the Time Office to ask for a pass to Swindon. He said he had a temperature, a headache and great stiffness in his joints. The people in the Time Office had no time for him and found his repeated complaints and insistence for a train pass annoying. The official report stated: 'He gave trouble at the Time Office and worried the staff.' A first-aid man escorted him back to his bed in the coach and Dr Robinson was sent for. The doctor found that Bennet had a temperature of 103°F and ordered him into Park Royal hospital. He remained in his damp bed for three days, until 2 June, before the people in charge at Old Oak Common shed were able to find a means of conveying him to the medical centre. Bennet spent nine weeks at Park Royal, suffering from an accumulation of fluid on a lung. After this period he was well enough to travel to Swindon to see the GWR doctor at Park House, Dr Bennet. Fireman Bennet was clearly an enthusiast – he wanted to go back to work but he also wanted compensation for the illness he contracted in the damp old coach. Dr Bennet put him on six months' light duties, but neither the GWR nor Western Region would agree to give him compensation for his misery.

He was abandoned by those who should have cared. Perhaps Fireman Bennet was not a member of ASLEF or the NUR. The report makes no mention of trade union intervention. Some other occupant of the coach must have brought him water and food during the ten days he suffered in the coach but no-one whose job it was to care for him fulfilled their duty.

No 4020 *Knight Commander* running into No 2 Platform Exeter St David's at Easter 1947. (Peter Pescod/Transport Treasury 348)

No 3832, a powerful, if scruffy, freight engine running into Platform 3 at Exeter St David's pressed into service for a Bristol–Paignton excursion in June 1947. (Peter Pescod/Transport Treasury 347)

Solving Problems

During May the Intermediate Block signals were removed from the Severn Tunnel. There was a signal box just outside the east and west ends of the tunnel – Severn Tunnel East and West boxes. A block section of 4 miles is a long one for a heavily occupied main line and especially so because of the great awkwardness – for trains of loose-coupled, un-braked wagons – of the steep gradients. Loose-coupled freight trains, coal or coal empties, were scheduled 15 minutes from Tunnel East to Tunnel West. Because of the intensity of wartime traffic the length of block section had to be shortened in order to increase the capacity of the line through the tunnel.

This was done in November 1941 by installing on both tracks an 'Intermediate Block Section' (IBS). A Stop/Proceed IBS Home signal – an electric colour-light signal – was placed 1 mile inside the tunnel. The westbound signal was controlled from the Severn Tunnel East signal box, the eastbound from the Tunnel West signal box. Two hundred yards to the rear of each Stop signal was a repeater Stop colour light. There was an Automatic Train Control (ATC) ramp at the repeater and at the actual Stop signal – probably a unique occurrence on the GWR to have an ATC ramp at a Stop signal. At the Welsh and English entrances to the tunnel was a semaphore Starting signal, with a semaphore Distant signal below the Stop arm. There was an ATC ramp at this signal. This Distant signal advised the driver whether he 'had the road' right through the tunnel or if the IBS Home signal was at 'Danger – Stop'.

Provided the rear vehicle of a train in the tunnel was more than 440yd ahead of the IBS Stop signal – this was proved by a track circuit – a second train could enter the tunnel. Under those conditions the Distant signal at the tunnel entrance would show 'Caution' (meaning get ready to stop at the Home signal). I have been told by Swindon footplatemen who worked through the tunnel from 1941–47 that the Tunnel IBS signals were detested by drivers because they made the men 'wait for the road' in the smoky and icy cold murk of the tunnel instead of letting them wait outside in the fresh air. When the IBS signals were removed the footplate crews were not the only ones to be pleased. It was also much to the satisfaction of the Signal & Telegraph Department men who no longer had to trudge into the pitch-dark, sulphurous, wet and icy waste of the tunnel to carry out maintenance and repairs.

During May there were forty-five incidents of goods trains breaking couplings. Twelve involved GWR wagons, while thirteen LMS wagons, five LNER wagons, two SR

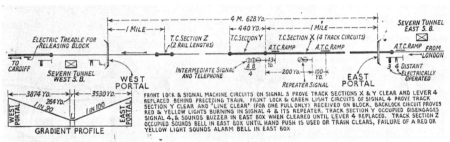

Diagram of intermediate advance section signalling installed in the Severn Tunnel, Great Western Railway.

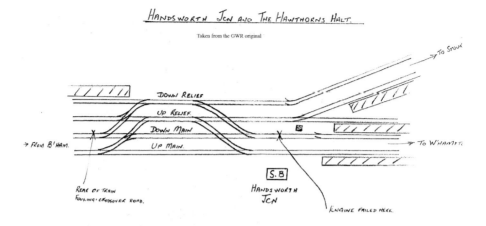

and thirteen Private Owner (PO) wagons were affected in this way. Three of the GWR partings were caused by the 'Instanter' coupling on the guard's brake van, and one was a brake van's drawbar hook snapping. Three drawbars broke. Seven LMS wagons broke three-link couplings, three drawbar hooks and three drawbars were pulled apart. The five LNER wagons that broke away suffered two, three-link couplings breaks, three drawbar hooks and three drawbars breaking. Of the thirteen PO wagons, four had broken drawbar hooks. The rest were caused by three-link coupling problems, and one was bad enough for the record to become a little personal: 'Atkinson & Prickett, Hull. Bad flaw – very rusty.' Mileage run by engines hauling goods trains in May totalled 1,834,726.

On 5 May GWR 'Aberdare' class 2-6-0 No 2640, shedded at Banbury, was hauling forty-two wagons of the 3 a.m. Taunton–Oxley goods train. It came toiling up the 2 miles at 1 in 100, north of Birmingham Snow Hill, and just as it reached the summit at Handsworth Junction, at 5.5 a.m., one of its coupling rods broke off. The train came to a stand with the engine outside the signal box on the Down Main blocking the Main to Relief and Relief to Main junctions. The Stourbridge line was not affected but single-line working was necessary over the Up Main between West Bromwich and Handsworth station box. It took an hour to find a man sufficiently competent to be a pilotman – and two hand signalmen – and the temporary single line came into use at 6.5 a.m. The West Bromwich shunting engine came Up on the Up main, to Handsworth station, crossed to the Down Main and went north to the train. The forty-two wagons were drawn back, crossed to the Up Main at Handsworth and were taken into Queen's Head Yard close to Winson Green station. The shunting engine returned for the 'Aberdare' and brought that back to Queen's Head. The Down Main was clear and normal working resumed at 7.35 a.m.

For No 2640 it was the end. It was scrapped in June.

On 9 May LMS 0-8-0, No 9247, an ex-LNWR inside-cylindered goods engine, hauled the 1.5 a.m. Coleham (Shrewsbury) to Abergavenny, comprised thirty-seven wagons. The driver was Jack Clarke, and the fireman's name was not given. The Guard was

Mr Harvey. These were LMS men, stationed at Abergavenny. The train left Hereford Barrs Court at 8 a.m. At 8.10 a.m. it was passing Rotherwas Junction, on the Down Main, going towards Redhill Junction. About a mile beyond Rotherwas the right-hand connecting rod broke away, smashing the valve gear and tangling with the sleepers for 88yd before the big-end cap broke and the rod fell away onto the track.

Single-line working was necessary. A competent man to act as pilotman was soon found at Hereford station. He had the use of the Station Pilot engine and went out to Redhill Junction via Brecon Curve Junction. There the 7.35 a.m. Cardiff train was waiting for him, travelling on the Up Main. He countersigned the signalman's entry in the Train Register concerning the opening of single-line working and left a single-line working form with the Redhill Junction signalman. He could now travel over the right line, Up Main, through to Rotherwas. He carried out the same duties there whereupon single-line working – Down trains over the Up line – commenced at 9.30 a.m.

The failed engine was attended to by the Hereford breakdown gang, rigged to be safe to move, and shunted clear of the Down Main at 11.30 a.m. Eighteen badly damaged sleepers were replaced in 1 hour and normal working resumed at 12.30 p.m.

During May there were six incidents of passenger trains becoming uncoupled. The average delay caused was 26 minutes. Passenger train mileage was 2,649,883. On 10 May, a Plymouth–Crewe train with thirteen coaches, hauled by No 7006 *Lydford Castle* with Driver Waters of Shrewsbury, was starting off from Bridgwater when the pull

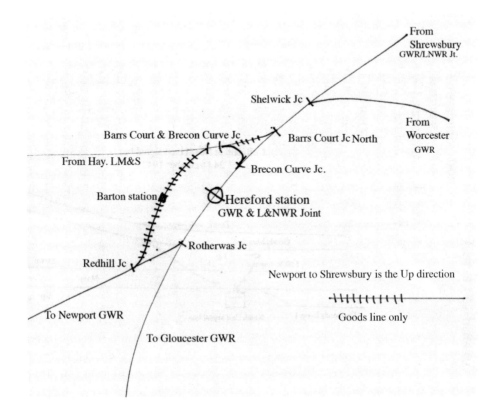

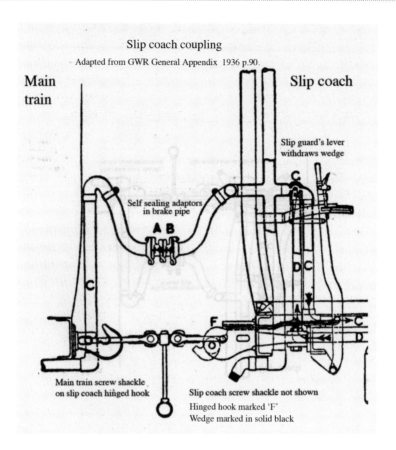

Slip coach coupling

Adapted from GWR General Appendix 1936 p.90.

Main
train

Slip coach

Slip guard's lever
withdraws wedge

Self sealing adaptors
in brake pipe

A B

C

D C

F

C

D

Main train screw shackle
on slip coach hinged hook

Slip coach screw shackle not shown

Hinged hook marked 'F'
Wedge marked in solid black

from the engine was too great for the drawbar on an LMS Brake Third. The headstock burst and the drawbar was ripped out of the carriage frame.

On 21 May the 8.30 a.m. Plymouth–Paddington train made its booked call at Westbury. The engine was No 6017 *King Edward IV*, with Driver Hayward from Old Oak Common, with fourteen coaches behind his tender. The 8.30 train had the Reading slip coach at the rear and as this was the last stop before the slip was made, the guard re-coupled the slip coach to the main train using the slip coupling and put the self-sealing valves onto the brake pipes. As the train set off on its journey, the pull on the hinged slip hook dragged it out from below the wedge, which was supposed to hold it in place until the slipping lever was pulled. The train stopped in a few yards. The slip coach was re-attached to the train using the normal coupling of the coach ahead and the whole train stopped at Reading.

On 8 May the 9.5 p.m. Birkenhead–Cardiff 'D' headcode train was approaching Craven Arms Long Lane Crossing[5] at 1.20 a.m. on the Down Main line. The train was formed of forty-one wagons, the leading eleven being vacuum braked, with the pipe connected to the engine brake. The engine was No 5919 *Worsley Hall*, with Driver T.H. Webb, and Fireman C.W. Pearce, both of Pontypool Road. The train was normally a 'C' headcode – which required a minimum of fourteen[6] vacuum-braked wagons and was then allowed to run at 45–50mph. Only eleven wagons were fitted with the vacuum brake so it had been downgraded to a 'D', restricted to 35mph. Driver Webb must have had it in his head that they were 'C' headcode. The 13-mile climb from Shrewsbury to Church Stretton summit was over and the route then fell at between 1 in 100 to 1 in 130 for many miles. The engine was running on a breath of steam at about 50mph and his mate was having an easy ride.

Three-quarters of a mile before Long Lane Crossing, on a left-hand curve, on well-laid track, the right-hand leading wheel of the twelfth wagon – an LNER box van – rose up over the right-hand rail, dragging its partner onto the sleepers while itself running over the chairs on the outside of the rail. Twenty-five yards further on, the trailing right-hand wheel went over the rail.

Seven hundred yards ahead were the facing points, set for the main line but with rails diverging left into a Goods Loop, 300yd beyond the points was Watling Street Crossing and 350yd beyond that was Long Lane signal box standing alongside the Down Main. When the derailed twelfth wagon's wheels hit the points its coupling to the eleventh wagon broke. The front part continued at speed. The twelfth wagon was pushed forward by the rest. It passed over Watling Street crossing and finally crashed into Long Lane signal box. The four wagons behind it were derailed by the crossing timbers. Three were scattered about the tracks – one jumped the Up Main and landed on its side in the front garden of the crossing keeper's house.

The Long Lane signalman, George Tunks, watched the headlamps of the train approaching in the darkness and, in his own words:

> After giving 'Train entering Section' for this train I was standing near the window to watch it coming past and noticed sparks and a series of bumps as the train approached. I went towards the Block Bell to send 'Stop & Examine' to Central Wales Junction[7] but before I could do so the box collapsed. After crawling from under the debris the Guard told me that he had advised Central Wales Junction of the mishap.

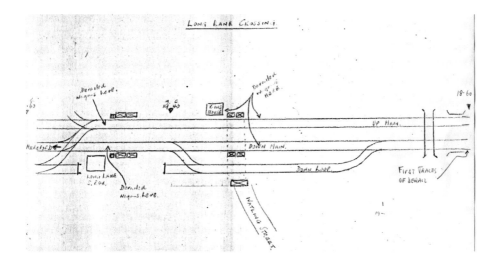

The footplate crew felt no irregularity in the track and had no idea that their train had become parted until they had Onibury Crossing's[8] Distant against them, looked back along the train and could not see the side lamps of the guard's van.

The Up and Down lines at Long Lane box were blocked with four derailed wagons and thirteen more that were variously damaged. The signal box, a timber construction dating from 1931, was demolished. Two telegraph poles had been knocked to the ground and another was leaning at an acute angle. The twelfth wagon, the LNER van, was suspected of some defect which, together with some modest irregularities found in the curved track, could have caused the mayhem. The van was too badly damaged to be examined for faults. No official blame was attached to it and the cause was judged to be faults in the alignment of the curved track. As a result the GWR was obliged to carry the entire costs of restoring the damage, which of course included an entirely new signal box with all necessary equipment and the restoration of 300yd of telegraph wires with three poles. The estimated total cost of restoring everything to working order was £3,800, of which £500 was the estimated cost of replacing 'like for like' the 1931 wooden signal box and equipment.

The GWR steam cranes at Wolverhampton Stafford Road and the LMS steam crane from Shrewsbury were both under repair, and so cranes were ordered from Cardiff and Crewe. Meanwhile the re-laying gang started work on restoring the damaged track. The cranes arrived on site at 8 a.m. and 12.35 p.m. respectively on 9 May. By 4 p.m. all thirteen shattered wagon bodies, buffers and wheel-sets, had been cleared away. The Engineering Department handed the tracks back to the Traffic Department at 5.35 p.m., subject to a 5mph speed restriction.

Through passenger trains booked over the 'North and West' line were diverted throughout the day via Wolverhampton and Worcester. Local trains were replaced by Midland Red buses between Craven Arms station and Church Stretton. Freight traffic had to be held in the yards at Shrewsbury, Hereford and Newport because the Wolverhampton–Worcester route could only take the North to West passenger trains. There had been a derailment at Wombourn, Shrewsbury and Worcester footplate crews were fully engaged, leaving no-one spare who knew the road over the Shrewsbury–Bewdley line.

Signalman Tunks was 57 years old in May 1947. He entered the service of the Great Western railway in 1911 and was appointed a signalman in 1919. Mr Tunks escaped from the demolition of his signal box with a cut forehead, a sprained wrist and severe shock. He applied to the company for the replacement of the two most valuable pieces of his property. I think he stated his claim with great honesty, taking no advantage of his experience by demanding restitution for the 'severe shock' he suffered. Gilbert Matthews' letter to Sir James Milne, dated 14 July, states:

> Further to my memorandum of 28th ult. Enquiry has been made in regard to the claim the signalman at Long Lane Crossing with a view to ascertaining whether the amounts he claims may be considered reasonable, bearing in mind that some allowance must be made for wear and tear.
>
> I am informed that the cycle in question was a 'Swift' machine purchased about 7 years ago and the fountain pen was a 'Summit' with a 14-carat gold

nib purchased 18 months ago. In view of the cost of replacing these articles the amount claimed is considered reasonable and I shall be obliged if you will kindly say whether the man can be reimbursed to the extent of his loss.

Sir James Milne agreed and on 15 July a cheque for £10 10s was sent to Signalman Tunks.

On 20 May the 1.25 a.m. Crewe–Cardiff express was approaching Long Lane signal box, Craven Arms, at 3.20 a.m. The train consisted of twelve LMS coaches hauled by engine 6903 *Belmont Hall*, with Driver Rowdon of Hereford. The train was coming down a 1 in 106 gradient and was slowing for a speed restriction over new track – the aftermath of the derailment of 8 May – when the shackle coupling of the ninth coach, a brake-third coach, broke. The front and rear parts of the train stopped 2yd apart with the vacuum brake pipes of the eighth and the ninth coach ripped apart and useless. The train backed up and was re-coupled using the shackle of the eighth coach onto the ninth coach's hook. The vacuum pipes between the seventh and the eighth coach were undone and the pipe of the seventh coach placed on its 'stop'. The train was then worked forward at reduced speed to Hereford, 31 miles away, the vacuum brake working only on the seven front coaches. The guard rode in the brake van at the rear, looking out of the window, ready to screw down his handbrake immediately if another coupling should break.

On 13 May the 3.55 p.m. Bristol Temple Meads–Melksham passenger train was brought to a stand by signals at Bradford Junction at 5.00 p.m. The guard, Bill Cox, looked out of his window on the off-side to see what was the matter and saw a door opening and a passenger getting down onto the track. Cox quickly opened his door and climbed down onto the track and tried to get the person to go back up into the carriage but very quickly realised that the passenger, a man, was 'helplessly drunk'. The inebriated man shoved Cox aside and staggered across the Up line and promptly fell down the embankment. He was crawling back up the embankment when the driver, who was unaware of what was going on behind him, gave a 'toot' on the whistle. The signal had cleared. Cox dashed for the footstep up into his van and left the man to his own devices. However, Cox did not abandon his duties; he knew he had a colleague on the train who would be getting off, with his bicycle, at Staverton Halt, which was 400yd beyond Bradford Junction. So he asked his associate to cycle back to the junction signalman and warn him that there was a very drunken civilian, who might possibly be staggering about on the track near his box. The off-duty railwayman did this. When the train got to Holt Junction station Cox got out onto the platform and saw another very drunken passenger get off. He approached him to ask him if he had lost a mate. He had. The two friends had been drinking in Bristol and caught the train together. Both had intended to get off at Avoncliff Halt but hadn't noticed it, and had been over-carried.

Meanwhile the first drunk had managed to crawl up the embankment but was unable, on reaching the trackside footpath, to get up off his knees, so he lay down on the gravel. Within a few minutes Lengthman Parfitt, who was walking home, found him and, telling him to remain lying down, went to tell the signalman that the drunk was safely at the side of the line. The signalman had already telephoned Trowbridge station. The

Station Master telephoned the police and a constable came to the station. By that time, the Trowbridge shunting engine had been brought into the platform and the policeman, with a shunter, had a footplate ride to Bradford Junction. The drunk was arrested and all three rode the engine back to Trowbridge.

On 26 May the 10.10 a.m. Hartlebury–Bewdley train was formed with the Worcester-based GWR diesel rail car No 22. It left the beautiful station of Stourport-on-Severn 'right time' at 10.20 a.m., packed with forty happy 'excursionists' looking forward to a nice walk in the country and a meal in a pub. At 10.25 a.m. the guard telephoned Stourport North signalman to say No 22 was a total failure at Burlish Halt – 1½ miles away – and that he was walking back to him with the single line token in order that an assisting engine could enter the section and rescue the failure. The guard was a very fast walker, getting back to Stourport North at 10.40 a.m.

The Hartlebury–Stourport 'Trip' engine was available, and this went into the section with the rail car's guard and the single line token. At 10.56 a.m. the guard phoned in to say that No 22 could not be moved without some dismantling, and fitters from Worcester would be required. As there was going to be a very long delay, the guard told the passengers that they could get down from the car and walk back to Stourport. This they did. The Station Master made arrangements for a bus to take them to Bewdley, but before it arrived he discovered that all the passengers had left the station and had made their own way. The Worcester locomotive fitters arrived at 11.45 a.m. They got the car into a fit state to be moved and the Hartlebury 'Trip' engine brought it back to Stourport at 12.10 p.m.

On 30 May the 12.35 p.m. Weymouth–Bristol passenger train was working hard on climbing Bruton bank, and was near Bruton when the leading section of the water scoop beneath the tender dropped, as if to pick up water. The other end of the scoop remained attached to the tender. The driver brought the train to a stand and got down to inspect. The leading end of the scoop was hinged, held to the lowering and raising screw by a nut and bolt. The nut had worked itself off the bolt, resulting in the fall of the scoop. There was slight damage to the scoop and the ballast was disturbed for some hundreds of yards. The driver crawled under the tender and managed to fix the fallen section up securely. This took him 10 minutes. The following Penzance–Paddington express lost 1 minute.

On Saturday 31 May, George Morgan was fireman to Driver Bill Taylor, both of Bristol. They had charge of 0-6-0 tank engine No 8714 with the Lawrence Hill–Stoke Gifford 'Trip' engine. They left Ashley Hill station at 5.10 p.m. and were put into Filton Loop at 5.30 p.m. While they were standing in the loop Fireman Morgan went out along the running plate to see how they were for water and came back to say they needed more, and then went to the signal phone to inform the signalman that they needed to get to Stoke Gifford as soon as possible for water. As he climbed back onto the engine he gave an exclamation and said he had felt a severe pain in his head. Bill Taylor thought that Morgan looked very pale, and said he would 'cut the engine off' and go at once to Stoke Gifford. But as he said this the signal came off for them to leave, which they did.

On arrival at Stoke Gifford yard at 6 p.m. Morgan got down off the engine and went to the Yard Master's office to report that he was unwell and could not carry on. No sooner had he spoken than he vomited at the Yard Master's feet. The Yard Master sat him down and sent for Shunter Williams, who was the St John's Ambulance first-aider, while one of the men in the office brought a glass of water. Morgan took a mouthful, spat it out, and then poured the rest of it over his head. Shunter Williams saw that Morgan was getting worse by the second and told the Yard Master to call an ambulance. Morgan called for Bill Taylor to come and hold his head because his pain was intense. The St John's Ambulance vehicle arrived at 7 p.m. but did not leave until 7.30 p.m., when Fireman Morgan was taken to the Bristol Royal Infirmary. He died at 10.10 p.m. The cause of death was a ruptured congenital aneurysm at the base of the brain. This was not in any way the result of his work as a locomotive fireman.

Fireman Morgan's father lived in Fishguard and the very sad news was broken to him by the night sister at the Bristol Royal Infirmary, who had already been in touch with Mr Morgan. Later that evening someone from Fishguard station, or from the locomotive depot, went to see Mr Morgan. There were no trains out of Fishguard that late at night so on Sunday morning Mr Morgan, who was not in good health and so was accompanied by Mr Williams, a close friend of the family, took the first fast train to Bristol. The return train fares of both men were subsequently refunded by the GWR. The ASLEF local branch secretary wrote to Leslie Edwards, the Assistant Divisional Superintendent at Bristol, asking that this be done, but I think it very likely that the refund would have been paid without the request. As they had to be in Bristol all day it is very likely that Edwards, a very well respected man in Bristol, made sure they were fed and cared for. They made their way to the Bristol Royal Infirmary, where they had an interview with the doctor who had attended to Mr Morgan's son. Edwards must have been aware of their presence in the city because the two men were taken to meet the locomotive shed Chief Foreman at Bristol Bath Road, Mr H. Brown. At the end of the meeting Mr Brown handed over to Mr Morgan his son's footplateman's serge jacket, overcoat and food bag, together with the £4 11s 4d that was in the inside pocket.

Notes

1 *Great Western Railway Staff Magazine*, November p. 223.
2 See Appendix II.
3 The *Staff Magazine* consistently spells his name 'Edric'.
4 See Appendix III.
5 Renamed Craven Arms Crossing in March 1956.
6 GWR Regulations in 1947.
7 Craven Arms Station signal box was switched out. It was 628yd from Long Lane Crossing. Central Wales Junction was 308yd beyond Craven Arms Station box.
8 Onibury Crossing signal box was 2¾ miles south of Central Wales Junction.

GREAT WESTERN RAILWAY
MAGAZINE

MIDSUMMER · 1947

VOLUME 59 · NO. 5

Pride in the Job—4
(See Page 106)

PRICE ONE PENNY

JUNE

Fifteen directors met on 15 June. A clause in the Transport (Nationalisation) Bill restricted the amount of money owned by the companies which could be distributed to their shareholders. The companies felt that the clause was unduly harsh and unfair, and negotiations were conducted with the government. The June Minutes contain the announcement that the restrictive clause in the Bill had been relaxed and the effect for the Great Western was that they now had an extra £574,000 to distribute amongst their investors – and there were several large hospitals in London and others around the country who were shareholders.

The General Manager reported the outcome of another meeting with the railway trade unions. He had not been able to agree to increase wages and reduce hours of work in a way that would satisfy the National Union of Railwaymen (NUR) and Associated Society of Locomotive Enginemen & Firemen (ASLEF).

The Company's annual census, held on 29 March, showed that it employed the equivalent of 113,601 full-time staff, a decrease of 1,369 on the census of 1946.[1] The Traffic Department had lost the most, 1,251 men; signalmen found the overtime useful but tiring. The cost of living was rising continuously and the railways were trying to hold down their wage costs. Because railway wages/salaries were relatively low, all four railway companies found it very difficult to recruit and retain staff in London and major centres. Not only were railwaymen's wages lower than for comparable work outside the rail service, but railwaymen worked a 48-hour week while in other types of employment, the 44-hour week was common. There was also a shortage of housing in London. The old Great Central Railway Hotel at Marylebone was being converted into a hostel for 900 to 1,000 railwaymen, with 160 'places' allocated to the GWR. The accommodation should have been ready in June but a shortage of builders and materials had slowed down the work of conversion.

In the case of engine drivers and firemen there were the 'double-home' or 'lodging' turns. These were the long-distance jobs where the men had to stay overnight at the far end of their journey. ASLEF wanted these turns abolished, and both unions wanted a 40-hour week.

A Court of Inquiry was set up in early June under the chairmanship of Mr C.W. Guillebaud to investigate the unions' claims and the company's financial reasons for refusing them.

Evidence for the four railway companies was presented by Sir William Wood, President of the London Midland & Scottish Railway. His brief was to provide Mr Guillebaud with factual information as to the financial position of the companies but not to discuss or argue the merits/demerits of the unions' claims.

Meanwhile the railways' clerks had been awarded pay rises by the Railway Staff National Tribunal. Grade 'A' clerks starting at aged 18 would now receive wages of £190 p.a., which would rise to £470 at 36 years of age if the person was still, by that time, a Clerk Grade 'A'. A Grade 'B' clerk would earn £475 annually, rising to £515 and a Grade 'C' clerk would get £525 p.a. rising to £573. These increases would cost the GWR £10,000 annually.

Dock workers in all railway-company-owned docks and harbours wanted to cease to be regarded as casual labour – meaning they were paid only for the exact time they worked. They wanted to be classed as railway employees, with a guaranteed weekly wage. The railway companies would not agree to this. Professor Sir Hector Hetherington, Professor of Moral Philosophy and Principal of Glasgow University, was appointed by the Minister of Labour to look into the men's claim. He recommended that the railway dockers should receive a guaranteed minimum wage of £4 7s 6d per week. The companies objected to this minimum wage and the dockers objected to various other provisions of Hetherington's report and so the whole dispute was referred to Mr John Cameron KC. The outcome of that was an extra 6d on the guaranteed week's wage suggested by Hetherington, and a reduction from 6s to 5s for the daily allowance for dockers who report for work but then are not required.

MARLBOROUGH HOUSE
S.W.1.

18th June, 1947.

My dear Wyndham,

      Thank you for your letter of the 16th June which I showed to Queen Mary. Her Majesty knows Mr. Charles Cox, your London Divisional Superintendent, well and is sorry to learn that the time of his retirement is approaching after so very many years in the service of the Great Western Railway.

      Queen Mary remembers especially Mr. Cox's kindness in arranging many journeys for her between Badminton and London during the years of the war, and is most grateful for his unfailing help during those difficult times.

      By Queen Mary's commands I am enclosing a signed photograph which Her Majesty hopes that Mr. Cox will accept as a small token of her grateful remembrance of his services to her and with her best wishes to him for the future.

           Yours ever,

             Jack Windham.

The
    Viscount Portal, D.S.O., M.V.O.

Mr Guillebaud published the conclusions of his Court of Inquiry on 26 June. His recommendations were that the basic wage or salary of all adult weekly or annually paid adult workers should be be increased by 7s 6d a week, or £19 a year, with smaller increases for juveniles; a 44-hour week should be introduced for all wages grade staff without loss of pay, clerical workers to have a 42-hour week; and there was to be no increase of the rates for overtime pay. The railway unions accepted the report and the Minister of Transport asked the companies for their observations on the findings.

Seven GWR senior managers were given small pay rises. For instance, the pay of G.W. Gaut, New Works Assistant to the Superintendent of the Line, rose from £973 p.a. to £1,100; H.A. Alexander, Divisional Engineer, Bristol, increased from £1,600 to £1,750; and R. Hodges, Assistant to the Chief Signal & Telegraph Engineer, had an annual rise from £823 to £950.

Mr Christian Barman, aged 48, was appointed as a Publicity Officer in April 1947, at a salary of £2,000 p.a. – much more than a Divisional Traffic Superintendent's salary. In June 1947 he applied to be granted pension credits as if his contributions had started in 1942, and the directors agreed. Mr Barman's book *Next Station: A Railway Plans for the Future* – which described what the GWR planned to do if they were not nationalised – was published in 1947.

The Great Western Railway was – apart from occasional lapses – a good employer and offered a worthy career path. As a result, most employees joined as boys or teenagers and spent the rest of their working lives 'in the Service'. The Board of Directors were usually long-serving members. The London Division Traffic Superintendent, Mr C.T. Cox MBE, retired in June after fifty years' service with the GWR. The Chairman of the Board, Viscount Portal, knowing of Cox's friendship with Queen Mary, wrote to her private secretary informing him of Cox's retirement. Queen Mary replied, through her Secretary, to Portal (see picture).

Mr Cox's place as London Division Superintendent was taken by Mr C.W. Powell. He came to the GWR in 1915 and served in the RAF in 1918–19. Returning to the GWR he worked his way through many positions in the clerical and operating grades. He came to the Paddington office from his post as Superintendent of the Swansea Division.

The Chief Accountant of the Company, Mr C.R. Dashwood, was awarded the CBE, and the Old Oak Common Passenger Carriage Yard Chief Inspector was awarded the BEM in the King's June Birthday Honours List. Mr K.J. Cook OBE, MIMechE, was Swindon Works Manager when he was promoted to Works Assistant to the Chief Mechanical Engineer in June 1947. Mr Cook began his service as an apprentice at Swindon Works in 1912. He served in the Army Service Corps[2] in France and the Balkans in the Great War.

His replacement as Swindon Works Manager was Mr H. Randle. Mr Randle started as a Swindon Works apprentice in 1916. He served in the Royal Naval Air Service and the Royal Flying Corps in the Great War before returning to Swindon Works. In 1939 he formed and commanded 5th Workshop Company Royal Army Ordnance Corps and was released in 1941 to assist Kenneth Cook at Swindon Works. These were serious men, men who knew their GWR business inside out, and who were used to command.

The estimated income of the GWR for June amounted to £4,911,000, a decrease of £179,000 or 3.52 per cent on the same period in 1946. Passenger income was down by £353,000 (12.58 per cent), while general merchandise income increased by £38,000 (2.28 per cent) and revenue from coal haulage went up by £136,000 (22.1 per cent). The receipts for the twelve months June 1946 to June 1947 amounted to £22,781,000, down £2,408,000 on 1945–46.[3]

During June the GWR carried away 1,579 cars from the Cowley works of Morris Motors, and 702 Austin cars from the Longbridge factory. These were taken to London or Liverpool for export. In the six months from January to the end of June, the GWR had carried 10,647 cars, 600 fewer than the corresponding period in 1946.

Expenditure on the maintenance and improvements of the railway continued, some of which are detailed in the following. Repairs to the river bank at Brentford docks cost £3,500, and also providing a larger staff canteen at Cardiff Newtown (£7,615), repairing the steam tug *Benson*, the dredger *Mowbray* and the Plymouth Millbay tender *Sir Richard Willoughby* (totalling £14,636). Renewing and modernising the Intermediate Block signals between Tilehurst and Cholsey added up to £20,000, re-glazing and repairing the carriage shed roof at Old Oak Common (£3,500), and removing loose rock from the cliff face on the Easton–Portland section cost the company £4,000.

The GWR were permitted by the Minister to bring into use their Summer Timetable on 16 June, and this enhanced level of service was to last until 5 October, but it was not permitted to be a totally pleasurable experience.

Overcrowding was going to be so great in the summer months that it was actually considered to be an incitement to unruliness for passengers to stand, whilst looking at an empty – but reserved – seat. An equally confrontational situation might occur if someone who had reserved a seat was to find it occupied by someone who had not. The reservation of seats was banned by order of the Railway Executive on 16 June 1946, and was not resumed until the introduction of the 1947 winter timetable.

The General Manager's report stated:

The Minister of Transport has directed that the summer services are to be based on the reduced mileage in operation immediately prior to the summer timetable and it is therefore necessary to continue the suspension of a number of the more lightly loaded services and the withdrawal of trains run solely for holiday traffic during the summer season. The 'Cornish Riviera' and 'Torbay' expresses will be retained but, on Saturdays Only, the former train will stop at Exeter to pick up and the latter to leave Paddington at 11 a.m. and make stops at Taunton and Exeter as it does during the week. In the Up direction the 'Cornish Riviera' will call daily at Exeter and, on Saturdays only, at St. Erth and Par as it does on weekdays.

The 'Torbay Express' will be combined at Newton Abbot with the 5 o'clock train from Penzance, scheduled to reach Paddington at 4.35 p.m. with stops at Exeter, Taunton and Reading. This arrangement will enable the 1.25 p.m. train from Penzance to Paddington to be restored and thus provide an afternoon service from Cornwall and Devon to London. The 2.35 p.m. Paddington to Bristol via Newbury and Devizes will be restored[4] and in view of heavy weekend traffic the 1.15 p.m. Paddington (SO) will also run on Friday.[5]

Appropriate arrangements will be made in connection with the steamer services to and from the Channel Islands and Eire (those ships being entirely GWR owned) but in the former case carriages will be attached – on Tuesdays, Thursdays and Saturdays – for boat train passengers to the 4.15 p.m. and 6 p.m. Paddington–Weymouth expresses.

This will remove the need for special boat trains. There will be an additional service to Fishguard Harbour leaving Paddington at 11.35 a.m. on Tuesdays, Thursday and Saturdays in place of the existing arrangement under which through carriages are attached to the 8.55 a.m. Paddington in connection with the tri-weekly sailings to Cork. In the reverse direction a train will leave Fishguard Harbour at 5 a.m. on Tuesdays, Thursdays and Saturdays conveying through carriages to Cardiff to connect with the 8.15 a.m. thence to Paddington.[6]

There was a speed limit of 75mph, with relaxations to 85 on some lengths. The passenger train services were reasonably frequent. The needs of the passengers had to be set against the need to provide 'paths' for cumbersome but vital loose-coupled freights as well as the partly and fully vacuum-braked express freights, parcels and milk trains and empty stock trains. The railway was still carrying a large part of the nation's output.

The GWR did not reinstate their showcase expresses, the 'Bristolian' and 'Cheltenham Flyer', although the 9.5 a.m. Paddington train stopped only at Reading on the 118¼ miles to Bristol via Chippenham, slipping a coach at Bath and taking 138 minutes for the 118¼ miles. Slip coaches had been reintroduced in the summer timetable of 1946.

The 10.30 a.m. Paddington train, known as the 'Cornish Riviera Express' was restored with the commencement of the summer 1947 timetable. Milne (see above) stated that it will be 'retained' but he meant 'reinstated', according to his statement to the Traffic Committee for April. The schedule was 280 minutes for the 225½ miles from Paddington to Plymouth North Road via Westbury, an average speed of 48.4mph. From 1933, after the final improvements had been made to the West of England main line by the opening of the Westbury and Frome by-pass lines, and until the outbreak of war in 1939, the schedule had been 244 minutes, an average speed of 55.4mph.

The time allowances for all express trains were greater than they had been pre-war, which is understandable. From Paddington, taking 40 minutes to pass Reading was the 1947 timing for the best trains against 37 minutes in 1936. In summer 1947 the 2.30 a.m. Paddington–Bristol newspaper train, the 10.30 a.m. to Penzance, the 11.55 a.m. to Milford Haven and the 1.15 p.m. (SO) to Weston-super-Mare passenger train were all allowed 40 minutes to pass Reading. The 9.5 a.m. Paddington train and some other expresses were allowed 41 minutes to *stop* at Reading, which was a harder schedule to meet than taking 40 minutes to pass the town.

The point-to-point timings west of Reading, either down the 'Berks & Hants' or the Bristol road, required average speeds of less than 60mph. The 9.5 a.m. Paddington train was the most tightly timed train between Paddington and Bristol: 46 minutes from a stand at Reading to passing Swindon, 41¼ miles in 46 minutes – 53.8mph; Swindon to pass Chippenham, 16¾ miles in 17 minutes, including going down Dauntsey bank; Chippenham pass to Bath pass, at 30mph because of the curve,

13 minutes for 12½ miles; Bath to a stop at Temple Meads, 11½ miles in 16 minutes. So for the most part the train was cruising at 60–65mph.

The maximum load which a single locomotive, goods or passenger train, could haul over any GWR route – as shown in the tables at the back of the Working Time Table – was almost the same in 1947 as in 1937. There were a very few, minor, increases. In 1947 a 'King' was allowed to haul 530 tons between Swindon and Paddington rather than the 500 tons of 1937, but the schedules were slower. Goods trains could be made of up to seventy wagons between Swindon and Paddington in 1947, as against sixty in 1937.

Sir James Milne wrote a lengthy article first published in the *News of the World* on 18 May and reprinted in the 'Midsummer' edition of the *Great Western Railway Magazine* explaining the problems that all the railway companies faced. This was entitled 'Holiday Travel will be no picnic'. In abridged form it reads:

> The railways anticipate a record holiday traffic this summer. But all hopes of providing the public with any better facilities than last year were shattered when, in accordance with a decision of the Cabinet Fuel Committee, the Minister of Transport directed that, in order to save fuel, the summer timetable services must be reduced by 10% as compared with 1946. With fewer passenger trains the difficulties experienced last year regulating crowds at stations will be greatly increased. At peak periods some of the main stations will have to be closed for long intervals to prevent dangerous overcrowding ... All holidaymakers must be prepared to run the risk of having to stand for long journeys in corridors and in the compartments and this may happen to people who have had to stand for hours in queues before they can get to the train. Facilities for the reservation of seats have had to be withdrawn because experience has shown that the system invariably breaks down in overcrowded conditions (because) labels are removed and the seats occupied by other passengers.
>
> Time keeping of passenger trains will be adversely affected by speed restrictions made necessary by the lack of new rails and sleepers; by the priority to be given to the movement of coal; by the heavier loading – the greater number of coaches required to convey more passengers in fewer trains. These circumstances are quite outside the control of the railways and that is why I am writing in the *News of the World* to obtain the widest possible understanding of the situation. This, I hope, will not only prevent much unjust criticism of railway administration but will help to reduce public inconvenience by encouraging people to plan their holiday travel accordingly.
>
> Before winter sets in the railways need a minimum stock of two weeks' supply of coal. Today the coal stock held by the railways is equal to 5 or 6 days' consumption. To bring that up to the required minimum of two weeks supply by the end of October an additional 500,000 tons must be put into stock during the next five months.

The movement of lumbering – but utterly vital – coal trains had, from 1945, something like the same priority over other traffic that the 'Jellicoe' coal trains had when they were supplying the Royal Navy in the First World War. The Minister of Transport had restricted the winter passenger timetable to release engines and men for coal traffic and banned, from 9 January, all excursion trains for any purpose. In June he eased the ban, insofar as the GWR were permitted to use their diesel rail cars for excursion traffic provided that these did not hinder the movement of coal.

The situation as regards the availability of motive power on the GWR was actually very slightly better in blizzard February than in summery May/June. This suggests utterly heroic efforts, in the terrible winter, on the part of the shed maintenance staff and the footplate crews.

In the four weeks ending 22 February, the GWR had 3,932 steam locomotives on their books. Excluded from that total were the sixteen GWR engines on loan to the government or private firms and included in that total were sixty-nine engines on loan to the GWR from the LMS, and nineteen from the government. Of that total of 3,932, 78.56 per cent were daily available for use – the others were under repair or having their boilers washed out or undergoing other maintenance. Of those available, 97.26 per cent were in daily use. Those engines that worked passenger, milk and parcels trains ran 2,811,161 miles in traffic and 402,718 miles in shunting and running 'light'. Freight train mileage was 1,602,207 miles in traffic and 1,940,681 miles shunting and running 'light'.

In the four weeks ending 14 June, there were 3,930 locomotives in stock, of which 78.5 per cent were available for use, 97.18 per cent of which were at work, daily. Engines on passenger, milk and parcels trains ran 2,705,610 miles and 398,946 miles shunting and running 'light'. Freight train engines in the May–June period ran 1,719,776 miles with loaded trains and 1,848,479 miles shunting and running 'light'.

In the four weeks ending 22 February the average miles per day run by all engines in use was 70.12. The average hours at work each day for those engines was 12.6. The average miles run in each hour for passenger, milk and parcels trains was 12.38 and for freight trains was 7.42.

The four weeks ending 14 June produced an 'average miles run per day' of 96.13 and 'average hours at work per day' of 12.95 for passenger, parcels and milk trains and 8.56 for freight trains.[7]

In the course of the month of June 188,733 loaded wagons of coal were hauled away from collieries on the GWR system. This was 10,177 more than in June 1946.

A new class of mixed-traffic engine was introduced in June. This was the '9400' class 0-6-0 pannier tank, a modernised version of the '5700' class pannier tank of 1929. Like the latter class, the '9400' was used for local main-line and branch passenger train working. Both classes had the 4ft 7½in driving wheels, which was the standard GWR size for freight working. Below the boiler the '9400' class was identical to the '5700' class – the improvement over the '5700' class was in the fitting of a No 10 standard boiler – and a much more commodious cab than that on the '57s'. The No 10 boiler was fitted to the '2251' of 0-6-0 tender engines – but the latter class had 5ft 2in driving wheels. Ten '94s' were built at Swindon but a further 190 were built by contractors – including Robert Stephenson & Co., the company that built the *North Star* in 1837, the GWR's first successful engine.

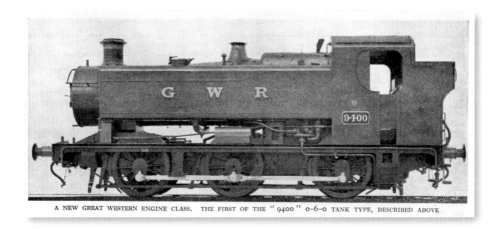

A NEW GREAT WESTERN ENGINE CLASS. THE FIRST OF THE " 9400 " 0–6–0 TANK TYPE, DESCRIBED ABOVE.

There were 7,000 more staff employed in the Locomotive Department in 1947 than in 1938. During the four weeks ending 11 December 1937 there were 39,315 men employed by the Department. Twelve months later this number was decreased to 37,544. From the outbreak of war, numbers employed in the Department began to rise to reach a peak of 48,967 on 30 December 1944. Thereafter numbers fell, but in June 1947 there were still 44,678.

The company's annual 'Horse and Harness' competitions took place at Bristol, Cardiff and Birmingham during May and June. The beautiful horses harnessed in gleaming leather and embellished with gleaming brass enthralled large crowds at the parades and inspection. The RSPCA awarded medallions and diplomas to proud draymen and the directors provided £45 in prize money. Two pairs of GWR Paddington-based horses entered for the Trade and Agricultural Heavy Turnout Class at the Royal Windsor show on 26 to 28 June. Both pairs were awarded Commendations.

The GWR hauled 310 wagon-loads of merchandise and feedstuff to the Bath & West show held on Cheltenham racecourse from 28 May to 31 May. Fifty-four loads of livestock and 280 consignments of large packages came by passenger train. The racecourse had its booked service of passenger trains, but several express and local passenger trains not scheduled to call made special stops at the racecourse station. A total of 103,000 people visited the show compared to the 56,000 who went to the Bath & West show at Bridgwater in 1946.

At the other end of the scale of haulage – and demonstrating the enthusiasm with which the GWR served their very various localities – the Cheddar Valley strawberry traffic was handled in June with van-loads going to major cities, and the first French strawberries since June 1939 were landed at Plymouth on 1 June. Between then and 26 June, 1,450 tons of the fruit were carried away from Millbay docks in thirty-seven full train-loads. Meanwhile at Weymouth, Channel Islands tomatoes were landing and 650 wagon-loads were taken out by the GWR.

The Cornish broccoli season was in progress during June. The GWR had for decades provided express goods trains to carry the season's crop to London, Bristol and Birmingham. GWR express goods trains that were fitted with the vacuum brake on

GREAT WESTERN RAILWAY
MAGAZINE

July · 1947   Vol. 59 · No. 6

Faster Handling of Freight

THE GOODS DEPARTMENT DISPLAYS SOME OF ITS MODERN LOADING APPLIANCES

SPEED, safe transit and economy in manpower—these are dominant factors in the Goods Department's constant search for ways of improving its service to traders and the public generally in the conveyance of all classes of freight.

Recently the department issued a visual progress report, by staging at Paddington a demonstration of modern mechanical appliances designed to simplify and speed up the handling of goods.

Some of this equipment is already in daily use; many of the other appliances will be introduced into regular working as soon as the makers can execute the orders placed by the Company, while others are still being tested in service.

The demonstration was held at St. Ervans Road depot. Traders and representatives of trade papers were invited, many of the Company's principal officers attended, and in view of the great interest of the Company's staff in new appliances for their use, members of Sectional Council No. 4 were specially invited to the demonstration.

Prominent among the exhibits were three new type containers—a far cry from the original S.L. type first introduced in the early nineteen-twenties, and from which so many variations have since been made.

Our new collapsible type of container clearly proved its value for conveying market " empties." Compact and economical of space, the model is a light frame construction with a loading capacity of one ton; and can take a maximum load of 120 fish " empties." Two loaded containers or six empty ones (collapsed) can be stowed on one open wagon, and are craned on or off the vehicle. The contrast between a lorry carrying collapsible containers and a horse-drawn dray laden with stacked empties secured by ropes was most marked.

The second exhibit in this particular field was the covered bulk container, expressly designed for carrying cement, lime, china clay and kindred traffics which are susceptible to climatic conditions. The container is completely weatherproof.

A prototype of this model was sent to the Aberthaw & Bristol Channel Portland Cement Company, who will supply approximately 70,000 tons of cement for use in building the Claerwen Dam project at Rhayader, North Wales. The Cement Company approved the design, subject to minor alterations, and asked the Company to build 72 of the containers. A valuable saving in time, manpower and material will be effected, as it is estimated that well over a million cement bags will be saved by using the covered bulk

CONTAINERS FOR MARKET EMPTIES.   THE TRAILER IS CARRYING TWO—ONE LOADED AND ONE COLLAPSED.

125

each wagon and the brake under the control of the driver were signalled as a 'Five bells' and had no top speed stipulated in the 'Is Line Clear?' Regulations. Express goods trains having not less than one third of the wagons vacuum-braked ran at 35mph and were belled through the signal boxes '4-4'. The vegetables – broccoli or potatoes – were packed in crates in the vans. The crates of vegetables had to be unloaded and carried to road lorries and on 3 June and the following day a series of demonstrations were held at Paddington to show off the latest inventions in mechanical handling adopted by the company.

The demonstrations were attended by public works contractors, greengrocery wholesalers and GWR staff. The four companies were continuing to develop co-operation between themselves, and also the co-ordination of road/rail passenger services, a policy which began in 1930. On show was a standardised, refrigerated rail/road container, which all four railway companies would use. This was to carry ice

The 'Loco Pulseur'. This was a Belgian State Railways device. It ran on rail or plain ground, and moved a maximum of 150 tons at 2–4mph given a level surface. It was powered by a petrol-electric motor.

Spectators from other railways and the road hauliers came to view the demonstrations.

cream, quick frozen foods and pancreas glands for the medical profession. There were new, standardised containers for the bulk conveyance by rail of cement and roadstone, returned empty crates and pallets, loading elevators, and a petrol-engine shunting locomotive. This was a four-wheeled machine running on standard-gauge axles. The demonstration was successful because four of them were built – Nos 23, 24, 26 and 27: two of them were in use in the large, low-level, goods yards at Reading in 1948–50, these being 23 and 24, as I recollect.

The Great Western started a 'Suggestion' scheme in May 1941, with a money prize if the suggestions were adopted by the company. Since the start of the scheme Driver John Drayton, up until June 1947, had 100 of his suggestions adopted by the

The 'Scott' tractor was battery powered. It was an early form of fork-lift for use in large goods sheds. The items were handed out of a wagon beside the goods shed platform, onto the table; the tractor backed its lift beneath the table.

A Bedford-Scammell articulated lorry.

company and with the acceptance of his hundredth suggestion he was awarded £10 for his persistent ingenuity.[8]

Foreman F.J. Herbert, holding this post at the GWR bus depot at Slough, designed an 'Improved jig for boring connecting rods of petrol engines' and was paid £25. R.G. Short, a signalman at Barnstaple, sent in a revised method of working light engines between Barnstaple Junction (SR) and Barnstaple (GW), and was awarded £10. Writing as an ex-signalman – I guess that the *ad hoc* passage of light engines between Barnstaple (GW) and Barnstaple Junction (SR) was immensely irritating to the signalmen, hence the incentive to devise a rational system.

On 20 June 1947 the Annual Inter-Railway First Aid competition was held for the first time since 1939. Each of the four companies sent two teams. The Great Western were represented by the Swindon Works team and the team from Cardiff Docks. It would be fair to say that the Swindon Works team had more experience of injuries than any other team on the GWR. Old-hand Swindon Works people have said to me: 'I don't suppose there was hardly a day went by when the ambulance wasn't called to the factory.' Looking at it in another way, one has to remember that 14,000 men were employed on a 200-acre site containing thousands of cutting, stamping, forging, drilling and boring machines, and they were pouring molten metal and constructing locomotives. Between them the Swindon Works and Cardiff Docks teams gained second place out of the four companies and were awarded the Corbett-Fletcher Cup.

The heat wave, which began in late May, baked the country until early September and temperatures were as hot – and in places hotter – than anything previously recorded. The heat led to some buckled track and to fires. Burning cinders from engines' chimneys set the lineside grass on fire, and also ignited straw and paper left in wagons, wagon sheets and even carriages, specifically the canvas of the corridor connectors between carriages. In the middle of the month thunderstorms occurred, bringing torrential rain, resulting in some flooding and landslides. On 3 June, a Tuesday morning, five cases of buckled track were reported to the Superintendent of the Line.

At 3.30 p.m. on 2 June the 2.55 p.m. Evesham goods train ran over the buckled Up Main line near the Starting signal of Aldington Sidings signal box, which was switched out of circuit at the time. The driver stopped at Littleton & Badsey and reported that he had run over some very rough track which needed looking at. The signalman at once sent 'Obstruction Danger' – 6 bells – to Evesham South signal box. The 2.55 p.m. Evesham train went on its way.

Driver Haynes with 'City' class engine No 3406 *Melbourne*, with the 1.15 a.m. Oswestry–Avonmouth freight train that had forty-four wagons, was approaching Evesham. Haynes was stopped at Evesham South as a result of the receipt of the 6-bell warning signal. He was told to go into the section to Littleton & Badsey under Regulation 15, to proceed cautiously in the vicinity of Aldington sidings and report what he found at Littleton.

As Haynes brought his train to a stand in the platform at Littleton, the coupling between the eighth and ninth vehicles from the engine – a pair of an empty GW 'Fruit A' vans – broke. The train's brakes were well on and the train had almost stopped. The two parts ended up stationary, 20ft apart, the vacuum-pipe couplings pulled apart without damage. The driver went to the signal box to report that the track was buckled at Aldington but had no idea that his train had parted. It was the Foreman in the station sidings that saw what had happened. The front portion reversed and the vans re-coupled using the undamaged coupling of the other vehicle. Fifteen minutes' delay was booked to account for this.

The Littleton signalman reported to his Station Master, a porter was sent along to line to advise Ganger Leadbetter, and an off-duty signalman was contacted at home

First Aid Competitions

HIGH PERFORMANCE STANDARDS REACHED IN REVIVED ANNUAL EVENTS

This year the Great Western Railway First Aid competition finals were held for the first time since 1939. Both events took place at Porchester Hall, Paddington, and were attended by many of the Company's principal officers, including the Chief Medical Officer.

Eight teams, survivors from 93 original entries, took part in the men's final. The test was staged in a restaurant setting, with scenery loaned by Pinewood Studios. Contestants had to render first aid to a waiter who had fallen while carrying a loaded tray.

Swindon " B " team won the Directors' Shield, scoring 202 marks out of a possible 300. Cardiff Bute Docks (188) were second, and won the " Carvell " cup, and Reading No. 2 team (178) were third. Other placings were:—4, Stafford Road; 5, Newport High Street " A "; 6, Taunton " B "; 7, Weymouth No. 1; 8, Old Oak Common Locomotive.

The Rt. Hon. Viscount Portal, P.C., D.S.O., M.V.O., who presided, said how delighted he was, as Chairman of the Company, at the keenness and interest displayed by the staff in this competition. Last year we celebrated the jubilee of the establishment of the Great Western Railway as a Centre of the St. John Ambulance Association, and that was a great record. Congratulating the Swindon members on their success, Lord Portal expressed the Company's appreciation of all its staff who are members of the valuable First Aid Movement.

The Chairman then presented trophies and prizes to the winners, and handed medals and certificates to staff who had rendered exceptionally efficient first aid during 1946. He thanked Dr. H.H. Cavendish Fuller, Chief Medical Officer, for his invaluable services

to the Movement. The Hon. Sir Edward C. G. Cadogan, K.B.E., C.B., a Director of the Company, proposed a vote of thanks to the adjudicators, Major White Knox, O.B.E.,

Planet News photo.

STAIRCASE MISHAP. PLYMOUTH LADIES' TEAM IN ACTION.

M.C. (who spoke congratulating the teams on the excellent standard they had attained) and Dr. G. S. Phillips.

Five teams entered for the women's competition which was held a fortnight later. A feature was the close scoring—only $26\frac{1}{2}$ marks separating the first four teams. Plymouth won the competition, scoring $226\frac{1}{2}$ marks out of a maximum 360, and were awarded the " Florence M. Lean " cup, individual miniature cups and prizes. Paddington were runners-up, with $219\frac{1}{2}$ marks, and gained the " Mabel A. Potter " cup and prizes. Two Swindon teams were rivals for third position, " B " scoring 215 marks against the " A " team's 206, while Teignmouth were adjudged fifth, with 165 marks.

Mr. H. Adams Clarke, Chief Staff and Establishment Officer, who presided, expressed his keen pleasure at the resumption of the women's contest. He congratulated each team on its enterprise in taking part.

After Mr. Adams Clarke had conveyed Mrs. Lean's regrets that she was unable to attend to hand the cup personally to the winning team, he introduced Mrs. Adams Clarke who presented the trophies and prizes. The event concluded with votes of thanks to Col. E. J. Selby, O.B.E., who adjudicated, and to Mr. and Mrs. Adams Clarke.

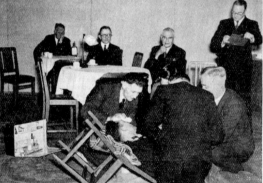

Fox photo.

WAITER SLIPPED WITH TRAY, BUT HAD INSTANT FIRST AID FROM HIGHLY QUALIFIED DINERS.

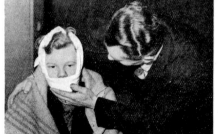

Dominion Press photo.

A FRACTURED JAW. ANOTHER TEST OF FIRST AID SKILL.

and asked to go to Aldington Sidings box to switch into circuit to protect the damaged track. The ganger and his crew arrived at Aldington at 3.50 p.m. They had the track straightened and normal working resumed at 5.5 p.m.

On the same afternoon, over at Warwick, the Permanent Way Inspector reported buckled track at 4.07 p.m. This was in the Up Main at the south end of the station platform. The rail was badly distorted and had to be removed. This proved to be difficult. Single-line working was put into force at 5.20 p.m., affecting all trains over the Down Main, between Warwick station and Leamington North box. Normal working was resumed at 9.17 p.m.

The GWR recorded forty-two occasions when goods trains broke couplings during June and also the parting of seven trains, carrying either passengers, parcels or milk. There was a tendency for there to be fewer breakaways in good weather. Passenger train mileage in June was 2,705,610 and goods trains ran 1,719,726 miles. Seven GWR wagons broke away including two 20-ton brake vans: one of them had a broken link on the 'Instanter' coupling, and the other had a broken draw hook. Eight LMS wagons in GW trains broke away, one because of a broken drawbar, one with a broken draw hook. Nine LNER wagons broke away, two with broken hooks and four with drawbars which pulled apart. Nineteen Private Owner wagons broke away, three with broken hooks, and three with broken drawbars.

That same day the 10.55 p.m. Banbury–Severn Tunnel Junction via the North Warwickshire route had sixty-two loose-coupled, un-braked wagons, with a 20-ton brake van occupied by Guard Harry Bircher. The train was hauled by engine No 2887, with Driver George Sykes and Fireman Len Baker, all three men from Banbury. The locomotive was a Severn Tunnel engine working home. Having worked hard up Hatton bank, the train turned towards the North Warwick line at Hatton East Junction and joined it at South Junction. It was here that the fifty-eighth wagon from the engine broke away. The wagon was owned by 'Fountain Burnley' and was loaded from Port Clarence (a district of Stockton-on-Tees) to Mountain Ash high up in the Cynon Valley, South Wales. The guard heard the coupling break and signalled to the footplate crew – who were looking back as they came around the chord line – that the train was divided.

The crew remained completely calm and in charge of the situation. They were perfectly aware that they were on a falling gradient of 1 in 100. The guard applied his handbrake gently; the driver kept his part of the train going. He stopped his train within the protection of signals at Bearley East Junction, where it was reversed into a siding. Harry Bircher brought his part of the train to a stand at Claverdon Halt – 2 miles from Bearley East. He then walked back three-quarters of a mile and put down three detonators, 10yd apart, and stood there with a red flag just in case, somehow, another train was allowed into the section. The train engine was uncoupled and returned on the other track, the footplatemen looking out in case there was a derailed wagon or wagons. They passed their guard protecting the rear of the breakaway and arrived at Hatton South Junction. Here they were crossed over to the obstructed line and entered the section, cautiously, stopped to pick up their guard and his detonators and went onto the rear of the breakaway. The wagons were propelled to Bearley East, the train re-coupled and off they went – with 40 minutes' delay.

A rather more desperate occasion arose at 3.45 p.m. on 14 June at Little Mill Junction, 1¼ miles north of Pontypool Road. The 5 a.m. Croes Newydd (South Fork) to Pontypool Road stopped at Little Mill Junction to put off traffic. There were forty-one un-braked wagons with a 20-ton brake van at the rear, hauled by engine 'WD' 2-8-0 No 77049, driven by Bill Hancock of Hereford. The train came to a stand on a 1 in 104 rising grade, ahead of the points which led into No 1 Siding. The wagons had come to a stand – unusually for a train on a rising grade – all buffered up tight against the engine. The guard, Fred Price of Hereford, had screwed his handbrake on, which kept the wagons tight up together. The points were pulled over for the siding and the ground signal cleared. Fred Price unscrewed his handbrake. His van immediately started to roll back on the grade; each three-link coupling was slack, thus allowing a foot or so of movement until the links became taut. By the time the backwards movement had reached the front of the train it was moving briskly and several hundred tons of train gave a destructive tug on the coupling on the fourth wagon from the engine, an LMS 'open' with thirty-eight wagons. Unleashed from the engine, it gathered speed back down the incline towards the buffer stops.

Fred Price was unaware of his predicament – but was alerted to the danger by the signalman as he passed the signal box. Fred jumped for his life and was uninjured. A shunter had seen the parting and, reacting quickly, realised that the inevitable collision with the buffers at the end of No 1 siding would cause wagons to tumble all over the branch line to Monmouth and Ross-on-Wye. He ran to a set of hand points in No 1 Siding and, in the nick of time, got them over, thus diverting the runaways in to No 7 Siding which was empty except for an LNER cripple wagon that was against the buffers.

Fred Price and the shunter tried to pin down wagon brakes as the wagons passed but the vehicles moved too fast. The collision took place, completely demolishing the LNER wagon and severely damaging the brake van and four wagons behind it as they smashed the buffer stops out of the way. But no-one was hurt and the Monmouth branch remained clear. Fred Price was held responsible for the mishap because he did not work his brake properly as the train was stopping, and he was 'dealt with under disciplinary procedure'.

On 9 June at 2.25 p.m. at Sampford Peverell, the 10.15 a.m. Hackney (Newton Abbot yard) to Avonmouth freight train, hauled by engine No 2829 (driver not recorded) arrived on the Up Platform Loop. The engine was uncoupled and went into the sidings to shunt and collect wagons. This required a lot of movements and lever pulling because access to the sidings was gained only from the Down Platform Loop. In the sidings there was shunting to do, but after nearly an hour engine 2829 emerged pushing some wagons, across all four tracks, out onto the Down Main, back through the crossover, along the Up Main and back into the Up platform. The train now had seventy-nine wagons, equal to eighty for length, all un-braked – except for the guard's van. The man in charge of this enormously long, difficult, train was a porter acting as a temporary Goods Guard, H.G. Tapley.

The engine and a few wagons were still out on the Up Main after coupling-up had occurred and the train needed to be set back along the Platform Loop to get the engine 'inside clear' of the Up Main. Temporary Guard Tapley waved the engine back – and

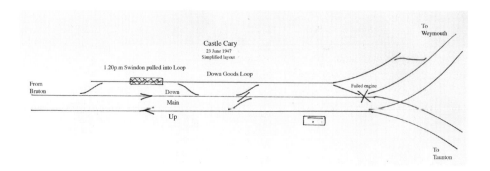

back – and the engine moved seventy-nine wagons, even though the handbrakes of the last four wagons, and that of the 20-ton van, were all tightly pinned down or screwed on. Back went the train and 'onto Olde England' at the end of the Loop. The brake van tipped over and fell across the Up Main at 3.25 p.m. 'Obstruction Danger – 6 bells' was sent for the Up Main and the breakdown vans were ordered from Taunton at 3.30 p.m. They left Taunton at 4.44 p.m. after a fresh brake van had been found and attached to the train. The vans arrived at Sampford at 5.08 p.m. The fresh brake van was attached and the 10.15 Hackney train left at 6.19 p.m.

On 21 June a powerful 2-6-2 tank engine, No 5192, was working the 12.30 p.m. passenger train from Leamington to Birmingham Snow Hill. When the train stopped at Lapworth station the driver reported a broken spring and thus a failure. The 9.30 a.m. Bordesley–Banbury goods train was standing in the Up Refuge siding with engine *Dean Goods*, No 2409, in charge. This engine was quickly commandeered. No 5192 came off the passenger train, No 2409 was put on, and they went away, with 12 minutes' delay. Engine 5192 ran 'light' to Tyseley locomotive shed.

An 'auto' train at Princes Risborough, 27 July 1947. The driver could drive the train from the outer end of the coach. He had a regulator handle in the coach cab which operated rodding back to the regulator handle in the locomotive's cab. On the engine the fireman had to be a qualified driver ('passed fireman'). His job, apart from firing, was to adjust the 'cut-off' screw for admission of steam to the cylinders and also to 'blow the brakes off' after the remote driver had allowed air into the system to apply the brakes.

The Up Main Starting signal at Castle Cary with 'Calling-on' arm below for permitting the bank engine onto the rear of a train; signal on left routing to Up Goods Loop. In the right distance is the Down Goods Loop to Down Main Starting signal with left-hand arm for continuing along the Loop. The signal arm lowered is the Down Main Inner Home. (R.C. Riley/ Transport Treasury)

The 1.20 p.m. Swindon–Weymouth goods train, with forty-seven wagons, stopped on the Down Main, outside the signal box at Castle Cary at 6.5 p.m. on Monday 23 June. The signalman feared the worst. The road was set and the signals were 'off' for the Weymouth road. The driver went up into the box and reported mechanical problems with his engine and said he was going to attempt to put matters right. This was decidedly inconsiderate of the driver, who ought to have stopped 'outside' at Cary and whistled-up to be put into the Loop. The driver tinkered with his engine, couldn't mend it, and came back to report a failure. Now he was stuck, the engine on the Weymouth/Taunton junction and the brake van at the platform.

The following train, the 5.10 p.m. Melksham–Yeovil 'auto', was standing at Bruton station awaiting a clear road. The engine was uncoupled and went 'light' to Castle Cary. It arrived at the brake van of the 1.20 p.m. Swindon train at 6.44 p.m., hooked on, and drew the train backwards into the Down Loop, clearing the main line at 6.54 p.m. The little engine then unhooked, went out of the loop at the Bruton end, onto the Down Main, ran past the goods train, dropped into the loop at the station end and ran past the engine, out onto the Weymouth line, backed onto the engine and took it forwards, clear of the points and back into the Loop and pushed it back onto its train. Having got matters sorted, it crossed to the Up Main, dashed back up to Bruton, rejoined its coach and continued its journey. The passengers had suffered 37 minutes' delay. Behind that, 'waiting the road' at Brewham, the 5.03 p.m. Bristol train had been delayed for 12 minutes.

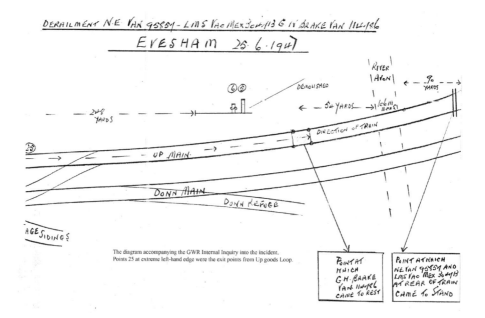

The diagram accompanying the GWR Internal Inquiry into the incident.
Points 25 at extreme left-hand edge were the exit points from Up goods Loop.

Late on a summer evening, on 25 June, Mr Sidney Trout, who had served in the Royal Navy during the Second World War, was working in his garden in Philips Cote, off King's Road, Evesham. He was a Temporary Porter at the LMS station alongside the GWR. His garden was 400yd south of the line, close to the east bank of the River Avon.

At 8.55 p.m. he heard a GWR whistle from the station and the sound of a goods train starting: a goods train was easing itself out of the Up Goods Loop. The engine came under the Birmingham Road bridge and moved slowly towards the Avon bridge. The wagons followed – seemingly endlessly – through the arch. The train was the 6.50 p.m. Worcester–Cardiff, 'C' headcode, with sixty-four wagons. It was hauled by engine No 5992 *Horton Hall*, with Driver R. Kimble and Fireman R. Burton, of Worcester, and Guard Mr Marklove in the brake van. The driver was carefully moving forwards to 'pick up' the slack couplings and get them all taut before putting on steam for acceleration. Sidney Trout unbent from his gardening and watched with an interest that was appropriate to a railwayman – even if he was classed as 'temporary'.

For the subsequent inquiry, Sidney's statement was:

> I saw the guard's van dancing about and at once assumed that it was derailed. I immediately got on my bicycle and rode about half a mile along the pathway of some grounds[9] and got to a pathway alongside the railway line. The engine had already passed that point so I cycled along the path and shouted and succeeded in attracting the driver's attention.

The exit from the Up Goods Loop was close to the South signal box[10] and the signalman received a great shock as the box suddenly shook and shuddered, accompanied by banging and crunching noises. As the brake van came out over No 25 points it was lurching from side to side, obviously derailed. The shock which shot through him in the first instant galvanised him into action – rather than paralysing him. He sent 'Obstruction Danger' – 6 bells – to Littleton & Badsey, and replaced his Up Advanced Starting signal to 'Danger'. The engine had already passed it at 'All Right', of course. He then contacted Control and explained what was happening and finished off by phoning his Station Master, letting him know that he, the Station Master, would have to institute single-line working.

The line curves fairly sharply to the left as it goes through the Birmingham Road arch, but the van remained in sight long enough for the signalman to see it collide with, and demolish, his Up Advanced Starting signal. That was 248yd from his box and close to the River Avon bridge. Guard Marklove was on the verandah of the GWR brake van, watching the train out of the loop. The lurching threw him painfully this way and that but he managed to get the side door open and jump – for his life as he then thought – off his van, then picked himself up and watched his train going away over the bridge. He saw the rearmost wagon was bouncing about on the track. Finally they became still – two more wagons off the road – about 90yd in advance of Aldington Sidings Distant signal. Aldington Sidings box was switched out and the signals were thus showing 'All Right'.

The badly shocked Marklove, with his uniform ripped and his limbs cut and bruised, limped back to the South signal box, carrying out his duties under Rule 179: to put down his 'shots' to ensure that no train was allowed into the section. In so doing he came to the signal box and reported to the signalman at 9.18, giving all the details he had witnessed.

Driver Kimble was unable to see any of this owing to the curvature of the line, but he realised something was wrong. His description of events is:

> My vacuum gauge dropped a few inches and the train seemed unusually heavy but after a few yards the vacuum was alright and the train moved better but was still dragging although the vacuum gauge was correct.[11] I could not have seen the van side lights until after Aldington box but I was very much on the alert. Between the river bridge and the two overbridges I saw a man cycling along the pathway of market garden grounds. He was waving to me, pointing backwards and clearly endeavouring to attract my attention. Acting on his signals I stopped the train. He climbed over the fence and came to the engine and informed me that some rear vehicles were wrong because the van was dancing about. I asked this man – whose name was Trout – if he thought the opposite road was blocked and he said 'Yes', so I sent my fireman forward to Badsey, to protect the opposite road. Afterwards I found that the opposite road was clear.
>
> I would add that Mr Trout had cycled very hard to give us the message and although in an exhausted condition when he approached the engine, he was anxious to render all the assistance he could.

Mr Trout was interviewed by an Inspector from the Worcester Chief Inspector's Office. At the end of his report he wrote:

> A man who can think and act as this man did is worthy of a better position than he has and I would very much like, in addition to anything this Company might do, his action to be brought to the attention of the LM&S Company.
> Yours truly,
> H. Healey

The Littleton & Badsey signalman called up the Honeybourne banker to go through the section to Evesham South to examine the line under the provisions of Regulation 14A and when it was established that the Down line was clear the 6.5 p.m. Paddington–Great Malvern passenger train was allowed to leave Honeybourne at 9.45 p.m. It was travelling on the correct track and did not need special permission. Before Up trains could travel over the Down line the requisite staff had to be gathered at Evesham South and Littleton & Badsey. Single-line working was instituted at 10.50 p.m. with the empty stock of the 10.10 p.m. Stratford-on-Avon–Honeybourne passenger train.

Examination, by lamplight, of the Up Main revealed severe damage to the track for about three-eighths of a mile up to the Advanced Starting signal. Beyond that point there was considerable damage, though not as severe as that caused by the heavy brake van. Practically the whole of the signal wires and point rodding at the south end of Evesham station were demolished. The Worcester vans and crane – together with wagons loaded with new chairs and sleepers – arrived at 11.04 p.m. They were reversed into Evesham yard while the remaining sixty-three wagons of the 6.50 Worcester train had been examined by the Carriage & Wagon Department and then drawn into the sidings at Littleton & Badsey.

Various passenger and important freight trains, which had been stacked up at Worcester awaiting events, had then to be passed through the single line. When the more important Up line traffic had passed, the 6.50 Worcester train left Badsey for Honeybourne and Cheltenham at 12.34 a.m. The train had a fresh guard in another brake van – all these vehicles and guards were ordered in the middle of the night and were promptly supplied.

To repair the damaged track at Evesham not only were the men of the Evesham permanent-way gang called out just after they had gone to bed, but they were reinforced by the Worcester Station permanent-way gangs. The Worcester breakdown vans and Permanent-way Department wagons loaded with sleepers left Evesham at 12.34 a.m. on 26 June, on the single line, unloading materials and men to repair the track before proceeding to Badsey where the permanent-way wagons were put aside and the breakdown vans reversed to the Up line and went back to attend to the derailed wagons.

The two derailed wagons were re-railed at 4 a.m. and hauled to Badsey, where their content was trans-shipped. These vehicles were an LNER box van and an LMS cattle truck, each loaded with fruit and vegetables.

At 7 a.m. a Relief Signalman opened Aldington Siding box so as to reduce, by about half, the length of the single line. The railway always had back-up resources on which to draw. The Up line was repaired sufficiently to be handed back to the Traffic Department at 1.18 p.m. on 26 June, subject to a speed restriction of 15mph over a distance of 1,474yd.

The actions of Sidney Trout did not go unrewarded by the GWR. Gilbert Matthews sent memos to the LMS as well as to his own General Manager stating:

It is considered that the man displayed considerable initiative and promptitude in taking steps to inform the driver of what had happened and his action prevented further damage.

In the circumstances it is recommended that Trout be awarded a gratuity of £5 5*s* in recognition of his actions. The Chief Mechanical Engineer and the Chief Operating Manager of the LMS Railway are in agreement and I shall be glad if you will say you concur. I may add that Mr. Fisher[12] has stated that when he is advised that the award has taken place he will send Trout a personal letter of congratulation.

Sir James Milne – with his usual strict formality – replied coldly but fairly, noting that Matthews had omitted to date his memo:

> Derailment at Evesham 25.6.47
>
> With reference to your undated memorandum in regard to the above matter. I agree to L.M.S Temporary Porter Trout being awarded a gratuity of £5 guineas in recognition of his prompt action on the occasion of the above occurrence.
>
> The amount may be paid out of Petty Cash and my reference quoted as your authority.
>
> Yours truly,
>
> J. Milne.

This note was also sent to Mr Dashwood, Chief Accountant, for his information.

Notes

1 *Rail* 250/482 June.
2 The Corps was given the prefix 'Royal' in 1918.
3 *Rail* 250/469 June.
4 In the Working Time Table this train's schedule was shown as 'Suspended'.
5 In the Working Time Table this train was not scheduled to run on Fridays.
6 *Rail* 250/469 June.
7 *Rail* 250/281.
8 John Drayton wrote about his railway life in *On the Footplate* published by Bradford Barton in 1976.
9 In 1947 there was a market garden and a hospital there.
10 Evesham South signal box was on the Downside, just off the platform end with the main road bridge a little distance to the south. It was abolished on 9 March 1957.
11 The vacuum pipes, having been torn apart by the breaking away of the van, had been almost sealed again by the pipe ends being crushed together by the coiled wire reinforcing preventing the ingress of atmosphere, and the rest of any air leaking in was drawn out by the action of the engine's air pump.
12 The Evesham (LMS) Station Master.

GREAT WESTERN RAILWAY
MAGAZINE

JULY · 1947

VOL. 59 · NO. 6

Pride in the Job—5
(See Page 134)

PRICE ONE PENNY

JULY

Seventeen directors met at Paddington on 18 July, under the chairmanship of Viscount Portal. The recommendations of Mr Guillebaud's Court of Inquiry into railwaymen's wages, salaries and working conditions were discussed. Guillebaud recommended that the unions' claim for a 44-hour week for wages grades and 42-hour week for salaried staff be granted, together with an extra 7s 6d a week for wages grades and a £19 10s increase on the annual pay for salaried staff, with lesser amounts for juveniles. Guillebaud stated that his report 'could only be considered as a short-term solution because in a very short time the transport industry will be nationalised and may well then be considered as one unit and thus relative wages and conditions between the various sections will be a matter requiring careful consideration'.

The GWR directors did not believe that they could take any responsibility in implementing the report, since they were about to be abolished. A letter was sent to the Minister suggesting, very diplomatically, that the Minister should take responsibility for matters which would be his headache long after the GWR had been abolished. Here is an extract:

> In view of the magnitude of the financial issues involved, the railway companies could not assume the responsibility of dealing with the claims put forward by the Unions. In these circumstances, and bearing in mind that the recommendations of the Court of Inquiry involved negotiations with the Unions, it has been suggested to the Minister that the Railway Executive Committee might be asked for their observations on the Report, following which, consideration could be given to the issuing of such directions to the railway companies through the REC as the Minister may decide.[1]

At this meeting they approved the expenditure of £19,121 on accounting machines at the Mineral Accounts Office in the GWR Barry docks, and £684,297 for the supply of fifty articulated tractors from Scammell and Burrell & Edwards, together with twenty insulated containers. Fifteen mobile cranes were ordered, costing £33,278. The amount of £111,200 was allocated for the replacement of the boiler at the Sudbrook pumping station, £141,045 for staff hostels at Banbury, Southall and Westbury, £10,600 for renewing the telegraph poles and wiring between Camborne and Gwinear Road and Stow-on-the-Wold to Kingham. The list goes on. Salary increases were awarded to six divisional officers including R.G. Pole, Divisional Manager at Bristol, who got an additional £50 a year added to his annual £1,700 (equivalent to £54,423 in 2012). Pole's assistant Leslie Edwards had a larger rise, from £928 to £1,200 p.a.

(equivalent to £38,304 today). Both men had – of course – spent their entire working lives on the GWR. They were legends in their own lifetime and their fine reputations lingered for years: I heard them spoken of with admiration at various times between 1960 and 1975.

Details of revenue earned in July are not reported in the Company Minutes, because each month's figures are reported as 'estimates' in the General Manager's report to the Traffic Committee of the following month. There are no Minutes for August because all the directors of the GWR went on holiday during that month.

Although coal trains were top priority, freight trains additional to those scheduled in the Working Time Table *were* run in order to clear cargoes coming into GWR ports. The government concluded an agreement with the Spanish for the importation of 60,000 tons of salt. This was for distribution to British highways authorities for use in winter. The first 3,000 tons arrived in Cardiff GWR docks at the end of July and was hauled away by the GWR.

The General Manager reported to the Board on 17 July that the Winter Timetable would commence on 6 October. The arrangements for passenger trains had been planned to meet the directions of the Minister of Transport. The timetable was to revert – almost – to what had been agreed with him for the previous winter's train service. A number of winter trains which had been lightly loaded in the January to April timetable remained in the timetable but were shown 'suspended' – the 'paths' were there 'if required'.

Paddington station on Saturday 26 July, the week prior to the bank holiday weekend.

GREAT WESTERN SUMMER ACADEMY. TWO SPECIMENS OF THE COMPANY'S NEW SERIES OF PICTORIAL POSTERS.

The 'Cornish Riviera' and 'Torbay' expresses would be allowed to run. The 'Cornish Riviera' would stop at Exeter on Saturdays to 'pick up only'. The 'Torbay' was a 'Saturdays Only' train in the summer and would continue as it had done, leaving Paddington at 12 noon and calling at Taunton, Exeter and Newton Abbot. In the Up direction the 'Cornish Riviera' would call every day at Par and Exeter and on Saturdays it would call additionally at St Erth. The Up 'Torbay Express' would be combined at Newton Abbot with the 5 a.m. Penzance–Paddington train, scheduled to arrive at Paddington at 4.35 p.m. with stops at Exeter, Taunton and Reading. This arrangement made it possible to restore the 1.15 p.m. Penzance–Paddington train, calling at main stations.

The 1.15 p.m. Paddington–Bristol train (Saturdays Only) was introduced and the 2.35 p.m. Paddington–Bristol train – famous for travelling the Great Way Round via Newbury and Devizes – was restored.

Channel Island steamer services out of Weymouth were restored in April 1947 and an operationally expensive, dedicated boat train service was introduced to convey Channel Island passengers. These did not serve Weymouth Town terminus, but, having changed the express locomotive for a small tank engine, went directly to the quayside along the tramway and through the town. In the summer timetable, the 6 p.m. Paddington ran to Weymouth Town station with coaches at the rear for Channel Island passengers. Coaches from the quay were attached to the 4.15 Weymouth–Paddington. A restaurant car was included for the winter service from 5 October.

The re-worked Winter Timetable entailed 86,083 steam-hauled train miles and 4,853 diesel-rail car miles per day, which was a decrease of 11,813 steam-hauled miles and 168 diesel-rail car miles per day compared with the Winter Timetable which commenced on 1 October 1946.

The company's internal social amusements and entertainments – amateur dramatics, music, football, rugby, cricket teams, first-aid competitions and exhibiting their cart

BRISTOL COMPETITIONS: (*Left*) MR. H. BOLTON AND (*right*) MR. R. G. POLE CONGRATULATING PRIZE WINNERS.

LLANELLY TRADESMEN'S AGRICULTURAL SOCIETY'S SHOW. LLANELLY GOODS HORSES GAINED AWARDS.

ROYAL WINDSOR HORSE SHOW. A GREAT WESTERN PAIR IN THE ARENA.

horse teams at county shows and at inter-Divisional parades, plus horse and harness competitions – started in March and filled the succeeding months. Twenty-six teams from the Birmingham Division took part in the final parade at Moor Street station in July, where they were judged by the Company's Birmingham veterinarian, Captain Dawes, the GWR Divisional Goods Manager, Mr Warren-King, and the Traffic Superintendent, Mr A.V.R. Brown. Parades and judgings took place at Bristol, Cardiff and Paddington.

Two teams of GWR horses, carters and carts were sent to the Royal Windsor Horse Show. The GWR teams did not win any official prizes – those went to brewery teams from around the country. Those horses were expensive, pedigree animals worth £250 or more, whereas the GWR's cart horses cost around £90. However, the representative of a Birmingham cartage company – who regarded the GWR horsemen as 'amateurs', sent this letter to the company:

> I was extremely impressed with the manner in which your two drivers conducted themselves and their turnouts at the Royal Windsor Horse Show that I am sending £5 as a gift from me to be shared between them. When I see such excellent work and interest taken by amateurs whose daily work is to carry on, as opposed to professional drivers I think it is only fair that they should have some special reward.

The Annual Swindon Works Holiday – Swindon Trip – was permitted to take place by the Minister of Transport. Twenty thousand Swindon factory workers and their families were taken to the seaside resort of their choice on 5 July. Twenty-four special trains were required for them, and these left between 11 p.m. on 5 July and 8 a.m. on the following day. Some families stayed on holiday until 12 July and thirteen 'specials' were needed to bring those people home, while the folk who were able to stay on holiday until 19 July had eleven 'specials' to bring them home. The

Sawing white-hot metal. (Hubert Cook)

The Welder. (Hubert Cook)

Heating metal prior to forging.
(Hubert Cook)

Hydraulic riveting. (Hubert Cook)

engines and carriages came from major depots on the GWR and ran 'empty stock' to Swindon, arriving on Friday evening and continuing to do so into the early hours of Saturday. Some trains started from Swindon station, but to cope with this astonishing peak, trains were brought onto the Carriage Works sidings alongside the main line. The passengers, men, women and children, climbed aboard in lamp-lit darkness using short ladders. That was all a part of the excitement and the great ritual of the 'Trip'.

Excursion trains for the general public were still forbidden – except that, since June, diesel rail cars could be used, provided that the excursion trip did not take them off their booked duties.

Swindon Works was a world in itself. It was a great community of men and women – and their families at home – all bound together in the common purpose and yet full of individuality. The work was certainly not for the faint hearted and the resulting characteristic 'Swindon Works humour' was dry and sarcastic, but also very funny. There was a male-voice choir of sixty-one, and many other talented people in clubs for drama, debating, sports and the arts. The camaraderie of Swindon Works illustrated that life is, indeed, 'what you make it'.

In 1934 Hubert Cook, a gifted artist who was working as a machinist in Swindon Works, was attending to his lathe by day and attending art classes at the Swindon School of Art in the evenings. Cook's talent was noticed and was encouraged by the GWR Staff Association, always there to assist talent of any kind, and he was given a monetary grant by the directors to pursue his studies at the Royal College of Art. The result was the blossoming of a unique artist – one who was able to 'see' and paint the peaceful beauty of landscapes as well as the dramatic power of scenes around Swindon Works.

At 9 a.m. on 5 July Driver Len Baker and his fireman booked on at their home depot, Severn Tunnel Junction. The morning was warm and looked set to become hotter. The two men walked to the Goods Lines and relieved the men on the 3 a.m. Radyr–Moreton Cutting Yard. Their engine was an ex-Great Central Railway, ex-War Department 2-8-0, No 3028, allocated to Wolverhampton (Oxley) shed, and the load was 51 tons of coal. Len Baker's engine was a Class E locomotive – the most powerful grade of goods engine on the GWR – but it was still eleven wagons over the load for the climb from under the River Severn to easier grades after Patchway. While Baker and engine No 3028 stood in Severn Tunnel yard, Severn Tunnel pilot engine, 2-6-2 tank No 4137, with Driver Tom Parry, backed down and was hooked on to the front for extra power.

At the English end, illuminated by daylight, was a trap point to derail the rear part of a train which had broken away further on. Breakaways in the tunnel were fairly frequent but, given the frightful nature of the place, it was remarkable they didn't happen more often.

The engines had blasted out of the tunnel and into the hot sunshine at the English end and were going on up the hill when the three-link coupling on an LMS wooden coal wagon, fourth from the engine, broke. A gang of ten track men – the Ganger, Sub-ganger and eight Lengthmen – who were working on the Down line, saw and heard the event and dashed the few feet to the wagons while they were still – just – moving forwards. All of them worked hard to pin down the handbrakes of the wagons and got enough down to stop them running back into the tunnel. The guard was sheltering in his van from the choking fumes and saw none of this and only realised his train had broken away when it came to a stand in silence.

The Chief Civil Engineer of the Great Western Railway, Mr A.S. Quartermaine, was informed of his men's prompt action and wrote to the General Manager, Sir James Milne, to say: 'these men prevented a serious derailment with subsequent interference to traffic and their action merits recognition'. That meant a 'gratuity' should be paid to the men. Milne was pleased to oblige. The Ganger, W.E. Williams of Pilning, received a guinea (£1 and 1s) and each of the eight men got half a guinea. They were: Lengthmen G.I.R. Tudor, S. Jefferies and J.A. Strickland, all from Pilning; Sub-ganger A. Oakhill from Patchway; Lengthmen E.W. Croxon and J. Thomas of Patchway; G.R. Tudor and B. Roddy of Severn Beach.

The heat wave intensified in July, causing tremendous thunderstorms and torrential rain, flash floods and landslides. On 3 July the signalman for Tonmawr Junction cycled in darkness through heavy rain to get to his signal box for the booked time of opening – 4 a.m. This was to enable the passing of the 3.15 a.m. Duffryn Yard (Port Talbot)–Glyncorrwg goods train. Tonmawr Junction box was remote from any road or lane, in a deep valley between thousand-foot hills and very close to the rushing Afon Corrwg. He wheeled his bike along the trackside path to his signal box, and then crossed the bridge over the river – the signal box was a few yards beyond the bridge and the same distance before the portal of Tonmawr tunnel, which was 1,109yd long.

While crossing the bridge the signalman was alarmed to hear the sound of the swollen river flooding just below him, the noise of thousands of tons of roaring water. He knew that the tunnel had been driven through some unstable strata (there was a history of landslips) so, having switched in his signal box at 4 a.m., he decided to check the tunnel. He found a landslide blocking the line. He ran back to his box and sent 'Obstruction Danger' – 6 bells – to Glyncorrwg at 4.05 a.m., and telephoned for the Ganger. The latter fetched his men out of bed rather earlier than they would have liked, but they came quickly, arriving at 5 a.m., and, using their picks and shovels, had the mud and rocks thrown to one side and the track cleared at 5.45 a.m. The 'Obstruction Removed' bell signal, 2-1, was then sent and normal working resumed.

At 10.30 p.m. on 6 July there was another fall of rock at the tunnel mouth. The Gang was called. They worked through till 4 a.m. the following morning to have the line open for the 3.15 a.m. Duffryn Yard.

At about 8.55 p.m. on 13 July, just after a train had passed, an estimated 100 tons of earth and rock fell at the tunnel mouth, filling the cutting to a depth of 8ft. The 6-bells signal ('Obstruction Danger') was sent and the Glyncorrwg Station Master was made aware of the situation at 9 p.m., and he called the Ganger. The Station Master arranged for traffic out of Glyncorrwg Colliery and the South Pit to travel to Port Talbot docks via Cymmer and Tondu.

The Port Talbot to Tonmawr Junction–Glyncorrwg branch was closed while the Divisional Engineer decided what to do about the very unstable strata at the tunnel. Mechanical digging equipment was necessary to clear the line and there would be great difficulty in getting heavy plant to the site. There was an alternative route to the ports for Glyncorrwg coal, and so Tonmawr tunnel and the line beyond to North Rhondda was abandoned.

There were more very heavy thunderstorms and massive rainfall from 16 July to 19 July. From just south of Shrewsbury to just north of Wolverhampton, the rain fell 'whole water' for hours. Track circuits became occupied because of the water short-circuiting the rails. Landslides blocked the rails, buried signal wires and damaged point-rodding by bending it. At Madeley Junction all these disasters happened at 2.34 p.m., but by 7 p.m. the local permanent-way gang and the Signal & Telegraph Department lineman had the railway back to normal. At Stanwardine Halt, near Haughton, at 7.30 p.m. the embankment slipped away, exposing the sleeper ends. The Engineering Department declared the site safe for trains at 5mph at 9.30 p.m. A man was stationed on the site all night to keep an eye on it and the signalmen on each side stopped trains and warned the drivers.

At Condover, south of Shrewsbury on the Hereford line, hours of heavy rain flooded the tracks up to rail level and caused the failure of the track circuit ahead of the Down Home signal at 2.30 p.m. The signalman then noticed, looking through torrential rain towards Shrewsbury, that the embankment top and the rails had acquired a slight 'dip'. He called for his permanent-way gang. The track was declared safe for speeds of 5mph and a watchman was provided, who had to stand there in torrential rain. At 7.30 p.m. the Up line track circuits shorted out, locking the signals to the rear.

The rails were under 4in of water from Priestfield to Stow Heath and Bilston from 6 a.m. until 2.30 p.m. on 16 July. On 19 July a portion of the retaining wall of the Brook Street bridge at Bilston was burst open by the weight of waterlogged earth behind it. At Oxley the drains beside the track burst open and washed away the top several feet of the embankment, leaving sleeper ends in mid-air; there was 6in of water over the rails between Priestfield and Stow Heath. On the Halesowen branch monsoon quality rain fell and washed onto the line tons of debris from a slag heap belonging to Coombs Wood colliery. The GWR notified the colliery manager and men were sent to dig the slag off the rails.

On 13 July engine No 5510 attached to the 2.17 p.m. Bath–Chippenham stopping train failed at Box station at 2.32 p.m. While the engine's brakes were being applied a shaft in the brake gear broke, rendering the brakes inoperative, but not interfering with the operation of the brakes on the train, which brought coaches and engine to a safe stand at the station. The Box signalman made inquiries and found that there was an engine shunting in the Royal Naval sidings at Thingley. He requested this to be sent to Box. It arrived at 3.03 p.m. Having taken engine No 5510 off the train and placed it in the sidings, the fresh engine took the train on to Chippenham.

On 17 July engine No 4925 *Eynsham Hall* on the 9.45 p.m. Stonehouse (Glos.) to Crewe train failed at Didcot North Junction signal box at 1.53 a.m. The left-hand valve spindle gland had fallen out, so the engine was working on one cylinder. The signalman set the points for the Down Goods Loop to Appleford Crossing box. Engine No 4925 was able to struggle into the Loop and get the whole train inside, clear of the main line. The signalman contacted Didcot shed, explained No 4925's problem and asked for a fresh engine. A fresh engine went out with the Didcot Yard Pilot coupled *behind* it. This was good thinking. The pair arrived at Appleford at 2.30 a.m. and uncoupled on the Down Main line. The Yard Pilot engine, nearest to the Loop exit points, went into the Loop, coupled to No 4925 and drew it out onto the Down Main and from there propelled it into the Up Loop. The fresh engine could then back onto the train. The 9.45 p.m. Stonehouse train left at 2.53 a.m. and the failed engine was propelled back to Didcot North and the shed along the Up Loop.

The loss of the valve spindle gland was blamed on the driver who had not seen that the nuts securing it to the cylinder casting were very loose when he examined the engine before taking it out.

At 11.45 p.m. on 17 July the 8.10 p.m. Swindon–Paddington passenger train, hauled by the venerable 'Bulldog' engine 4-4-0 No 3375 *Sir Watkin Wynn*, failed at Langley Up Relief Line Starting signal. The guard advised the signalman of the failure and asked for a fresh engine. This arrived from Slough on the Up Main at 12.24 a.m. on 18 July. After working its way across all four tracks this engine took No 3375 into the sidings and then took the train on, leaving at 12.49 a.m. Engine No 3375 was cut up in September 1947.

When there was no rain the baking hot weather created ideal conditions for fires on the line. Sparks from passing engines landed in empty open wagons and set light to the rubbish or straw lying inside. There were fire-related incidents of this kind occurring on railways lines around a wide area. On 20 July the driver of the 10.10 p.m. Oxford–Henley, with empty coaches, stopped at Goring at 11.10 p.m. to report to the signalman a wagon on fire in the sidings at Cholsey. The signalman phoned his mate at Cholsey and he sent the porter into the siding to deal with the fire. The wagon was a big one – an LNER bogie bolster No 93804, empty, and labelled 'back to the LNER via Banbury'. In the dark, and with only a couple of buckets of water, the porter could not do a lot but the 4.40 p.m. Exeter–Kensington milk train was signalled on the Up Relief Line. The Cholsey signalman stopped it at 11.20 p.m., and pointed out the fire in the siding adjacent to the Up Relief Line, 100yd along the line. The driver drew his train up alongside the fire. Turning on the feed water to the boiler he was able to use the coal watering hose, supplied by the boiler water injector, to hose the flames. The fire was out at 11.45 p.m. The bogie bolster was examined and found to be rather charred in its timbers but otherwise safe to travel. It went away from Cholsey on 24 July.

On 24 July Brewham signal box was destroyed by fire. It was freshly painted outside and inside, including its 14 levers. The signal box stood on the Downside of the line at the summit of the steep 6½-mile climb from Castle Cary. Witham signal box was 2½ miles further east. The signal box was an all-wooden structure set onto the ground without any foundations. It was brought into use in March 1907 with 9 levers and given a 14-lever frame in 1920, when a siding to stable the banking engine was introduced. There was no piped water, no electricity, no flush lavatory – or indeed any lavatory, since the surrounding fields afforded personal privacy. About 200yd to the west of the box was the Strap Lane bridge, on the west side of which was a wooden 'halt'. It was remote – a lovely place to work amid beautiful countryside, with the bank engines to attend to as well as the main-line trains steaming hard uphill from both sides of the summit.

Temporary signalman William Kingdon was on the night shift on 24 July. He was aged 19 and had been working Brewham box for eighteen months, and he cycled to work. At 11 p.m. he had the 3.45 p.m. Penzance Perishables train coming up the bank and he knew there would be a gap of time after that to have a cup of tea in peace. To boil water the company provided a 'Valor' paraffin stove. This was a circular tank of fuel with the burner set into the top. A tower-like, metal cylinder encompassed the burner and rose 9 or 10in to a platform on which the kettle stood. The 'Valor' was placed on a locker top – and inside that locker was the two-gallon paraffin can. That was a fairly common thing to do because the stove lived in the locker with the fuel can. The kettle was an ancient GWR cast-iron vessel, very considerably heavier than the paraffin stove, even when empty. Kingdon lit the stove and put the kettle on top.

The Penzance train came blasting past the box at 15mph. Kingdon stated at the subsequent inquiry that as it did so, the stove toppled off the locker onto the floor, and immediately the fuel caught fire. He grabbed the doormat and tried to smother the flames with that, but the mat started to burn and he realised that the blaze was out of control and he had no alternative but to leave. He ran down the steps, got on his bike, intending to raise the alarm with the Witham signalman by using the telephone beside the Up Home signal. As he pedalled he heard the fog signal 'detonators' stored in the signal box exploding. From the Witham's Up Home signal phone he reported what had happened, gave 'Obstruction Danger' and asked for the fire brigade. He then cycled on to Witham box to collect detonators to place on the Down line in accordance with 'Obstruction Danger' and then returned to his blazing box.

By the time the fire brigade arrived from Bruton the signal box was a pile of hot charcoal – in the midst of which was the blackened, heat-distorted ruin of the once brightly painted, silver-handled 14-lever frame.

With the signal box destroyed there was no bell or block instrument communication between Bruton and Witham signal boxes, but the overhead telephone lines were operating, so permission for trains to proceed would be carried out under Regulation 25 (a) (iii). All signalling messages normally sent by bell and block instruments were sent by telephone. The Signal & Telegraph Department at Frome were roused from their beds in order to restore the Block Telegraph circuits between Bruton and Witham.

The 3.50 p.m. Milford Haven–Yeovil Pen Mill fish train was held at Witham for 121 minutes and the 11.20 p.m. Taunton–Wolverhampton parcels train was held at Bruton for 115 minutes. Behind those only the 6.20 p.m. Penzance–Kensington milk train and the 12.15 a.m. Paddington–Penzance newspapers train were delayed, for 9 and 11 minutes respectively – which suggests that Control acted very quickly and diverted West of England traffic via Bristol.

The officers inquiring into the loss of an entire signal box and all it contained wrote:

We find it difficult to accept Signalman Kingdon's statement that the vibration of a passing train – at low speed – caused the stove to fall. We made a test with a 'Valor' stove at Blatchbridge Junction – which is a small wooden box similar to Brewham and where trains pass at speed – but there was no noticeable effect when a Down express and an Up freight passed simultaneously. However, it must be recorded that Blatchbridge is a much newer box than was Brewham.

We have found no evidence to refute Signalman Kingdon's statement that he was replacing signal levers and signalling the train on to Witham when the stove fell. The signal levers in the frame show that the Up Distant and Home had been replaced and the Starting signal lever was still over.

We are of the opinion that Signalman Kingdon showed a lack of initiative in dealing with the outbreak.

Relief Signalman George Coleman of Frome, with thirty-three years' GWR service, twenty-seven of those as a signalman, worked the early turn in Brewham box on 24 July and he stated: 'I use the oil stove whenever I am at Brewham. I place it on the oil locker top and find this a very suitable place. I have not noticed any undue oscillation at Brewham.'

The final word goes to the investigators, H. Pearson of the Engineering Department, R. Whittington from Bristol Division Superintendent's Office and R. Lane of the Signal & Telegraph at Frome. They wrote: 'It does seem necessary that some kind of fire-fighting appliance is provided at signal boxes.' A new signal box, all wood but standing on firm foundations, was brought into use on 17 August. But it had no fire extinguisher and no signal boxes along that line ever had such appliances.

A fire which descended into farce – and had nothing to do with the heat wave – began at High Wycombe on 26 July. Signalman Cooper had walked to High Wycombe station from West Wycombe signal box at the end of his shift. At 6.50 p.m. he was astride his motorbike on the platform. He pedalled down on the kick-starter and flames burst out from the vicinity of the engine. Dismounting with some urgency, he pushed the flaming machine rapidly through the booking hall, hitting and breaking open a wooden cage designed to hold fish boxes awaiting collection. Outside the station he hauled the bike backwards onto its stand. He had in mind the fire buckets in the Gents' lavatory. He rushed in, grabbed two buckets, ran out and dashed the contents over the engine. All this activity had not gone unnoticed: passengers in the booking hall were astonished and people outside were staring and wondering what to do. While Mr Cooper was running to and from the Gents' lavatory a postman and a GWR lorry driver started to move.

Just as Mr Cooper had poured the second bucket of calming water upon the fire – almost but not quite dousing the flames – the postman arrived, gave the bike a hard shove and knocked it over. Petrol leaked from the tank, followed by a mighty explosion. The GWR lorry driver was parked further away from the fire than the postman. He arrived with his GWR fire extinguisher just as the motor cycle went up in a ball of flame. The flames were extinguished and order was restored – but the sad result was a smouldering wreck. There is no mention of Mr Cooper being charged for the damage to the fish storage cage.

On 22 July the 1.30 a.m. Cardiff–Banbury freight train, with forty-three wagons, was hauled by a 'WD' engine, 2-8-0 No 77106. It drifted through Newport station, passing the East signal box at 9.22 a.m. but then, with a clear road signalled ahead through the Maindee junctions, the driver put on a little steam. Three-quarters of a mile further on, approaching Maindee East Junction signal box, No 77106 had the full weight of the train. The engine had just passed over the junction points when the right-hand connecting rod became disconnected from the crosshead, dropped onto the sleepers, and penetrated the ground. The engine vaulted over the embedded rod, giving the engine a heave to the left, and causing the crew to have an awful fright and, continuing to run along the rails, pulled the rod out of the ground and dragged it along the sleeper ends. The driver braked and the train came to a stand outside the signal box at 9.27 a.m. The signalman had been observing the train according to the Regulations, and he saw the frightening lurch to the left and at once sent 'Obstruction Danger' signal – 6 bells – to the three signal boxes with which he worked.

The line between Maindee East and Newport East was examined on foot at 9.49 a.m. and found to be safe for Down trains. An engine entered the Newport East–Maindee East Junction section under the provisions of Regulation 14 and went to the rear of the goods train, coupled on, and drew it back 100yd so that the leading end was clear of the points from the Up Main to the Up Goods Loop. An engine working at East Usk Junction, the next box east of Maindee East, came Down the Up Goods Loop under the provisions of a Wrong Line Order and was thus able to get onto the front of the goods train waiting on the Up Main just clear of the Loop points. The goods train was then drawn into the Loop, and the engine from Newport crossed to the Down main to return to the station. That left the disabled engine standing on the Up Main outside the box. While all these manoeuvres had been taking place, an engine with fitters on board had come out of Ebbw Junction locomotive depot, through Newport station, and turned onto the Abergavenny line at Maindee West. At the north end of the triangular junction it stopped, crossed to the other side of the line and as soon as the disabled engine was standing on its own, this engine came around the east curve and onto the Up Main.

Passenger trains needing to get away eastwards from Newport could then get past the crippled engine by using the Up Goods Loop at Maindee East Junction. The Goods Loop was normally worked under 'Permissive Block' regulations – permitting more than one train at a time to occupy the section. A 'Block Conversion Ticket' was written out at Maindee East Junction and was carried to East Usk Junction by a man on foot. Once this had been delivered the Goods Loop came under 'Absolute Block' regulations – one train at a time only in the section.

The dropping of the connecting rod was due to the little-end gudgeon pin locking plate falling off because the head of each of the three bolts securing it to the rod had sheared from the threaded part. As a consequence, the plate fell and the gudgeon pin worked its way out. The Chief Mechanical Engineer, Mr Hawksworth, stated that a failure of that nature cannot be seen under a driver's inspection and that the design of this locking plate was being reviewed to facilitate a plan to fit better plates in future.

Cradley Heath station was the hub for a complex of industrial branch lines serving iron foundries, brickworks, steelworks and collieries. On 9 July a Mr Stacey of 90 Graingers Lane, Cradley Heath, wrote a letter of complaint to the Great Western Railway at Paddington and the letter found its way to the office of David Blee, Chief Goods Manager. The subsequent correspondence reveals the tolerant, literally fatalistic, attitude of the railwaymen on the spot compared to the top Management at Paddington. Mr Stacey wrote:

Dear Sirs,

I wish to make a complaint regarding the way some of your employees leave the trucks on the siding from Cradley Heath station to Corngreaves Works. On Wednesday night I was at home and saw some of the trucks running down the line endangering life. This I found was caused through children releasing the brakes. I went and stopped them but in so doing I got injured making it impossible for me to carry on my employment. Also it has caused me to have my teeth extracted, besides doctor's attendance, having two stitches in my lip.

I trust that you will see your way clear to compensate me in some way.

Yours truly,

S. Stacey.

Mr Stacey had no legally enforceable claim on the company but David Blee sent a memorandum and Mr Stacey's letter should be sent to the General Manager, Sir James Milne.

I enclose a copy of a letter received from the above named in regard to the action he took in connection with the stopping of runaway wagons in Cradley Heath goods yard on 9 July ... The siding upon which the trucks had been standing is on an incline and Mr. Stacey recognizing the possibility of an accident proceeded to the spot which entailed his climbing our fence and the embankment. He found that children had released the brakes. In order to reach the wagons to stop them he fell sustaining injury to his face and teeth.

The following morning Inspector Barrett and Checker Partridge observed that the wagons had been moved but apart from that there is no evidence to corroborate Mr. Stacey's statement. Nevertheless there is no reason to doubt him.

I recommend that Mr. Stacey be allowed an amount of £6 to cover his loss of wages and in view of the action taken by him, that he be granted a gratuity of two guineas.

Will you kindly consider the matter and let me know if you concur?

Signed 'For David Blee'

A GWR Official, Mr G. Howard, perhaps the Cradley Heath Goods Agent, was sent to talk to Mr Stacey. This official wrote a memorandum to the General Manager, detailed here:

I have had a talk with Mr. Stacey. He explained that he was shaving that evening and he saw, reflected in his shaving mirror a number of youths attempting to set trucks free on our line which runs along an embankment at the end of his garden. The line is on a falling gradient (towards the Corngreaves and other Works) and he was fearful that there would be a disaster. He at once rushed from the house to chase the boys away and in mounting the embankment he slipped and fell cutting his upper lip and dislodging a number of teeth.

He has insurance for his doctor and dentist's attention but he has lost four days pay from his regular employment and a number of hours as a gardener for his employer who pays him time and a quarter at his day time rate for this additional work. Mr. Stacey says he has lost £6.

I told Mr. Stacey that the Company appreciate his action and regret that he hurt himself so badly.

I recommend that he be given a gratuity of £10.

Checker Partridge was asked for a statement and this captures perfectly the casual 'live and let live' attitude of those times. At one point he might imply that he thought Mr Stacey an interfering busy-body:

I left three wagons for repair on Corngreaves siding. The brakes were properly secured when I left them but next morning I saw that the brakes had been eased and had moved away about six wagon lengths and then stopped. They had grease boxes and the gradient was slight, they would not have run far.

The Fireman on No. 6 shunting engine told me that some man – I now know as Mr. Stacey – saw the trucks moving and ran to stop them and fell down and suffered a cut lip and two teeth loosened. I had forgotten about the incident until asked to make this statement.

I would like to add that trespassing in Corngreaves Sidings is a continual thing, in fact, if I look on the sidings and see no trespasser I am surprised. The sidings are in fact a playground for children – and grown-ups too.

Yours truly,
Checker Partridge

The General Manager's Office gave consideration to the recommendation to reward Mr Stacey. On 15 September a letter went back to Blee's office asking: 'Does Corngreaves Sidings belong to the GWR and do we have any responsibility for them?' David Blee's office replied on 16 October: 'Corngreaves Siding is in fact a Branch Line and is the property of the Company.' The memo concluded:

... Regarding the final paragraph of your communication, the sidings are enclosed with a 5-strand wire fence and beyond the exhibition of a notice prohibiting trespassing I do not know what other measures can be adopted to prevent unlawful entrance, particularly by children and youths. The local Officer is, however, communicating with the Divisional Engineer on this subject.

In the General Manager's Office this paragraph was given a pencilled double line and the word 'Police?' added. And there, as far as prevention of trespass was concerned, the matter rested.

As to Mr Stacey, four months later, on 22 October, he was awarded a gratuity. The time lapse since the event had obscured the reason for paying it – but at least he got it. The General Manager's Office invented a reason for paying. The letter of authorisation from the General Manager's Office to David Blee's Office was headed thus:

MR. S. STACEY, 90 GRAINGERS LANE CRADLEY HEATH;
STOPPING A RUNAWAY HORSE CRADLEY HEATH GOODS YARD 9.7.47

I have received your Memorandum of 17th inst. and although there is no liability attaching to the Company, in view of Mr. Stacey's action on the above occasion, I agree to him being paid an amount of £8. 2s 0d. as a gratuity.

I shall be glad if you will arrange accordingly the amount being paid out of petty cash and my reference quoted as authority.

Yours truly,

for J. Milne,

Leslie Doughy.

Copy sent to C.R. Dashwood for information.[2]

Notes

1   *Rail* 250/482 July.
2   C.R. Dashwood was Chief Accountant.

GREAT WESTERN RAILWAY
MAGAZINE

AUGUST · 1947

VOL. 59 · NO. 7

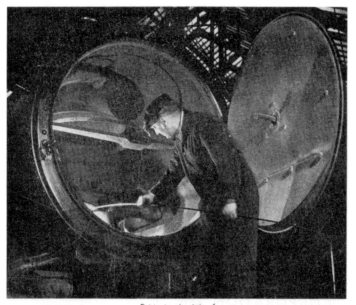

Pride in the Job—6
(See Page 156)

PRICE ONE PENNY

AUGUST

There are no Board or Committee Minutes for August. The directors were on leave but the Minutes for September throw some light on the events of August and the *Great Western Magazine* is useful in this respect.

The Chairman, Viscount Portal, did carry out at least one official function in August when he opened the 'Industrial Wales' exhibition at Kensington Olympia. This was a 'shop window' for the products of the growing 'light industry' sector in South Wales.

Viscount Portal became a director of the GWR in 1927, and took a particular interest in developing the great commercial potential of South and West Wales after the Great Collapse of the British economy 1928–33. Because the Great Western was a unified organisation, owning land and all necessary facilities for running a railway business, the directors could devote their large resources to assisting economic improvements and thus help the profits of their own organisation. In 1933 the Milk Marketing Board (MMB) was formed. The GWR at once provided the land and the sidings for MMB milk collection depots at Whitland and Pont Llanio, as well as the modern tanker wagons to cater for traffic.

In 1934 Viscount Portal, at the request of the government, produced a monumental report which was the blueprint for a revival of the fortunes of the people of South Wales, which he called *The Lifelines of Industry*. In 1934 there was barely one 'light' industry in South Wales. Portal's report suggested six districts that would be ideal to receive a number of light industry factories, all of which could be connected or were currently close to the railway. The first of these was the Treforest Trading Estate, but then the war intervened, curtailing the project.

After the war Portal immediately set to work to continue the pre-war process, bringing dozens of new industries and thousands of new jobs into South Wales. His energy in pursuit of this was astonishing. Between 1945 and 1947 he had enabled thirty-six factories to start, twenty-four of which were opened between January and August 1947. They were located around Cardiff, Merthyr, Llantarnam, Porth, Treorchy and Hirwaun, and produced electrical goods, clocks and watches, lingerie, radios, bus bodies, cardboard boxes, plastics and plasterboard. And of course a great steelworks was under construction at Margam Abbey.

The GWR and LMS companies co-operated in their efforts to encourage industry. In October 1946 the two companies made an experimental agreement with the millers and animal feedstuffs manufacturer Spillers Ltd. This was to carry flour and animal feed, formerly travelling by road from Spillers' mills in Birkenhead and Ellesmere Port, in bulk by rail to selected railhead stations in Central Wales for delivery to customers by GWR or LMS road lorries. The scheme had been a great success and in August it

GREAT WESTERN RAILWAY

MAGAZINE

| August · 1947 | Vol. 59 · No. 7 |

Maiden Voyage

THE GREAT WESTERN'S NEW SHIP "ST. DAVID" ENTERS THE ROSSLARE SERVICE

ON the 41st anniversary of the inauguration of the Fishguard–Rosslare service the Great Western Railway's new 3,500-ton mail steamer, St. David, made her maiden voyage. Launched at Birkenhead last February, this St. David replaces her gallant namesake which was bombed and sunk in Anzio Bay in 1944.

Gaily dressed and flying the tricolour, St. David entered Rosslare Harbour two hours and fifty minutes after leaving Fishguard, and received a gala reception. All the ships were beflagged and greeted the newcomer with sirens and whistles. Captain Kelly, master of the new vessel, who is a native of Waterford, has been with the Great Western for 26 years and his ship's company includes four survivors from the crew of the lost St. David.

Among the passengers on the maiden crossing were the Earl of Dudley, M.C., Deputy Chairman of the Great Western Railway; Sir Edward C. G. Cadogan, K.B.E., C.B., the Hon. A. W. Baldwin and Mr. W. M. Codrington, M.C., Directors of the Company; Sir James Milne, K.C.V.O., C.S.I., General Manager, and many of the principal officers. Among the welcoming committee were Mr. T. D. Sinnott, Wexford County Manager, and Mr. J. G. Maddock and Mr. T. J. Forde, Vice-Chairman and Secretary, respectively, of the Rosslare Harbour Development Board.

At a reception and luncheon on the ship, Lord Dudley said he first went to Ireland 42 years ago when his father was appointed Lord Lieutenant in succession to Lord Cadogan, whose son, Sir Edward, a Director of the Great Western Railway, was present at the luncheon. British Railways were to be nationalised in January, Lord Dudley continued; but whether under the Company's flag or that of the British Government, the Rosslare–Fishguard service

would still go on, and ever remain a link between Ireland and Britain. In response, Mr. W. E. Wylie, K.C., Deputy Chairman of the Fishguard & Rosslare Railway, said the Irish people welcomed " beyond words " the resumption of the Rosslare–Fishguard service. When proposing the toast of the Great Western Railway, Mr. F. M. O'Connor, Solicitor, Rosslare Harbour Development Board, congratulated the Company on their policy of recruiting 50 per cent. of the crew for the steamer from Ireland and the remainder from the English side of St. George's Channel.

Before returning to Fishguard, St. David visited Cork, where a dinner was given on board ship and attended by many prominent persons including the Deputy Lord Mayor (Alderman G. F. Brewitt). The Earl of Dudley presided and apologised for the absence of Viscount Portal, the Chairman. Proposing a toast to the City of Cork, Lord Dudley said how proud they were to have with them eight survivors of the sunken Anzio ship. Sir James Milne said the Company had spent £500,000 on St. David, and had St. Patrick coming out in a few months'

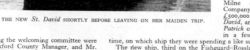

THE NEW St. David SHORTLY BEFORE LEAVING ON HER MAIDEN TRIP.

time, on which ship they were spending a like sum.

The new ship, third on the Fishguard–Rosslare service to carry the name St. David, was the first to enter Rosslare Harbour with radar equipment. Every detail of the coastline, the position of other ships, buoys and shoals, was visible on the screen.

An interesting feature of the design of St. David is the bow rudder, which permits the ship to manoeuvre with greater ease in congested space. She is also equipped with the latest type of ventilation—a system by which the air can be changed as often as every two minutes in the various compartments. St. David can accommodate 1,300 passengers, 52 motorcars, and 350 tons of cargo.

was extended to cover Central and North Wales and Shropshire in seventeen delivery zones. The GWR were negotiating with other millers to include their produce in the scheme.

There was a continuous campaign waged by the Traffic Department of the GWR to meet the manufacturers and ask how the company could help them move their produce. In August the company was working with the manufacturers of ice cream and frozen foods – and also the British Medical Association – with a view to making refrigerated rail-borne containers to carry the produce. In the case of the BMA, the railway wanted to carry human organs, at very low temperatures, for transplant; pancreas glands were also mentioned in the General Manager's report, and these were to be transported in small containers in the guard's compartment of a passenger express train.

The broccoli season in Cornwall ended in August. Practically all of it went by GWR to London and elsewhere, but owing to the disastrous weather of the first three months of the year only 21,770 tons were hauled, compared with 39,750 tons moved in 1946.

In July and August the company cleared 2,508 cars from Morris Cowley and 1,877 from Austin in Longbridge. This brought the total of cars exported by means of the GWR since the beginning of the year to 16,032, an increase of 640 (3 per cent) on the previous year.

On 5 August the Minister of Transport announced that from 1 October he would allow the four companies another increase in their charges: passenger fares up 16¼ per cent and 24 per cent for freight. Railway charges would then be 55 per cent above those of 1938. This was because the estimated total revenues of the four companies would fall short of what they were legally entitled to receive under the Control Agreement of 1940. The estimated shortfall in 1947 would be £59 million and £65 million in 1948. The increases were expected to yield approximately £15½ million in 1947 and about £65 million in 1948.[1] Tolls of shipping using railway docks were also increased. The increases were necessary because of the reduction in the purchasing power of money and to cover the costs of the increased wages as a result of the Guillebaud Report.

The railways were still considered by government as the main arteries of transport for the country and the GWR continued to do all they could to fulfil that role.

During the ten weeks ended 13 September 1947, the GWR took away from collieries 316,856 wagon-loads of coal. This was a decrease of 16,445 wagon-loads, 3 per cent down on the same period in 1946, and this decrease was attributed to the introduction in the mines of a five-day week.

In connection with the Royal Cornwall Show, the Three Counties Show, and the Royal Welsh Agricultural Show which were held in Truro, Hereford and Carmarthen respectively during July and August, the company hauled 566 wagon-loads of traffic by merchandise train, 93 wagon-loads of livestock and 1,900 miscellaneous consignments by passenger train. The total attendance of people at the three agricultural shows was approximately 158,000. During July and August GWR trains hauled to various ports for export 2,508 motor cars from Morris Cowley works and 1,877 from the Austin works at Longbridge. The GWR had taken 16,032 cars to the ports since January – a welcome increase of 4 per cent compared to 1946.

Contrary to Mr O.S. Nock's statement on page 146 of his book *The Great Western Railway*: 'In recent years the number of passengers wishing to leave Paddington on Friday nights and Saturdays has grown increasingly formidable', Sir James Milne told the directors that passenger figures for the summer of 1947 were less than those for 1946, and 1946 carryings were less than for 1945.

Although passenger numbers were reduced compared to 1945 and 1937, the number of passengers handled by Paddington and the other great stations such as Bristol, Cardiff and Birmingham Snow Hill during August was indeed 'formidable' especially given the relatively worn out state of the locomotives, carriages and – even – the staff. At peak weekends in July and August there were queues equivalent to 2 miles long going out of Paddington station, four abreast, from the tight-packed 'Lawn' out onto Praed Street in front of the Great Western Royal Hotel and along Eastbourne Terrace to Bishop's Road.

A REGULAR CUSTOMER AT CARDIFF REFRESHMENT ROOMS DREW THIS AS A TRIBUTE TO THE COUNTER STAFF.

In 1947 the railway was losing passenger and general merchandise traffic month after month. In the ten weeks ending 14 September, income from those traffics had decreased by £10,300,000, a 7.5 per cent decrease on the same period in 1946. This implies a drop in income throughout August of £1,300,000 per week. Receipts for the year to 14 September were reduced by £33,082,000 compared to the same period in 1946. In the nine weeks ending 14 September 1947, 343,000 passengers departed from Paddington station – and that of course includes the Bank Holiday – and that figure was 35,000 less than the same period in 1946.[2] And that was in spite of petrol being rationed on the basis of 270 miles per motorist per month.[3]

In spite of the worsening financial condition of the Great Western, its directors were committed to provide accommodation for their staff. This had been the company's policy since before the Great War. After that war the company formed a GWR Housing Association for the purpose of building not just a few houses here and there, but actual housing estates. Post-1945 the company had entered into discussions with many local councils with proposals for staff housing. In some councils' districts it was possible for them to grant the company planning permission for staff housing; in other districts the council would allocate some of the council-built houses for GWR staff. The great difficulty was the shortage of materials and the national lack of money with which to buy imported materials.

Another great problem was the rapidly rising cost of all materials. In some cases the GWR loaned money to councils, at a rate of 4 per cent. In the Acton area the GWR had its own Housing Association and that body wanted permission to build more houses on the Acton Estate but was prevented by government restrictions on the purchase of building materials.

In Banbury, the Great Western (Banbury) Housing Association was given permission to build fifty more houses on their Hightown estate after the GWR directors reduced the rate of interest on their loan from 4 to 2.5 per cent. At Oswestry, Swansea and Hayes, GWR housing schemes were in abeyance but at Didcot, in August 1947, planning permission for forty-four GWR houses – the first instalment of a larger scheme – were shortly to be approved.

The railway companies had been given a low priority in the allocation of steel and other building materials since 1945. At the end of August or start of September the Ministry of Transport informed all four railway companies that they must reduce still further their building plans 'until such time as the national situation improves'. Scarce materials could only to be bought for works that complied with the following conditions:

(a)   Works which contributed to the increase of exports or reduction of imports.
(b)   Improvements in the turn around times of ships.
(c)   Promotion of tourist traffic.
(d)   Improvement of transport of coal or other essential commodities.
(e)   Realisation of important expenditure already agreed, especially in the development areas.
(f)   Essential maintenance work.

And the Ministry would be reviewing a number of building schemes for which licences had been issued during the past eighteen months.

The *Great Western Railway Staff Magazine* reported the maiden voyage from Fishguard to Rosslare of the Royal Mail steamer and Irish ferry *St David*, which took place 'at the end of August'. The *St David* was a fast ship of 3,500 gross tons, which had been launched at Birkenhead in February. The 54 miles' passage from Fishguard to Rosslare harbour was

THE NEW *St. David* SHORTLY BEFORE LEAVING ON HER MAIDEN TRIP.

The Great Western had a considerable navy. At Plymouth Millbay dock there were two 'tenders', the *Sir Francis Drake* and this one, the *Sir Walter Raleigh*. Their purpose was to go out to just beyond the Breakwater of Plymouth Sound and meet the great and famous ocean liners coming in from New York. Those ocean passengers who wanted to get to London a day or more earlier than staying on the ship went down a gangway – intrepid folk – slung down the cliff-like side of the liner and boarded the tender to be ferried back to Millbay quay and the waiting, non-stop, express train to Paddington – the fastest, most prestigious train on the Great Western bar none.

ON *St. David's* MAIDEN VOYAGE.   (*From left*) *The Earl of Dudley, Sir James Milne, Captain J. J. Kelly, Mr. W. M. Codrington, the Hon. A. W. Baldwin and the Hon. Sir Edward C. G. Cadogan.*

Crew and passengers of the *St David*'s maiden voyage.

AT PRINCE OF WALES DOCK, SWANSEA. THE COMPANY'S NON-PROPELLED BUCKET DREDGER " TAFF " (*described above*).

Another kind of GWR vessel, inelegant but very necessary.

made in 2 hours 55 minutes. The new ship had cost the Great Western £500,000 and a brother ship, the SS *St Patrick* – costing another £500,000 – was being fitted out at the time of the *St David*'s maiden voyage. The new *St David* was a replacement for a previous SS *St David* which had been bombed and sunk when serving as a military hospital off the beaches at Anzio in January 1944.

At the banquet on board, in Rosslare harbour, the Deputy Chairman of the Great Western Railway, the Earl of Dudley, proposed a toast to the City of Cork, in the course of which he said how proud he was that eight survivors of the bombed *St David* were present at the feast. The *St David* was the first ship ever to enter Rosslare harbour equipped with radar. It was also the first Great Western ship to have a bow rudder for easier manoeuvring in confined spaces. It had a capacity for 1,300 passengers, fifty-two motor cars and 350 tons of cargo. Captain Kelly and 50 per cent of his crew were recruited from Ireland.

During the four weeks ending 9 August the GWR had in stock 3,946 steam locomotives and one diesel-electric shunter. The total included eight LMS engines on loan and eighty-one War Department 2-8-0 engines. The company had sent out on loan to the government and private firms ten engines, giving a grand total of locos in stock of 3,937. In addition to these there were thirty-seven diesel rail cars.

During that four-week period 3,110 engines – 78.99 per cent of the total steam stock – was available for work for all or part of every day, and of those engines 3,004 (97.28 per cent) were used. The average miles run per day of the 97.28 per cent of them in use was 92.72 and each of those engines worked an average of 11 hours. Engines working trains for passengers, parcels and empty coaches ran 13.18 miles per train-engine hour. The coal consumption per mile for locomotives employed on passenger services during the four weeks ending 9 August was 46.34lb, while freight engines burned 47.82lb. Oil consumed by locomotives expressed as pints per 100 miles was: passenger trains 8.04 and freight trains 7.73.

In the four weeks ending 9 August the Locomotive Department employed 44,539 men and women – the lowest number since 1941 – although pre-war the number was only 37,544. At the height of the war, on 30 December 1944, 48,967 people were employed.[4]

A large and continuous physical effort was required to prepare dozens of steam locomotives and hundreds of carriages for the road. To cope with weekend 'peaks' the major locomotive depots received loans of locomotives from other depots. These movements had to be planned and timetabled – or simply left to the signalmen to pass along the route without interfering with normal traffic. On Friday evening at Old Oak Common, or Tyseley, Bristol Bath Road, or Cardiff Canton sheds the inflated fleet of engines had to be got into steam, coaled, water, oiled – and got away to the carriage sidings on time. Shed labourers, enginemen and signalmen were working and sweating to do their individual jobs, but were secure in the knowledge that they were part of a team, a public service.

In the carriage sidings at Old Oak and Malago Vale, shunters were working at marshalling coaches into the required sequence of the train they were to form, and had to get in between the wagons, crouching down, having to couple or uncouple, draw off a coach, shunt it onto some other set, fit in restaurant cars where they were allowed, attach slip coaches and re-form coaches into planned trains. During the week most of this standard procedure was well known to the hard-working shunters, but on the Friday there were special preparations – they had to form up the extra trains to carry away hundreds of people who turned up so trustingly, expecting to find a train to take them to Weymouth or Weston-super-Mare.

At Bristol Temple Meads, or Birmingham, or at Oxford – in fact surely at any large station – the Chief Clerk in the Booking Office would be alert to the rate of ticket sales for a particular destination. At Oxford heavy bookings by football fans on a

CORNWALL
GWR

Saturday would be reported to Mr Price, the Station Master, and he would order a coach out of 'Jericho' sidings to reinforce the next passenger train in that direction. At Bristol, Weston-super-Mare was *the* great destination for a summer Saturday or Sunday on the beach. The Chief Clerk would call the Station Master and he would order the last remaining carriages out of the sidings, hauled by their shunting engine, into Temple Meads station to 'lift' the excursionists off the platform and away to the beach. The *Great Western Railway Magazine* called this 'Pride in the Job'. And that sprang from a personal pride – not to 'let the job down'.

In August lineside fires sprang up all over the railway, including several in the Paddington area. These had a serious effect because the signalling was done electrically for the 9½ miles out to

* Also awarded a gratuity.

The " Kerry Klub "

THE September *Magazine* carried the story of the opening night of the " Kerry Klub ", formed for the benefit of the London divisional locomotive office staff and named after its founder and patron. The club is now well under way, and the table tennis team which plays in the Acton & District League has won its first two matches in the " All-line " competition. The noble game of darts is greatly favoured, especially when the members' skill is pitted against that of other departments. Among the gentler arts much in demand is whist; a recent drive won much praise for the hard-working committee.

REPRODUCED BY KIND PERMISSION OF THE *Oxford Mail.*

Southall, and lineside fires could destroy the cables carried close to the line, which were often in wooden channelling.

On 31 August, at about 1.30 p.m., the two signalmen in Old Oak Common West box (OOC) saw that a lineside location box 100yd east of the signal box, containing eight transformers, was on fire. One of the men ran to the site with a fire extinguisher. The fire was so intense that he could not get near enough to use the appliance – and he felt that, even if he had got close, he would have done no good. OOC West contained a lever frame numbered to 112 levers – with seventeen spaces – controlling a large layout. This comprised a quadruple main line, the junctions between main-line tracks, the junction for the main line to Birmingham, goods lines and the western exit/entrance to the largest locomotive depot and carriage sidings on the railway. First of all, the Down Main and Down Relief Lines Homes and Distants were rendered lightless and then the main fuse melted, rendering all signals and points for OOC West inoperative. The signalling instruments also stopped working and signals at OOC East were affected. This is the problem with electric signalling – you have 'all your eggs in one basket'.

However, in those days there were plenty of skilled men available equipped to deal with such emergencies. There were initial delays as forces were gathered. Hand signalmen were appointed at the signals and more of them to wind the point mechanisms by hand. And thus the train service was maintained.

The Signal & Telegraph Department were on the scene at 2 p.m. The main fuse was restored at 3 p.m. The signalling instruments were all working by 4 p.m. One by one, signals were brought back into use. In shifts the S&T gangs worked all through the night and up until 12.20 p.m. the following day. Normal working resumed exactly 23 hours after the fire was spotted.

On the Downside of the railway at Hayes, 11 miles from Paddington, the GWR established a factory for the creosoting under pressure of wooden railway sleepers. It was brought into use during 1935. The place was always a fire risk. Special wagons to carry creosoted sleepers stood, loaded, alongside the Down Main. Their proximity to the main line was the result of thinking borne of the fact that they were the emergency store, held there to be available to repair any track after a derailment. In the baking hot drought of the summer of 1947, this was a fire waiting to happen – requiring only a hot cinder from a passing engine.

At 5 p.m. on 6 August Signalman Boyce, in Hayes signal box, saw a fire in one of these wagons. By 5.10 p.m. the employees at the factory had their hoses gushing onto the flames. At 5.15 p.m. the men of the Nestlé factory fire brigade – on the opposite side of the line – had come across to assist, just as the National Fire Service arrived and started to hose the fire with water, pumped from the canal on which the raw sleepers had arrived. The fire was extinguished at 5.45 p.m.

The report states: 'There was little damage. Superficial burning of the sleepers, scorching of a telegraph pole and the burning of some personal clothing belonging to the Foreman.'

Foreman Simmonds wrote to the Superintendent of the Line, Gilbert Matthews, to commend the contribution played by several railwaymen in their prompt and, indeed, courageous, actions in attacking the fire, holding it in check until the fire brigade arrived. Matthews was suitably impressed and wrote to the General Manager to say:

> It has come to my notice that Signalman S.W. Boyce, Leading Shunter H.A. Fish and factory labourers York and Neville rendered valuable assistance in connection with the fire at Hayes creosoting works. I recommend that they be commended and awarded a gratuity of one guinea in recognition of the part they played. The Chief Civil Engineer (Mr. A. S. Quartermaine) is in agreement. I shall be obliged if you will kindly say whether you concur.

Someone on the civil engineering side wrote to Quartermaine extolling the splendid leadership Foreman Simmonds displayed in containing what could easily have destroyed thousands of sleepers and, indeed, the entire creosoting works. Mr Quartermaine wrote to Sir James Milne recommending *three* guineas for Foreman

Simmonds and *two* guineas each for the labourers. The awards were duly made. But I wonder what happened to the trains. Hayes' signal box was single manned and the signalman was helping to fight the fire for perhaps 15 minutes – at least until the fire brigade arrived.

On 25 August at 11.35 p.m. the Bridgwater wagon sheet factory caught fire. The works fire pump could not contain the blaze. The National Fire Service appliance arrived and also a military engine but they could not cope with the fire. The large brick shed where the canvas sheets were coated in a bituminous substance burned as if a bomb had hit it, leaving some sections of wall standing, in a shaky state, and the sheet repair shop and office building had nothing left standing. The fire caused £36,000-worth of damage which sum included £13,200 in respect of 2,200 wagon sheets destroyed.

The Daily Report of the Traffic Department to the General Manager reports locomotive and diesel rail car failures. In the eleven days between 19 August and 30 August, for which I have GWR records, there were twenty-seven steam engine or diesel rail car failures. Whether that is the full total for the railway or just refers to those that came to be reported to the General Manager's Office is, of course, open to question.

Of those twenty-seven, four were diesel rail car failures and of the remaining twenty-three, all but three were 'locomotive short of steam'. Among these, two – the 4.09 p.m. Crewe–Bristol train on 20 August, and the 7.55 a.m. Blackpool–Bristol train on 25 August – stopped at Leebotwood. This is 9 miles into the 13-mile climb from Shrewsbury to Little Stretton. Each train stopped for 15 minutes for a 'blow-up' – to recover the water level in the boiler and attain full pressure to complete the climb. While standing there the driver informed Control that he would 'fail' his engine at Hereford. From Little Stretton the route falls downhill for almost the whole 38 miles to Hereford, so they could get there without much loss of time. At Hereford the engines were waiting and the change-over made within the time scheduled for the stop. There were three which were not ordinary 'short of steam' failures, detailed below.

The 6 p.m. Paddington–Weymouth train on 19 August 'stopped for steam' at Subway Junction, slightly less than a mile from starting. After 5 minutes it set off but at Old Oak Common East box the driver stopped and reported his engine a failure. The record does not give the engine number but it was an oil burner and the reason for the failure was 'oil burning apparatus not distributing oil properly'. A replacement was sent out from Old Oak and the train restarted after 18 minutes' delay.

On 20 August the 9.10 a.m. Manchester–Plymouth train failed at Exeter St David's station at 5.13 p.m. The failure was mechanical. Fitters were called to make the engine movable. Meanwhile the coaches were uncoupled from the engine, passengers for Exeter got off, and others got on. When all the doors were shut the train was drawn back from the platform to East box by the Pilot and then propelled forwards onto the Down Middle line where a fresh engine was waiting at the west end. That engine took the train away at 6 p.m. The failed engine was towed away to the shed at 6.25 p.m.

The third failure was the engine for the 9.45 p.m. Paddington–Worcester train, on 26 August. This engine was failed by its driver before leaving Old Oak Common. A fresh engine was found immediately and the 9.45 p.m. left Paddington at 9.59 p.m.

The four diesel rail car failures are described in the following.

The 6.12 p.m. Newbury–Reading train on 19 August was the first. The passengers on this were taken forward by the 6.15 p.m. Savernake–Newbury train, which was specially extended to Reading.

Secondly, the 6.40 a.m. Kingham–Princes Risborough via Thame failed on 27 August. That this diesel car was failing must have been known well in advance of its arrival at Oxford. When it got there it went into the Up Bay and passengers transferred to a specially arranged steam-hauled train, standing at the Up Main Platform. The third failure was also on 27 August: the 1.33 p.m. Henley–Twyford diesel car failed and was at once replaced with an engine and coaches.

Finally the 9.5 a.m. Kingham–Oxford diesel car failed in the section between Kingham and Shipton on 28 August. The report states – with tantalising brevity – 'Diesel car propelled to Shipton and attached to the 10.0 a.m. Moreton-in-Marsh to Oxford. 6.50 a.m. Wolverhampton to Paddington stopped specially at Shipton and Charlbury to cover diesel service.' What these brief details suggest is that the guard of the rail car walked 3 miles back to Kingham, putting down 'shots' along the way, to protect from failure. The express 6.50 a.m. Wolverhampton train was delayed at Kingham owing to the failure of the diesel in the section to Shipton. Once the diesel car's guard arrived at Kingham the express could enter the occupied section under Regulation 14 as an assisting train with the guard on the footplate to guide the driver to where his rail car had stopped. The engine of the Wolverhampton train propelled the rail car to Shipton. The puzzling part is the 10 a.m. Moreton-in-Marsh train which had arrived at Shipton *before* the 9.5 a.m. Kingham rail car. I suggest that this was a local goods Oxford–Moreton train returning early to Oxford. The passengers in the rail car got out and the goods engine took the car onto its train in a siding. The 6.50 a.m. Wolverhampton train then came in to the platform, collected the passengers, and went on its way. This showed great independent thought and initiative all round.

Bassaleg Junction was a complex junction where the old Brecon & Merthyr Railway forked away from the GWR up the valley to Machen. The signal box contained a frame of ninety-five levers. On 14 August 1947 at 3.10 p.m. the Bassaleg Junction's man gave 'Line Clear' to Park Junction, a signal box of 100 levers, a mile to the south, towards Newport. This was to permit the 12.15 p.m. West Mendalgief–Ebbw Vale Iron Ore train to approach Bassaleg. That train passed Park Junction at 3.19 p.m. and came to a stand at Bassaleg Up Dock Lines Home which was at 'Danger'. The Up Dock Line between Park Junction and Bassaleg was worked under 'Permissive Block' regulations, which meant that more than one train was allowed to occupy the track at the same time. At 3.24 p.m. the Park Junction signalman obtained Bassaleg Junction signalman's permission for the N.11 'trip', engine and van, to enter the Up Dock Line. Bassaleg accepted N.11 under warning, because there was already a train in the section.

In connection with re-laying operations certain signals and points at Park Junction were disconnected, the Up Dock Line Starting signal being one of these. The Park Junction signalman had a hand signalman working under his instruction, for the purpose of instructing drivers when they could pass the signal at 'Danger'. The signalman instructed his hand signalman to instruct the driver of N.11 to pass the

TWO CRANES AND A STRONG SQUAD OF WORKMEN SLIDING THE NEW CROSSOVER ASSEMBLY INTO POSITION.

The re-laying of Park Junction was spread over two months. The layout consisted of eight pairs of points and forty crossings, the latter so joined together by very long sleepers that they had to be moved in one block, 130ft long and 30ft wide. The planning of the removal of the old and the replacement thereof was meticulously organised. The great central block of track was pre-assembled on the lineside – using all available railway land and a portion of a famer's field which had to be excavated down to lineside level.

Up Dock Starting signal at 'Danger' and to proceed cautiously, as there was a train standing at the Home signal at Bassaleg.

The N.11 engine and van proceeded faster than it should have done. The guard of the 12.15 train actually heard it coming, got down from his van, and ran towards it in a fruitless attempt to attract the driver's attention and to make him stop. The N.11 hit the brake van of the 12.15 train with enough force to shove the train, which was carrying iron ore, forwards so as to cause its driver to fall backwards and injure himself. He died in hospital. And yet, the driver and fireman of N.11 were not hurt, there was no derailment and the damage to the brake van of the 12.15 train was not enough to prevent it going on to Rogerstone yard.

The company wanted to issue the N.11 driver with a 'Registered Caution' but he was not prepared to admit that he was at fault and the case was still being appealed on 25 February 1948.

At about 11.52 a.m. on 14 August, Churchward Mogul No 5312 was running north through Cricklade station chimney-first, as the 9.25 a.m. Andover-to

GREAT WESTERN RAILWAY MAGAZINE

THE DOUBLE SCISSORS CROSSOVER AT PARK JUNCTION, NEWPORT, WITH NEW ASSEMBLY AT RIGHT.

THE NEW ASSEMBLY (*left*) FRAMED UP ON SUPPORTS BESIDE THE EXISTING TRACK.

Cheltenham 'light engine'. Driver W. Denchfield was in charge with Fireman A. Phelps. They were having a delightfully leisurely ride on a nice summer day and had then covered nearly 40 miles of a pleasantly scenic route. One-and-three-quarters of a mile north of Cricklade station, at about 11.55 a.m., this engine collided with a tractor driven onto Stone Farm 'accommodation' crossing by Mr Freeth of Cerney Wick. Mr Freeth was not hurt but the tractor's radiator was smashed and the steering rods buckled.

According to Driver Denchfield's report, he was running at 25mph, he blew his whistle as he approached the crossing and was an engine's length from the tractor when it emerged from the bushes on his side of the line. Denchfield applied his brake at once but could not avoid a collision. After the engine had stopped he sent Phelps back to see if the tractor driver was hurt. No 5312 was undamaged.

The tractor driver was not hurt in any way. He told Phelps that he had walked across the line to open the far gate and had seen that the line was clear in both directions over a considerable distance so he felt it was safe to cross. No 5312 must have come into view just as Mr Freeth turned his back.

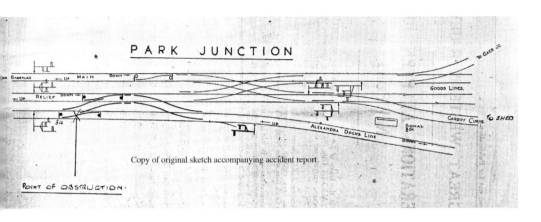

PARK JUNCTION

Copy of original sketch accompanying accident report.

A permanent-way gang was working a little way off and they came to the scene and all helped to drag and lift the tractor clear of the line. Phelps took the name and address of the farmer and, seeing there was nothing else to be done, he rejoined his engine and they continued on their way to Cheltenham at 12.08 p.m.

On 4 September a report – naturally biased in the company's favour – by inspectors from the Traffic, Locomotive, and Permanent-way Departments, A.J. Williams, R.T. Wade and E. Huxley respectively, was sent to Divisional Superintendent R.H. Nicholls at Gloucester and L.G. Morris at Worcester. This stated:

> This crossing is situated between the 40½ and 40¾ mile posts. The line is practically straight but any (GWR) driver would not be aware that the crossing existed until approximately 150 yards away in each direction and owing to undergrowth he would not see any vehicle crossing until the vehicle was practically on the four-foot.
>
> The gates are situated 6½ yards from the rails and it is impossible for the driver of any vehicle to see an approaching train from either direction until he is approximately 3 yards away from the rails.
>
> When standing in the four foot the users of this crossing have a clear view of an approaching train in each direction for 650 yards.

Besides that joint report, Locomotive Inspector Wade wrote his own report, which was rather more pointed, to the Locomotive Superintendent, L.G. Morris, at Worcester: 'The crossing is situated near the 41 mile post. The hedgerow is composed of bushes 5 to 6 feet high for a distance of half a mile in either direction and they come to within 3 yards of the rail. The crossing gate is 5½ yards from the rail.'

These reports reached the General Manager, Sir James Milne, on 11 September. The number of men employed on track maintenance on this route had been reduced in 1928 when the GWR introduced the 'motor trolley' system of track maintenance. The permanent-way gang had a petrol-engine rail trolley to travel on and so one gang could, in theory at any rate, maintain at least double the length of track than previously. But then came the war, and exceptionally heavy use of the route between 1939–45 made it impossible for the depleted gangs to keep the track in good order and keep the undergrowth at the sides cut back. So for this 2 miles – the bushes extended for a mile beside the line on each side of the gateway – rampant undergrowth had developed. The task of cutting it back would require the local gang to be reinforced with men from other districts and that would probably mean they would have to work on Sundays. Memos went back and forth and on 24 September, Gilbert Matthews, Superintendent of the Line, wrote to Milne:

Mishap between South Cerney and Cricklade.

14th August 1947.
With further reference to this matter, I am asked whether work on cutting back the undergrowth on both sides of the line to afford an improved view may now be put in hand with the Engineering Department. If you have no objection I will arrange accordingly.

On that memo, Milne wrote in pencil: 'No objection', and the work was ordered to start.

On Saturday 23 August there was a rear-end collision on the Down Relief Line between Swansea Loop East box and Swansea High Street box. Signalman Rowlands was working Swansea Loop East signal box. At 1.57 a.m. he had the 11.45 p.m. Margam–Swansea High Street goods train approaching him from Landore. The train consisted of thirty wagons and a brake van hauled by 0-6-2 tank engine No 6604. Rowlands reversed levers 30 and 31 to set the points from the Down Main into the Down Relief and pulled his Home signal, lever 64. The train passed him at 2.2 a.m. and he sent the 'Train out of Section' signal to Landore. The Down Relief Line worked under 'Absolute Block' regulations – only to be occupied by one train at a time.

At 2.34 a.m. Landore asked 'Is Line Clear?' for a light engine – 2–3 bells. This was the engine for the 3.10 a.m. parcels train to Carmarthen. The parcels train was standing in Swansea High Street station and had started from Swindon at 6.55 p.m. the previous evening.

With the road still set for the Down Relief Line and the Home signal still 'off', Rowlands gave 'Line Clear' to Landore and the latter at once sent the 'Train entering Section' signal. Rowlands then asked 'Is Line Clear?' to Swansea High Street box on the Down Main and High Street gave him the road.

The light engine was No 5963 *Wimpole Hall*, with Driver Talbot of Landore. It was running tender-first, on a curve, with the tender piled high with coal. Talbot was letting his engine freewheel at 15mph. He saw Swansea Loop East's Main to Relief Home signal showing a green light and he came coasting past the box and into the Down Relief. He did not see the rear lamps of the train 280yd ahead, the curve of the line was too sharp with the tender in front, and so he collided with the brake van of the goods train at 2.40 a.m.

The guard of the goods train was Cooper of Landore. He was aged 49 and had been a goods guard since 1922. His statement is an interesting account of the working practices. Here it is:

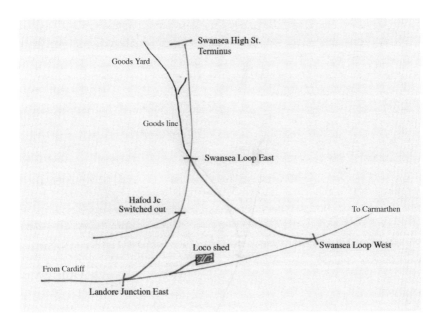

I booked on duty at 8.55 p.m. on August 22nd, having booked off duty at 4 a.m. that morning. I was in charge of the 11.45 p.m. Margan to Swansea High Street goods. It was a clear, still night. My train arrived. As I passed Swansea Loop East signal box I saw the signalman looking out of his window and when I was in clear on the Down Relief Line I lifted the near-side red shade a couple of times and then removed it.[5] I had worked this train all week and it had previously been accepted into the Yard within minutes of arrival. On this morning, about a quarter of an hour elapsed and no sign of a move being made I went down to see Yard Foreman Jones to give him the tally etc. Shortly after I got to him we heard a crash and I saw my train move forward slightly. I ran back at once and found that an engine had collided with the rear of my train. The Down Main was fouled by derailed wagons but the Up Line was clear. I went back at once to protect and met the fireman off the engine who told me he had put down detonators on the Down Main and Down Relief Lines. I asked him if he had protected the Loop Lines from West Wales and hearing that he had not done so I did that before reporting to the signalman at Loop East box. I questioned him as to the position of the instruments and levers and he assured me that everything was in order.

Signalman Rowlands did not hear the noise and no signalman was aware of the danger until the Yard Foreman telephoned a warning to Swansea High Street box. The signalman there sent the 'Obstruction Danger' signal to Swansea Loop East box at 2.46 a.m.

The Neath and the Landore breakdown gangs and the Landore steam crane were ordered at 2.50 a.m. Single-line working over the Up Main took an unusually long time to be put into action. The arrangements were not complete until 4.35 a.m. The coal wagons were cleared off the Down Main at 6.5 a.m. Single-line working was given up with the next train at 6.35 a.m. The wagons and van were re-railed and the debris cleared at 9.5 a.m. but the Down Relief Line was not cleared, owing to traffic movement on the Down Main until 11.27 a.m.

Signalman Rowlands was 46 years old and had been a signalman for 27 years. He had worked Swansea Loop East box for 14 years. He made no attempt to excuse himself except to say that he had had difficulty sleeping when coming off night shift because all that week the days had been so hot. He ended his report with these words: 'I very much regret my serious mistake in failing to carry out my signalling duties in a proper manner and I am afraid I cannot explain my lapse.'

Twenty-seven years' signalling *before* making the first mistake is surely a very fine record. He did say that he had had difficulty sleeping and I think he was very tired and became confused. The company was partly to blame because his block instrument was not wired up with the best circuitry: he should not have been able to peg up 'Line Clear' to Landore with his Home signal 'off'. That created the trap into which the sleepless man fell.

The Traffic Department's Daily Report for the General Manager also reports failures of rails and signalling equipment. Whether what is daily reported is the full total of such failures on 9,000 miles of track is open to question. I have the reports for eleven days between 19 August and 31 August. In that time failures of track circuits were reported at eighteen locations, there were twenty-one points failures, nineteen signal failures, five double-line block instrument failures, and two single-line electric key token or staff instrument failures. 'One-off' incidents reported were one broken rail, one failure of current to the power signalling at Ladbroke Grove, a fire in cable channelling at North Pole Junction and one buckled rail. Signal failures were due to broken wires, except in one case at Keyham where the red glass fell out of a signal spectacle. Points failures were often caused by the very hot weather expanding metal beyond what the expansion-compensating equipment in the rodding could accommodate.

The report for 19 August is typical:

Hayes. Points fail 2.10 – 2.15 p.m. 1.55 Padd. 2nd part. Delayed 2½ min; Little Mill Jc. Electric Staff failed. 4.15p.m – 5.15 p.m. Working by Pilotman; Dawlish. Up signal failed. Trains stopped. Instructed to pass signal at 'Danger'; Victory Siding. Up Block instrument failed. 7.23 p.m – 7.45 p.m. Trains stopped. Instructed to pass Starting signal at 'Danger'. Paddington Departure box. Track circuit failed. 12.55 a.m Paddington left at 12.57 a.m; Park Royal track circuit failure. 12.11 a.m. – 2.45 a.m. Up trains stopped. Instructed to pass signal at 'Danger'; Lydney West. Track circuit failure. 4.20 a.m – Time rectified not given; Wellington (Som) Track circuit failure. 6.15 a.m. – Time rectified not given.

Delays might be a few minutes or many; it depended on whether the men on the spot could sort it out or if they had to wait for a technician to repair something more technical. On 21 August a track failure at the power operated signal box at Newport East delayed the 12.25 a.m. Cardiff–Crewe train by 41 minutes, the 8.20 p.m. Crewe–Cardiff train by 48 minutes and the 8.40 p.m. Whitland–Kensington milk train by 53 minutes.

At 8.38 p.m. on 19 August, the signalman at Rushey Platt Junction, Swindon, had just turned a goods train into his Up Goods Loop. He was then unable to re-set the route for the Up Main. The following train was an express passenger, the 6.50 p.m. Weston-super-Mare–Paddington. Goods loops were worked on the 'Permissive' principle – more than one non-passenger train could be in the Loop at any one time. The 1947 Regulations allowed a passenger train to run over a goods loop without any special permissions being required. The signalmen at each end of the loop came to an understanding by telephone that a passenger train could pass, provided the loop was empty from end to end. The printed form 'Block Conversion Ticket – Permissive to Absolute' – which would have to be 'walked' from Rushey Platt to Swindon West – was a British Railways requirement.

The 6.50 p.m. Weston train was held on the Up Main Home signal at Rushey Platt for 16 minutes until the goods train had cleared out of the Loop at Swindon West box. The Rushey Platt signalman then 'asked the road' on the Loop for the passenger and until that train cleared off the Loop no other train could enter.

On 2 August the 7.37 p.m. Weymouth–West Ealing milk and empty coaching stock train was hauled by engine No 5985 *Mostyn Hall*, with Driver T. Miles and Fireman T. Griffiths, of Westbury. There were ninety wheels, and 340 tons behind the engine on a 1 in 190 falling gradient. They were stopping at Yetminster to pick up milk traffic when the drawbar of the last vehicle, an LMS eight-wheel brake van, broke. The vacuum brake pipe on the penultimate vehicle was undamaged. The crippled brake van had its brake released and was pushed back into a siding, its handbrake screwed down hard and left there. Five minutes' delay resulted.

I have thirty-five reports of goods trains breaking couplings, draw hooks or drawbars failing between 1 August and 30 August. Of those, ten were due to GWR couplings – including the drawbar breaking on 2-8-2 tank engine No 7215 – five were owned by Southern Railway and the rest were owned by LMS, LNER or Private Owners. Goods-train mileage for August was 1,794,327.

Most goods trains were lengthy, with between fifty and seventy wagons, the majority comprised of un-braked, loose-coupled wagons. To control this unwieldy procession so as to be able to stop – gently – at a 'Danger' signal, to run them fast enough to keep the schedule, and to understand the reaction of the wagons to changes in gradient, and to drive accordingly required experienced skill. There were bound to be incidents. There was no 'pattern' to the breakaways: they happened under any conditions. The locomotives involved were mostly belonging to GWR, but the 'WD' 2-8-0 and the LMS 0-8-0 types were also involved.

A couple of incidents are especially noteworthy since they give a taste of the skill and care of the train crews.

On 6 August the 1.10 a.m. Old Oak Common to Tyseley consisted of fifty-nine wagons hauled by oil-burning GWR engine 2-8-0 No 4854[6] with Driver Pearce and Guard Whitehead of Old Oak Common. The train passed through Princes Risborough station at about 3.25 a.m. at 35mph. Driver Pearce took advantage of the slight curve to look back at his train and saw a gap between the ninth and tenth wagon from his engine. He was running on a gently falling gradient after coming off the 1 in 100 falling grade of Saunderton bank, and the gradient was falling for miles ahead of him. He told his fireman to screw down the tender handbrake and cautiously reduced his speed by that alone, whilst watching the forty-nine wagons catching up with him. He felt the weight of the train push him forward and then applied his power brake. He brought the train to a stand in the section between Princes Risborough and Haddenham at 3.32 a.m. An examination of the wagon discovered that the drawbar had broken. GWR guard's vans were equipped with a 'short drawbar'. This was fitted, the wagon re-coupled, and the train proceeded to Haddenham where the defective wagon – an empty coal truck belonging to Birkenhead Corporation – was shunted into a siding.

On 13 August the 9.15 p.m. Cardiff–Hackney Yard (Newton Abbot) train set off for Devon from Severn Tunnel Junction. The train's engine was No 6815 *Frilford Grange*, with Driver Marion and Guard Knight, of Bristol. The load was fifty-two loaded coal wagons and a 20-ton guard's van to go up the 3 miles of 1 in 100 rising ground from tunnel bottom almost to Pilning. With the brake van, '52 of coal' would have weighed about 800 tons and this was twelve wagons more than the maximum unassisted load for a 'Grange' in the tunnel in 1936. In 1947 – conditions being what they were – Driver Marion asked for assistance and 2-6-2 tank engine No 3168 was coupled in front, driven by Driver Council of Severn Tunnel shed.

The heavy, cumbersome train left Severn Tunnel yard in starlight and entered the total darkness of the tunnel at 2.09 a.m. going down a 1 in 90 gradient. At some point, the engines must have accelerated to pull the couplings out taut and a 'tug' happened, breaking the coupling between the third and fourth wagon from the engines – so the drivers experienced a very sudden acceleration, realised what had happened, and kept speed going to keep away from the runaway portion. Guard Knight would have realised what had happened when he heard the diminishing sound of the engines and, with his handbrake on, he brought his 800 tons to a stand on the level 264yd at the lowest point in the tunnel in utter darkness. The mechanical railway required signalmen, and more particularly train crews, to use their initiative, courage and all five senses.

Mr Knight climbed down in total darkness with his oil lamps, groped his way to the tunnel wall, scrabbled about on the bricks to find the tell-tale wire and broke it. Immediately the alarm bells in Severn Tunnel East and West boxes began to ring. It was 2.25 a.m. Guard Knight then felt his way along, going towards the east end, counting the wagons, until he came to one of the telephones that were placed at intervals. He used that to phone the East box and informed the signalman that he was stationary at the bottom of the tunnel with forty-nine wagons, all of them safely standing on the Up Main, the Down Main clear. He then walked back to protect the rear of his train, putting down one detonator at a quarter of a mile, one at half a mile and three, 10yd apart, at three-quarters of a mile from his van. Then he just stood there, with a red light, in the freezing, sulphurous, cold and blind darkness.

The Tunnel Inspector at Pilning was informed of the situation by the Tunnel East signalman. He had two '3150' class bank engines coupled together there. He roused the crews out of their hut and at 2.42 a.m. the two engines had come the 2½ miles from Pilning and entered the tunnel. They ran through to Severn Tunnel West box, crossed to the Up line and crept back on the Up line. In the smoke they might not see the red light but they would certainly hear the three detonators, placed 10yd apart, going off. They exploded the 'dets', picked up the guard and reached the train safely. Then they started not less than 800 tons from a stand on a wet rail up the 1 in 100 gradient, out of the tunnel and on to Pilning, where the train was re-coupled. Wonderful railway work, skilled driving, courage and tremendous human endurance. All in a night's work.

Notes

1   *Rail* 250/469 September.
2   *Rail* 250/469 September.
3   *The Motor Car and Politics in Britain*, p. 326. William Plowden, Pelican, 1973.
4   *Rail* 250/282.
5   The goods train van carried three red lights, facing the rear, arranged as an inverted triangle. The Rule was that when such a train was on a line parallel to the Main Line, the side lamp nearest the Main Line had the red shade removed to leave the white light showing. This was a reassurance to any driver approaching on the Main Line that there was not a train in front on his track. Guard Cooper removed the wrong shade.
6   Renumbered from 3837 when converted to burn oil.

GREAT WESTERN RAILWAY
MAGAZINE

SEPTEMBER · 1947

VOL. 59 · NO. 8

Pride in the Job—7
(See Page 174)

PRICE TWO PENCE

INSURANCE EDITION

SEPTEMBER

On 3 September the directors of the GWR received a letter from Alfred Barnes, Minister of Transport. In it he expressed his 'appreciation of the services rendered to the transport of the country by the officers and men of the Great Western Railway'. He went on to state that he recognised the great traditions created and maintained by the company – and just when a reader might have thought he was going to say that he had decided against nationalising the company the letter concluded by saying: 'I am confident that those traditions would be maintained by those who will shortly become the Officers and servants of the British Transport Commission.'

Alfred Barnes had hoped that Milne would accept his, Barnes', invitation to become Chairman of the Commission – an idea which revolted Sir James. He gave notice at this meeting of his intention to retire from all work on 31 December.

The GWR Labour Committee Minute for September opens with a résumé of Alfred Barnes' reply to the letter the GWR directors had sent him in July. The directors were under the control of the Minister, but in July he had expected them to take responsibility for accepting and implementing the conclusions of the Guillebaud Report. The GWR directors had politely suggested that this was his responsibility. At this September Committee meeting Barnes' reply was read. Mr Barnes:

> had considered, in his capacity as Head of the Railway Executive and having regard to his Ministerial responsibilities for transport, the views they had expressed regarding the Guillebaud Report and had decided to take the responsibility of accepting the recommendations. Therefore he requested the Companies to put the recommendations into effect through the usual machinery.[1]

The GWR, in concert with the other railway companies, then put forward to the railway unions 'certain proposals for modifying certain agreements with a view to ensuring that the reduced number of working hours included in the new standard working week should represent *effective* working time to the greatest practicable extent'. That proposal was under discussion with the unions but only on the condition that no-one was committing themselves to anything at that stage. This was reported to the Minister of Transport and his decision was now awaited.

The 'Control of Engagement Order' was made on 18 September 1947. It was to come into force on 6 October. From that date it would be illegal for an employer to 'engage or seek to engage men between the ages of 18 and 50' and women between 18 and 40 except through the agency of the Labour Exchange. The order was to expire on 31 December 1948 – but not even trade union Members of Parliament believed that, and in parliament one trade union MP – Mr Rhys Davies – said the order was 'Industrial Conscription' and a denial of freedom.[2]

The GWR's staff census taken in March 1947 showed that 113,601 men, women and boys were employed. In September the Directors' Labour Committee minutes showed that 4,810 were disabled, 900 were over 65 and 'some 2,100 women are employed in wages grades on work normally done by men'. The Locomotive Department employed 44,613 people in September. The number of GWR employees serving with the armed forces on 13 September was 3,661. Since the start of 1947 1,530 staff had been conscripted into the armed forces and 1,233 GWR men had been released from military service and rejoined the company.

In his Fortnightly Report to the Traffic Committee, Sir James Milne estimated that receipts for the ten weeks ended 14 September amounted to £10,301,000, a decrease of £836,000 – 7.51 per cent down compared with the previous year. Passenger traffic receipts were down by £634,000 (9.2 per cent), general merchandise was down by £295,000 (8.46 per cent) and coal traffic increased by £93,000 (7.38 per cent).

It was announced in this report that the Yealmpton branch would have its passenger service withdrawn as from 6 October. This was with the agreement of the Ministry of Transport: 'owing to the decline of passenger traffic on the branch line and the fact that Yealmpton and District was served by the GWR/Southern Railway-owned bus company Western National. This will save 687 miles a week.'

Following this statement it was reported that the Atomic Scientists Association had chartered a train to haul an 'Atomic Energy Demonstration' exhibition around the country for five-and-a-half months, starting in Liverpool on 7 November. The train would visit Birmingham, Bristol, Cardiff and Paddington.

The oil-burning experiment, initiated by the Great Western Railway in October 1945, was an operational success. A 'Hall' could be the equal of the best performance of a coal-fired 'Castle'.[3] The other great advantage was that, without the need to empty cinders and piles of clinker from the smoke box, or remove half burnt coal and ash from the fire-grate, an oil-fired steam engine could be at work for more hours a day than a coal-fired one. In September the Minister of Transport 'requested' all the main-line companies to convert their steam engines to burn oil. This request came a month *after* the government had been obliged to default – on 20 August – on its obligation to make sterling convertible, tradable with the US dollar. That was the condition on which, on 15 July, the US government made their $4.3 billion (equivalent to $53 billion at 2011 values) loan to Britain. Oil could only be purchased with the US dollar and during the month in which sterling and the US dollar were tradable, the UK dollar reserves flooded out of the country. So now the GWR loyally set out to install oil firing throughout their locomotive fleet and depots when there were not enough dollars in the Bank of England to buy oil in sufficient quantities. Thus the scheme was doomed to extinction.

There was already a facility for dispensing oil fuel at Llanelly and Severn Tunnel Junction – the original installations – and now thirteen more were to be constructed at Old Oak Common, Reading, Didcot, Swindon, Bath, Bristol St Philip's Marsh, Westbury, Newton Abbot, Laira, Ebbw Junction, Gloucester and Banbury. The cost of all this was estimated at £127,938. The good news was that the entire amount was to be charged to the Ministry of Transport account.

Twenty of the '28xx' 2-8-0 locomotives had been converted between October 1945 and August 1947. The earliest conversions remained in service for three years; the last were in use for eighteen months before re-conversion to coal firing.[4] Five 'Castle' class express locomotives were converted to oil burning: No 5091 in October 1946, Nos 5039 and 5082 in December 1946, and Nos 100A1 and 5079 in January 1947. They all reverted to coal firing between September and November 1948. Eleven 'Hall' class mixed-traffic engines were converted during April and May 1947 and were re-converted between September 1948 and March 1950.

Before the war, coal for GWR engines was purchased at the start of each year. Approximately 2,184,000 tons annually was required to cover immediate use and to maintain the ground stockpiles at a high level. Ninety per cent of the coal came from South Wales, Eastern and Western and Rhymney Valleys. The vast tonnage was ordered in amounts according to its quality – the finest steam coal was for the engines of fast, heavy express passenger trains and for the fast, heavy, fully vacuum-braked goods trains, and lesser coal was used for lesser duties. Pre-war there was no difficulty in getting exactly the right types of coal for which GWR engines were designed. Around 6,000 tons per day had to be delivered to 130 engine sheds across the GWR system in amounts ranging from ten to 100 tons. Major locomotive depots received coal from eight or even ten different collieries so that all classes of engines, performing a variety of duties, got the correct grade of coal for their work. This finely tuned but rather expensive method of coal supply was abandoned when war broke out.

The volume of coal production declined and the distribution of coal was taken over, nationally, by the Ministry of Fuel and Power. The four railways were allocated a total tonnage of coal and that amount was divided amongst the four by their agreement based on their estimated requirements. Coal was transported in 'block loads' of forty-five to sixty-five 20-ton wagons, depending on the gradients of the route the train would take. Sheds would get a delivery in tons as the train moved along the route and this of course meant that the depots got what coal was available rather than the fine-tuned quality that had been the case pre-war. By 1945 the supply of coal was still dwindling and in 1947 coal supply was so little – or even non-existent – that there were days when some major depots had no more than three days' supply of coal in wagons and in their ground stocks. And of course, this was just any coal, rather than the correct coal for the jobs in hand. The locomotive depots telegraphed reports to Swindon daily at 9 a.m., giving the tonnage they had on hand so that coal could be shifted around between depots to keep all of them adequately supplied. And of course, all those wagons had to be promptly returned – empty – to the collieries. Oil firing would have had immense benefits but the dire British economic situation precluded it.

The first consignment of coal from the USA, under the Marshall Plan, arrived at Swansea on 24 July. All 9,000 tons was allocated by the Ministry of Fuel and Power to the GWR. A steady supply of coal developed and by 24 September 100,000 tons had been received at Plymouth, Avonmouth, and South Wales ports. The GWR had to shift this and at the same time in the ten weeks ended 13 September their locomotives and train crews had cleared from collieries 316,856 wagon-loads of Welsh coal. This was a decrease of 16,544 wagons compared to 1946. The miners' working week had been

GREAT WESTERN RAILWAY
MAGAZINE

September · 1947   Vol. 59 · No. 8

Industrial Wales
VISCOUNT PORTAL OPENS THE PRINCIPALITY'S EXHIBITION AT OLYMPIA

Last month we published an account of the gallant effort of the people of Wales in their climb out of the abyss of depression into the broad uplands of prosperity. The "Industrial Wales" exhibition at Olympia has since given abundant proof of their success. Industrialists from all over the world could look admiringly through this "Window of Wales" and see astonishingly varied evidence of how the Welsh people had put their house in order.

The exhibition was sponsored and organised by the Industrial Association of Wales and Monmouthshire, and a distinguished company met at the inaugural luncheon on August 29, at which Sir Gerald Bruce, K.C.B., C.M.G., D.S.O., President of the Association, was chairman. He said that until a short time ago there were two associations in Wales, but the recent amalgamation had made it possible for one authoritative voice to speak for the whole of Wales on all matters affecting her welfare.

Sir Gerald paid warm tribute to the work of the exhibitors and others behind the scenes, and said how fortunate they were to have Viscount Portal, P.C., D.S.O., M.V.O., Chairman of the Great Western Railway, to perform the opening ceremony, for he was the greatest friend Wales had ever had. It was as a result of his monumental report, made after the Commission's visit in 1934, that the special areas were constituted and the foundation laid for the Principality's industrial recovery.

Viscount Portal said how much he admired the enthusiasm and enterprise of Sir Gerald Bruce and his colleagues whose labours had made the exhibition possible. In 1934 there was hardly a single light industry in Wales; to-day there was practically no product of a light industry which that country could not claim, and Wales might almost be styled self-supporting.

It must be remembered, Viscount Portal continued, that these light industries were only ancillary to the great coal and steel industries, and in the matter of coal production Britain was up against a very difficult problem. We were a poor country at the moment, and we must admit it. There

AT THE "INDUSTRIAL WALES" EXHIBITION AT OLYMPIA, LONDON. THE G.W.R. AND L.M.S. COMPANIES' STAND.

Coal for our "Kings"
OUR PROBLEM OF GETTING 6,000 TONS A DAY FROM PITHEAD TO ENGINE SHEDS

THE DAILY RACE FROM COLLIERY TO GREAT WESTERN STOCK PILE. A TYPICAL LOCOMOTIVE COAL TRAIN.

In the floor of your coal cellar showing? How many days or weeks is your coalman overdue? If you are suffering from this sort of shortage you will find it easier to realise how great a daily anxiety it is for our Company to get enough coal for the "Kings", "Castles", "Counties", "Halls", and all the rest of our 3,000-odd Great Western engines. Being a railway enthusiast, you may like to know the general plan of the Company's locomotive coaling system.

With the great coalfield of South Wales on its system, it is natural that in normal times the Great Western should draw the bulk of its locomotive coal from this area; indeed, the fireboxes of our Company's engines have been designed expressly to get the best results from Welsh coals. The weekly requirement is in the region of 42,000 tons, so that about 6,000 tons have to be railed each day from collieries to the 130 depots on the Company's system.

Coal supplies are normally scheduled for fuelling locomotives on a "week to be performed" basis. This means that the higher grade coals—usually more costly—are allocated for the most important locomotive work, such as hauling express passenger and vacuum freight trains. Crack expresses like the "Cornish Riviera Limited", "Torbay Limited" and "Cheltenham Flyer", of course, would get the top-grade of all.

Before the war the Company could get, without restriction, the most suitable types of coal for all its various purposes. Locomotive depots had not to cope with to-day's shortage of and materials, so that the different grades of coal available could be used to the most economic advantage. At the major locomotive depots coals from as many as eight or ten different collieries could be used satisfactorily for their different purposes, ranging from express passenger engines down to pilots shunting in the yards.

Block Coal Trains

These pre-war methods, involving the allocation of specific coals for the various classes of locomotive duty, had largely to be revised when the entire working of railway traffic was re-cast to meet war needs. Instead of each colliery despatching locomotive coal for several depots in small consignments of anything from 10 to 120 tons a day—which involved much re-marshalling—"block coal train" working was introduced.

The initial approach to the change-over in practice was to legislate for the larger consuming depots first, appropriating the weekly tonnage required and including a high proportion of the better class coals. Having assessed these quantities, the number of wagons required to lift the necessary tonnage was worked out, and trainloads arranged accordingly; these were styled "block trains."

As every large user plant might not require a train load each day, the block trains were sometimes scheduled to run on only three, four or five days a week, as necessary. A combination of depots on a certain area could also have their requirements bulked, to enable a daily (or perhaps less frequent) train load of coal produced from adjacent collieries to be conveyed, detaching wagons as required en route. Two factors were essential to gain the full benefits from the operation of block train loads of coal, viz. (a) the daily output of a colliery or group of collieries

BERTHED AT AN ELECTRICALLY-DRIVEN COALING PLANT.

reduced from six days to five on 5 May and since that date the loaded wagons moved by the GWR had decreased by 21,039, a 3.1 per cent reduction.

The Great Western directors continued their efforts to improve their railway. Swindon Works was turning out new 'Hall' and 'County' class mixed-traffic 4-6-0 engines and an order for fifty 0-6-0 pannier tank engines was placed with Robert Stephenson & Hawthorns Ltd. Swindon Works built the boilers for them; the contractor did the rest for £457,350 – subject to increase on account of inflation. No 4972 *St Brides Hall* – renumbered 3904 – was equipped for oil burning and also had electric lighting installed in the cab in place of oil lamps.

Expenditure on new machine tools for Swindon Works continued. Purchases were approved by the Locomotive Committee but in the post-war famine of materials the flood of demands for new equipment could only result in a trickle of machines arriving. On 17 July an order for nine diesel-electric mobile cranes – for the benefit of the Goods Department – worth £23,618 was placed with Steels Engineering Products. In August the firm had to ask the GWR for an additional £2,348 4s 0d to cover their increased costs of production. In October 1945 the purchase had been approved of a 20in swing, sliding, surfacing and screw-cutting lathe from Messrs John Laing at a cost of £1,158. In August 1947 the lathe was purchased with £202 added to cover inflation of costs since October 1945.

In spite of all disadvantages, Swindon Works restarted a much-needed carriage-building programme in 1947. These were magnificent vehicles, designed by the Chief Mechanical Engineer, Mr F.W. Hawksworth, and surely with suggestions from his Chief Assistant, Kenneth Cook, OBE, his Carriage Works Manager, C.T. Roberts, and the Chief Draughtsman. The bodies were 64ft long on the best Swindon bogies. Inside they had a corridor with individual compartments, beautifully upholstered, accessed from the corridor by a sliding door. From 1942 the diminutive, art deco 'GWR' within a circle – aptly described as the 'shirt button' logo – had been replaced on locomotive side tanks and tenders by the noble and dignified 'Great Western' with the coat of arms of the company between. These new coaches were the first and last to carry this emblem.

The guard's compartment of 1,462 passenger brake vans were ordered to be fitted with a steam-heated radiator in place of a plain steam pipe passing under the guard's seat. This was estimated to cost £2 per radiator. Twelve six-wheeled milk tanks were ordered by United Dairies to replace twelve old ones at a cost of £7,020.

The Locomotive Committee approved the expenditure to demolish the old locomotive running and maintenance depot at Southall and build a new one, with modern facilities for the staff, at a cost of £195,000. The new facilities were brought into use in 1954.

Grants of money were awarded annually, each in September, by the directors to the ganger and his gang, for the 'Best Kept Length' in each Engineering Department Division. The track through the divisions was tested at high speed by a lightly loaded

A comparison of carriage bogie design. On the left the 10ft wheelbase 'Dean' bogie dating from 1895, and the ultimate development of a GWR carriage bogie under a handsome Hawksworth design coach of 1947. The 'Dean' coach has no pivot pin engaging in the bogie centre. The weight of the coach is transferred to the outside of the bogie by vertical posts from the main underframe to springs within those 'cups' down by the wheels. The Hawksworth bogie became the standard for the British Railways Mk.1 coaches of 1951.

Hawksworth 1947 designed carriage. A very handsome vehicle with the dignified title and arms of the Company along the waist. The bogies it runs on became the standard design for British Railways Mk.1 carriages.

'Special' with the 'white-wash' carriage at the rear. Separate containers of red and of white liquid marker were suspended beneath the carriage and any untoward 'bumps' or 'lurches' caused the coloured fluids to spill over onto the track. Those lengths which survived unmarked were then assessed for steadiness by examining the print-out on the moving roll of paper within the recording instrument on the floor of the coach. The best length, having been ascertained, was then visited by the Chief Civil Engineer, the Divisional Engineer and the Directors' Engineering Committee.[5] They came in their Inspection Saloon, hauled by a well-polished locomotive. Clearly, this was a vastly auspicious occasion for the gang concerned – and a jolly nice day out for the great ones of the GWR Engineering Department, for the saloon was well stocked with provisions.

The September issue of the *Great Western Railway Magazine* gave an account of some of the horticultural shows held across the GWR under the auspices of the Staff Association. Food production had always been a feature of the railwaymen and women, and their efforts to feed themselves were especially important during not one but two world wars.

At the Highbridge Flower and Vegetable Show a special feature of the event was the presentation of a silver cup, donated by Sir Felix Pole, to be known as the 'Edward Hadley Cup'. Edward Hadley was the founder of the GWR 'Social and Educational Union' – which was now the 'Staff Association' and also of the 'Freedom from Accident' movement. The cup was presented by Lt Col Brookfield to Mrs H.L. Godfrey, who had obtained the highest number of points of any exhibitor at the show. Other garden-produce shows were held at Newton Abbot and Westbury, and there was a two-day show at Swindon. On display at these venues were all the vegetables, together with fruit, cakes, poultry, honey and of course flowers and hand-crafted items. At Westbury there were athletic sports to enjoy as well.

The Swindon two-day event was opened by the Assistant Locomotive Works Manager, H.G. Johnson; £100 was given out in prize money. The 'Cyril Lloyd Perpetual Challenge Cup' (Lloyd was a director of the company) went to Mr A. Drew, who was the most successful exhibitor with ten 'firsts', six 'seconds' and three 'thirds'. The F.W. Hawksworth Cup, for gladioli, and the Royal Horticultural Society Silver Gilt Medal for chrysanthemums, went to Mr R.H. Brooks. There were several more cups. All were presented by Mrs F.C. Hall, wife of the Assistant Chief Mechanical Engineer. The exhibits were auctioned after each day's show and the proceeds placed in the 'Helping Hand' fund.

Beneath the account of the produce show in the September issue of the magazine is the report of an unusual honour bestowed on a GWR employee. Mr W. Stanley Smith was working in the Chief Goods Manager's Office at Paddington. He was a member of the 152 (GWR) Company Royal Engineers Supplementary Reserve. When war broke out he joined the regular army as a Royal Engineer. He went with the British Expeditionary Force to France and came back from Dunkirk. He went on the next ill-fated expedition – to Norway – and survived. In July 1944 he was a Captain RE and was sent to Ancona, a city and seaport on the Adriatic coast of Italy. The Allies had captured the city from the Nazis after a month-long battle. Stanley Smith's mission was to 'rehabilitate the railwaymen of the province' so that they could work again to transport soldiers and munitions.

Stanley Smith found them 'ragged, hungry, bereaved and seriously in need of leadership and friendship'. Captain Smith housed the homeless, organised supplies of food, opened canteens and other amenities and 'infused into them something of the Great Western spirit'. He became known as 'Signor Capitano del Genio Reale Smith'. In the summer of 1947 he took his wife and young son back to Ancona to see how his railwaymen friends were progressing and was astonished to be greeted by a formal civic reception, which included his being presented with the Freedom of the City inscribed ornately on a parchment 'Freedom Scroll'. This stated:

> Captain, W. Stanley Smith, Royal Corps of Engineers of Broseley, Shropshire, was of great service to the city from July 1944 to July 1945. He gave great assistance to the railway service, restored the railwaymen to their homes, provided them with food and clothing and aided their return to normal life. The City of Ancona, deeply grateful, confers on Captain Smith Honorary Citizenship. Ancona.

On 1 September 0-4-2 tank engine No 1450 was working the passenger trains – using an 'auto car' – on the Abingdon branch. It brought the 3.57 p.m. Radley train into Abingdon at 4.05 p.m. The engine was then to take over the working of an Abingdon–Oxford train, and the engine on the goods train was to take over the 'auto' train. No 1450 ran back along the Loop and into the Tank Siding. Then, without waiting for the signalman to set the route into the goods yard, the driver of No 1450 went forward and was derailed, all wheels at the still open trap point. The breakdown vans were ordered from Oxford shed at 4.10 p.m. The passengers for the 4.55 p.m. Abingdon–Radley train were taken to Radley station and on to Oxford by a regular service, Oxford City Motors bus. The breakdown vans arrived at Abingdon at 5.37 p.m. and No 1450 was back on the rails and ready to work the goods train at 6.10 p.m.

At 5.20 p.m. on 9 September at Paddington Departure box – where the signalling was operated by draw-slides switching current to point motors and signal lamps – the signalman set the route for empty coaches (ECS) to come from the sidings into Platform 4. When that movement was complete, the signalman restored the route and set the points from the Up Engine & Carriage Line (E&C Line) to No 4 Platform so that the engine for the train, No 6126, could go in and couple on. He drew out slide 94 – the signal for the route – and the driver received a proceed aspect with an illuminated indicator telling him he was routed into No 4. The engine set off but the route was set

This Freedom

CITIZENS OF ANCONA, ITALY, HONOUR THEIR GREAT WESTERN BENEFACTOR

SOON after war broke out in 1939, Mr. W. Stanley Smith, of the Chief Goods Manager's office, a member of the 152 (G.W.) Company, R.E. Supplementary Reserve, was back with the regular army—first in France, then Norway and eventually Italy. It was he who, as Captain Smith of the Allied Commission, was sent in 1944 to the Adriatic city and seaport of Ancona, charged with the task of rehabilitating the railwaymen of the province. He found them in a sorry plight—ill clad, poorly fed, many homeless and bereaved, and all of them sadly in need of leadership and friendship.

Captain Smith changed all this ; re-settled them, organised supplies, canteens and other amenities, and infused into them something resembling the "Great Western spirit." Thanks to his zealous welfare work, these stricken railway folk were welded into an energetic corps again. That is why the men, women and children of the now thriving railway colony in Ancona province still smile gratefully when anyone recalls "Signor Capitano del Genio Reale W. Stanley Smith ".

It also explains the sequel this summer. Wishing to see for himself how his old friends in Italy were faring,

CAPT. W. STANLEY SMITH.

"Signor Capitano" revisited Ancona with his wife and young son and had a great surprise—a civic reception, at which Ancona conferred the Freedom of the City on its Great Western benefactor.

The Freedom scroll (opposite) says that Ancona, in the sad times of war, had much sorrow and distress eased by the wise and humane work of Captain W. Stanley Smith, Royal Corps of Engineers, of Broseley, Shropshire, who was in service in the city from 1944 until July, 1945; how he gave great help to the railway service, restoring their homes to the railwaymen, helping them with food and clothing and, by his efficient and considerate provision, aiding their return to normal life; and that Ancona, deeply grateful, confers on Captain Smith Honorary Citizenship.

for No 2 Platform, which was fully occupied by the 5.23 p.m. departure. No 6126 was reversed back onto the E&C Line and the 5.23 left at 5.25.

As it did so the signalman set up the route for the ECS of the 5.37 p.m. departure to come from No 2 Up E&C Line to Platform 6 and drew slide 96 for the signal. The driver set off and he too found himself going towards Platform 2 and in so doing 'trailed' No 41 points. As this movement was taking place towards Platform 2, the engine which had brought in the stock of the 5.23 departure was moving along Platform 2 towards the Starting signal at the 'country' end. The signalman ran to the window with a red flag and hung it out to stop the movement off the E&C Line. The driver moving along Platform 2 line also saw it and stopped.

Points 41 were strained but usable. The Signal Lineman disconnected the electric connections and a hand signalman was provided to wind the blades back and forth as required with the hand crank. Points 69 were clipped and padlocked. An examination of the wiring and relays in the locking room below the operating floor revealed no evidence of faulty wiring which could have given false currents. The technicians did connect the necessary wires to produce the effects described but they could see no evidence that there were any bare wires to make a false connection. But they did replace the wiring which, had it been in contact, would have caused the malfunction.

Twenty-four hours after the emergency the wiring of Paddington Departure box had been renewed where required, the entire locking checked and signed off as safe. Mr A.W. Woodbridge, the Chief Signal & Telegraph Engineer of the GWR, wrote to the General Manager, saying: 'As certain wires in the Paddington Yard have been subjected to a considerable amount of interference I shall be asking the Board on 27th November for authority to put some renewals in hand as a precautionary measure against any undetected damage.'

On 11 September at Little Bedwyn at 8 p.m. the ganger's attention was drawn to a fire in the planking of the footbridge. With the assistance of Mr Mills of the Post Office at Little Bedwyn, a stirrup pump was obtained and the fire was extinguished. It is presumed to have been started by a spark from the chimney of the engine hauling the 6 p.m. Paddington–Weymouth express, which passed at about 7.42 p.m. One wooden post and two footboards were replaced at the cost of £5.

At 10 minutes to one o'clock on the morning of 13 September, the 9.45 p.m. Reading West Junction–Basingstoke goods train passed Southcote Junction on the Down branch line. The locomotive was No 3441 *Blackbird*. The next signal box after Southcote Junction was Burghfield, a box built because of additional wartime traffic, and opened in June 1941 to halve the original 5-mile section from Southcote to Mortimer. On 13 September Burghfield was switched out, so the old, long section remained. The goods train was in section for an unusually long time and the signalmen were alert, expecting some difficulty. At 1.30 a.m., the phone rang in Southcote Junction box. The guard of the 9.45 p.m. Reading train was ringing from Burghfield box – the door of which was unlocked as luck would have it – to report that the engine of his train was a failure. He had walked back to protect the rear in accordance with Rule 179 and had arrived at Burghfield signal box. He had put down one detonator a quarter of a mile to the rear of his train, another at half a mile and three at three-quarters of a mile, and would stand guard at that point with a red light.

The official report of this incident, which I have in front of me, states that the cause of the failure was that 'the driver's (water) gauge glass was broken and he was unable to replace it'. How this could be a reason to fail the engine is – superficially – a mystery. GWR locomotives have two water gauge glasses and each gauge has a shut-off cock so that if one breaks the escape of boiler pressure steam can be stopped simply by pulling down a handle.

A logical explanation would be that the other gauge glass was already broken and so now, with the second one burst, all they had left to check on the level of water in the boiler were the three test cocks. These were taps arranged one above the other on the back of the firebox. Turning a tap allowed scalding water to spurt out – so one stood well to the side when turning the tap – and so long as *water* came out the crew knew how high a level of water they had in the boiler, but if only *steam* came out then the men knew that water was lower down in the boiler and they tried the next lower tap. In darkness this method of checking water level was not possible and so the only thing to do was fail the engine and throw the fire out.

Reading Control was 'looking round' for a spare engine from somewhere to go to the assistance of the 9.45 goods train. At 2.40 a.m. the guard rang in to say that he was rejoining his train because the driver had not thrown the fire out and had decided he could work the train as far as Mortimer. The guard would return to his van, leaving the three detonators at Burghfield box and take up the other two as he walked back. While this was happening, Reading Control located an engine at Basingstoke which had a gap in its duties and could run out to Mortimer. It arrived there at 3.08 a.m. and reversed into a siding. The ailing *Blackbird* arrived at Mortimer on the Down line, the whole train complete with tail lamp at 3.40 a.m. It was then crossed over to the Up line, train out of section sent to Southcote Junction, and the 3.15 a.m. Reading–Basingstoke diesel rail car accepted. The latter had been standing at Southcote for 24 minutes. The Basingstoke engine coupled onto *Blackbird* and the train was worked away with 3 hours 34 minutes' delay booked to the failure.

On 13 September at 7.30 p.m., shunting operations were being carried out at Exeter West box between the Up Main and the station yard in connection with the 4.10 p.m. Plymouth–Paddington parcels train which was standing at the Up Main platform, the necessary headroom being obtained on the Up Main line.

In consequence of Up trains being due, Signalman Hamilton, who was on duty in Exeter West box, decided to divert the subsequent shunting movements out of the yard towards the Down Main line which amongst other lever movements necessitated reversing points 26 (Connection Up Relief to yard) before he could set up the new route. Whilst the shunting engine – tender leading at the signal box end of the train – was pulling six vehicles from the yard towards the Up Main line and the signal box, Signalman Hamilton hurriedly, and obviously without thinking, reversed points 26. He stopped the engine at the box and told the driver of the altered working and instructed him to set back into the yard so as to use the new route. But, in consequence of points 26 having been prematurely reversed, the engine had run through them. The consequence was that, when setting back towards the yard, the two rear wheels of the tender became derailed.

For causing the derailment Signalman Hamilton was 'verbally admonished'.

The General Manager, Sir James Milne, reading this wrote to Gilbert Matthews, Superintendent of the Line, on 23 September:

Derailment at Exeter St. David's 13.9.37

With reference to your report of the 18th inst it is observed that the signalman at fault in this instance was also held primarily responsible for the derailment of an engine and coach on July 28th and, in the circumstances, I shall be glad to know if you consider that the proposal to dispose of the matter by a verbal admonishment is adequate.

Handwritten at the base of that letter and dated 24 September 1947 is:

> Mr. Holmes will submit a communication setting out the nature of the disciplinary action taken in this instance.

On 6 October Mr Holmes wrote to Milne:

> Both cases – 28.7.47 and 13.9.47 – were taken into consideration when disciplinary action was taken. The Superintendent of the Line is satisfied that Hamilton may be allowed to continue his duties in the box.

Milne had to be content with that but clearly he would have preferred giving Hamilton a Registered Caution or even transferring him from the very, very busy Exeter West box to somewhere a lot quieter. Ralph Hamilton saw his career out to age 65 in Exeter West box without further upsets.

On 22 September the 8.30 a.m. Birkenhead–Paddington express was running 'in two parts'. That does not mean that the coupling between two carriages had snapped, but rather that there were so many passengers wanting to travel on this train that a second train was put on to carry the excess: that was how the railway ran in those days. The first part, hauled by engine No 6006 *King George I*, passed Aynho Junction signal box at 12.52 p.m. The signalman, W.G. Hucker, was observing the train and, with eyes as sharp as a hawk's, he saw a metal washer fall out from between the driving wheels. He sent the 'Train entering Section' signal – two beats on the bell – to Ardley and when that was acknowledged he sent seven beats – meaning 'Stop & Examine'. He phoned Ardley to report what he had seen and suggested to the Ardley man that he tell the driver to have a careful look around his engine. The train stopped at Ardley at 12.59 p.m. The driver examined his engine and reported it to be a complete failure – a spring under the leading nearside driving wheel had become displaced.

The Ardley signalman phoned Banbury at 1.5 p.m. and requested a fresh engine for the Birkenhead train. The fresh engine arrived at 1.53 p.m., removed the 'King', and worked the train forward at 2 p.m. The second part of the 8.30 a.m. Birkenhead train was stopped at Aynho Junction, the driver informed of what had occurred, and told to pass through the section to Ardley under caution.

Signalman Hucker's commitment to the job was reported to the Superintendent of the Line and it was agreed that he would receive a bonus of 1 guinea in his next pay packet.

Notes

1   *Rail* 250/482 September.
2   *Hansard* vol. 443 1947, cols. 1343–62.
3   *60 Years of Western Express Running* p. 264, by O.S. Nock.
4   *Locomotives of the GWR*, Part 8, RCTS.
5   See Appendix VI.

GREAT WESTERN RAILWAY
MAGAZINE

OCTOBER · 1947

VOL. 59 · NO. 9

Pride in the Job—8
(See Page 193)

PRICE ONE PENNY

OCTOBER

On 31 October, sixteen of the eighteen GWR directors met for their monthly Board Meeting in the Board Room at Paddington. They sat around the large, oval, rosewood table – which certainly looked as if it had been there since the opening of the new Paddington station in 1854 – and dealt with the problems of the railway of the present – and with those relating to the forthcoming demise. The first item was to note the contents of a letter sent from the Ministry of Transport on 23 October, informing them that:

> Messrs Deloitte, Plender, Griffiths & Co have been appointed as auditors to undertake the duties required by Section 20 of the Transport Act 1947 in relation to the Great Western undertaking and that the firm of Messrs Peat Marwick Mitchell & Co and Price Waterhouse & Co., have been appointed as a supervisory panel with the duty of signing an over-riding report based on the certificates given to them by the auditors of the individual undertakers.

The Chairman, Viscount Portal, then informed the Board that a final Annual General Meeting of the shareholders would be held in 1948 'when the amount receivable by the company under Section 20 of the Transport Act is known'.

The Minister of Transport continued to make the directors deal with the problems of the Guillebaud Report regarding the future:

> grading of railway workers and re-arrangement of inter-grade margin and in the event of it not being possible to reach agreement with the trade unions to consult with the British Transport Commission on the question of future procedure. The Companies' proposals have been sent to the Unions and will form the subject of discussion between the Railway Staff Conference and the Unions in due course.

'By which time,' I imagine the directors saying – thankfully – 'we won't be here.'

An Actuarial Report on the monetary value of the 'Great Western Railway Superannuation Fund' had been commissioned from Sir Joseph Burns and he submitted this to the October meeting. The balance sheet showed that, taking into account payments already made for deficiencies disclosed in previous valuations, the Fund had a deficiency of £1,904,413.

The reasons were: (1) on 23 December 1946 the conversion of the War Bonus (additional money paid to counteract the rising cost of living in wartime) into a permanent wage rise, (2) the increase in salaries of £19 10s, and (3) the transfer

I took this in the GWR Board Room at Paddington in 1962. Models of locomotives made by Swindon apprentices were ranged around the great oval table. Pictures of GWR directors are on the wall and there was a solid walnut cupboard.

to the Superannuation Fund of those former members of the Salaried Staff Retiring Allowances Fund and Female Clerks Pension Fund. Pensions had to be paid according to wages/salary and each individual's contribution was graded according to his/her pay. The deficiency arose from increases that were not covered by a similar increase in contributions to the Fund.

The British Transport Commission had moved its offices into the first three floors of the Great Central Hotel at Marylebone station. The hotel had been used as a railwaymen's hostel and a certain number were rendered homeless. The Southern Railway had the Craven Hotel as a hostel for their London staff accommodation and twenty-five GWR men evicted from the Great Central were accommodated at 'The Craven'. Meanwhile the upper four floors of the 'Great Central' were being converted to hostel accommodation 'as a matter of urgency'.

For the winter of 1947–48 the railway education programme was revived after its suspension during the war. Evening classes on railway subjects were to be held at the London School of Economics under the auspices of the London County Council. Classes were available in Railway Signalling and Operating; Station Accountancy; Goods Rates and Station Working; Railway Salesmanship; Dock Management and Operation; and Permanent-way Maintenance. The GWR (London) Lecture and Debating Society was another, but more relaxed, educational facility. Any London Division employee could join for 1s a year. Another such society was based at Bristol for the Bristol Division, and at Swindon, within the Bristol Division, there was also the Lecture and Debating Society of the Mechanics' Institute. Formal evening classes for GWR employees including Works Apprentices, were held at Swindon Technical College.

GWR officers gave talks on aspects of railway work, according to their own speciality. On 16 October the Manager of the GWR docks at Cardiff and Penarth spoke on 'The Trade of the Port of Cardiff'. Mr K.J. Cook, Works Assistant to the Chief Mechanical Engineer, addressed the London Society on 13 November on 'Locomotive Maintenance Problems'. All lectures were followed by discussion. The Proceedings of the GWR (London) Debating Society for the winter season 1947–48 were to be printed and bound for distribution to members of the society at an estimated cost to the GWR of £400.

The estimated receipts of the GWR for the five weeks ended 19 October were £4,925,000. This was a decrease of £38,000 (0.77 per cent) compared with the same period in 1946. Passenger traffic receipts were down by £205,000 (8.6 per cent), general merchandise traffic was down by £19,000 (1.02 per cent) and coal traffic

Experts of Tomorrow

GREAT WESTERN SIGNAL AND TELEGRAPH STAFF GO TO SCHOOL IN WORKING HOURS

LAST year the Great Western Railway was faced with the problem of filling a considerable number of vacant posts with key maintenance staff, such as signal and telegraph linemen and installers. To overcome the immediate staff shortage, as well as making provision for the future, the Company established signalling training schools at Bristol and Birmingham.

These schools have classrooms which contain full-scale crossing sections of permanent way, signals, levers, power-operated points and all types of telephone and block-working instruments.

A Three-months' Intensive Course

The training scheme enables both new entrants to the service and eligible men drawn from existing staff in all parts of the system to be given an intensive course over a period of three months. During this time the students learn how to install and maintain mechanical and electrical signalling apparatus, block telegraph instruments, electrically operated points, track circuits and telephones.

An essential part of the course is instruction in the rules and regulations associated with the type of work they will undertake, and in emergency arrangements and look-out duties. As a practical contribution to their training, the first intake of students at Bristol and Birmingham helped to install the new apparatus which they would later be using.

Signal Department's Jubilee

On August 2 this year the Signal and Telegraph Engineer's department celebrated its jubilee as an independent organisation. Prior to 1897 the department's activities came under the jurisdiction of the Company's Civil Engineer. We hope to publish next month an article dealing with the department's history and progress during the past fifty years.

STUDYING SIGNAL WORK UNDER REALISTIC CONDITIONS.

TWO CLASSES AT WORK UNDER EXPERT INSTRUCTORS AT BRISTOL SIGNALLING SCHOOL.

Classes to train Signal & Telegraph Department technicians were held at Bristol and Birmingham.

brought in an increase of £136,000, 25.69 per cent up on the same period in 1946. Taking the whole of 1947 up to 19 October, total income was £38,007,000, down by £3,282,000 on 1946. Over that ten months passenger traffic income had declined by £2,367,000 (11.23 per cent) and general merchandise decreased by £915,000 or 4.53 per cent.[1]

The General Post Office and the GWR had made an agreement on 29 August 1928 as to the annual sum the former would pay the latter for carrying the Royal Mail at high speed and with punctuality guaranteed on pain of a fine. That agreement was still in force on 30 September 1947 – in spite of years of decay in the value of money. On 1 October the GPO agreed to an increase of 52 per cent in the charge levied by the company. The total annual amount then paid to the GWR became £464,995.

The delivery of coal to homes and power stations was still difficult in October. A National Electricity Saving Scheme had been started in September. As far as offices, factories, docks and railway workshops were concerned this required a 'staggering' of starting and finishing times of people at work. More night shifts were to be worked so as to keep demand for electricity steady and thus avoid an overloading 'peak' demand, which could shut down a power station. The government hoped to 'spread the load' and reduce 'peak' demand by one third.

The GWR management made every effort to co-operate in the regional load spreading schemes but on the other hand the working of the schemes would have an adverse effect on railway and dock operations and the turnaround of ships. The four railway companies pointed this out to the Ministry of Transport and asked that electricity supplies to railway works, locomotive depots and docks should be considered as essential and that the regional electricity boards should be advised of this.

As a result of the 'staggering' of working hours, the railway companies were ordered by the Ministry of Transport that 'workmen's cheap tickets were now to be made available to artisans, mechanics and labourers who, by reason of the adoption of local rota schemes designed to spread the peak electricity load are required to travel between the time when the issue of workmen's tickets normally ceases and twelve noon'.

During the five weeks ended 17 October, 188,148 loaded coal wagons were hauled from collieries on the GWR. This was 1,752 wagons fewer than the same period in 1946. 'Loaded wagons cleared' had been decreasing since the miners' five-day week had been introduced on 5 May. This measure was not just applied to the coal mining industry alone. Throughout industry the five-day week was resulting in wagons which arrived on a Friday standing until Monday before they were opened. To unload the wagons on a Saturday required the payment of overtime wages.

This exacerbated the already critical problem of there not being enough empty wagons available for reloading. The shortage was caused by a depleted wagon fleet owing to unrepaired wear and tear during and since the war, the increasing age of the mostly wooden wagons and, in very large part, to the consignees using the loaded wagons loaned to them as if they were their own storage facility. The railway allowed a trader three days to clear a wagon and after that he was charged a 'demurrage' fee. The problem was not confined to coal wagons: any wagon under load would end up in the local station yard and could stand there for days awaiting release, and this was affecting imports at the docks because of a shortage of empty wagons.

In October the problem was urgently focused upon by the Ministry of Transport, the Railway Executive and a Sub-Committee of the National Production Advisory Council on Industry in an effort to speed things up before winter set in and the increased demand for electricity and coal made the railway supply system worse. The suggested ways forward shows why the amalgamation of all four railway companies into one nationalised operation was considered the best way forward.

Firstly, traffic was to be re-routed over the most direct route; all the old conventions from company days were to be abandoned.

Secondly, coal was to be conveyed by block trains, working through to destination, to avoid marshalling yard delays, and moved direct to the power station or to a central coal depot, from which lorries could distribute the 'penny packets' of coal to the hundreds of consumers.

Thirdly, places served by more than one railway were to have coal trains on the most convenient route.

The old arrangement of demurrage payments was not – and never had been – enough to ensure wagons were cleared promptly. To get the coal and merchandise wagons emptied quicker, the demurrage charges were increased and the railway companies agreed, in October, to employ men as 'wagon chasers'. These people were to go to the sidings at factories and local stations and, by whatever means they could, instil a sense of urgency into the consignees of the wagons.

The situation on the railway was so difficult that it was obvious there would be too few wagons available to meet demand in the winter. Delivering coal to power stations was the overriding concern and thus the railways would have to be relieved, as far as possible, of freight traffic of other kinds. The Ministry of Transport therefore requested the Regional Transport Commissioners to divert as much as they could off rail to the roads, canals or coastwise shipping.

Not only was there an open wagon shortage problem, there was an insufficient supply of coal. The National Coal Board was considering opening a new coal mine at Warmley, near Bristol, making a central washery at Tufts Junction in the Forest of Dean, and the Ministry of Works was proposing to purchase 17½ acres between Bridgend and Maesteg for an opencast coal extraction, which would yield 40,000 tons for the railway, road lorries or ships to carry.

Top priority was given to having enough covered vans available for the transport of new motor cars to the docks of Merseyside. During the five weeks ended 17 October the GWR carried away from Morris Cowley 2,292 cars for export as well as 921 vehicles from the Austin works at Longbridge. This brought the total number of cars shifted by the GWR since the beginning of the year to 19,245, an 11 per cent increase on 1946. The General Manager noted in this report that the GWR had also moved to Dover for export: 86 tons of photographic paper from Wooburn Green to Belgium, France and Switzerland, 188 tons of machinery from Mortimer station and Corsham to Belgium and 218 motorcycles from Birmingham to Switzerland.

The Great Western had an entirely different load to move on the night of Tuesday 28 October. The LMS Royal Train was brought into Paddington and King George and Queen Elizabeth set out that evening for a tour of the West Country. The train was put aside at Totnes, so that the royal party could sleep in perfect comfort, and was restarted

LAST SPECIAL TRAIN ON THE GREAT WESTERN RAILWAY (*see page* 5). *Photo: " Western Times" Co. Ltd.*

Their Majesties, King George VI and Queen Elizabeth, saying goodbye to officials at Kingswear before boarding their train, the 4.40 p.m. departure, on 30 October. This was the last Royal Train to be run on the GWR.

VISCOUNT PORTAL (*left*) BIDS MR. PARTRIDGE GOODBYE.

Chief Inspector Partridge and the Chairman of the Board.

the following morning, reaching St Austell at 10 a.m. on 29 October. The train went back to Devonport and was boarded by the King and Queen that evening. It set off from there for an overnight stay at Totnes and the following morning, 30 October, it took them to Kingswear, where it was stabled. That evening the royal couple were transported back to Paddington, arriving at 9.35 p.m.

That Royal Train was the last one to be supervised by Chief Passenger Train Inspector George Partridge MBE. George Partridge was aged 14 when he started his career on the GWR at Newton Abbot engine shed in 1895. From his two portraits in the *Great Western Railway Magazine* I guess that he found the filth of cleaning engines too much and he transferred to the Traffic Department of the London Division in 1899. Four years later he was promoted to Passenger Train Guard. This is an indication of his very spick and span personality and attitude to railway work because, in those days, a man had to be *recommended* for promotion to passenger guard. They wore very smart uniforms that can only be described as 'elegant' and their knowledge of good manners and railway regulations was expected to be first class. Partridge was a good organiser. In 1904–05 he supervised the inauguration of the company's first road motor and steam rail motor services, and by 1908 he was a Passenger Train Inspector. He ranged all over the GWR, carrying out investigations and doing his utmost for high standards of public service and punctuality. In 1926 he was Assistant Chief Passenger Train Inspector, which brought him into the work of organising royal trains and in 1927 he became Chief. From the outbreak of war he was involved in organising the special troop train movements, the trains evacuating children from Paddington and Ealing and the most remarkable operation, organised completely 'off the cuff', with only a few days' notice, of creating a pool of 186 sets of coaches from all four companies and feeding them to and fro over the Reading–Redhill–Dover route. Partridge was in the control office at Redhill and helped keep order as the fleet of trains made 620 journeys into and out of Dover, lifting 319,000 soldiers to rest camp. For his work between 1939 and 1941 he was awarded the MBE. His age was 65 in 1946 but at the directors' request he stayed on an extra year instead of retiring. He thus completed fifty-two years' service and had been in charge of seventy-seven royal trains since 1926. He retired to a house at Blue Anchor in October 1947.

At the end of the summer train service the GWR invited the famous locomotive performance recorder Cecil J. Allen to ride on the footplate of engine No 6012 *King Edward VI*, which was hauling the 10.30 a.m. 'Cornish Riviera Express'.

In charge of the engine were two of Laira shed's finest: Driver Gordard and Fireman Ball. The load was fourteen coaches weighing 450 tons, 495 tons with every seat taken on the train and the guard's van piled high with luggage. The full load was to be taken to Plymouth with a stop at Exeter and Newton Abbot. The company wanted to show Allen the best of what they had in the grimmest period of their history.

They passed Reading in 41 minutes from Paddington – 1 minute late – due to a temporary speed restriction, but all was well on the engine: they had a heavy train but good coal and an undemanding schedule compared to 1937. Just after Maurice Earley had taken the picture overleaf, Fireman Ball, digging into the fuel, building up the fire for the long climb through the Kennet Valley, found that the fine cobbles of Welsh steam coal were merely a decoration, hiding a tender-full of Welsh 'nutty slack'.

Ball had about 44 sq ft of fire-grate to keep covered with an 11ft throw to the front end. Good cobbles lay where he aimed them, with air space around them for burning but small coal and dust was a dreadful prospect, with 205 miles to go pulling a heavy train. But experience was all. Ball worked twice as fast with the shovel and Gordard realised

DOWN "CORNISH RIVIERA EXPRESS", WITH AUTHOR ON FOOTPLATE, NEAR READING WEST.   *Photo.: Maurice W Earley.*

Cecil J. Allen going west on the 'Cornish Riviera Express'.

what his mate had to deal with and handled the engine accordingly. Losing some little time on the climbs to Savernake, Brewham, Whiteball summits, and picking up time running on a breath of steam on the long, downhill runs, touching 75mph at the foot of the declines, Gordard gave his mate time to run the long pricker over the firebars to clear clinker, build the fire, and re-fill the boiler and get the pressure back.

At Newton Abbot they picked up the usual Pilot engine for the very steep banks between there and Plymouth: Dainton, Rattery and Brent. 'Bulldog' engine 4-4-0 No 3401 *Vancouver* coupled on ahead of the 'King' and with this assistance they kept time, skimming down the other side of the 'grades', dashing through Totnes and down Hemerdon. They arrived in Plymouth North Road at 3.09 p.m. 1 minute early, having covered 31.9 very difficult miles in 50½ minutes. The 225¾ miles from Paddington had taken 279 minutes – but this was with almost 500 tons behind the tender and with coal duff for fuel. In 1937 the schedule was 244 minutes, with a maximum 500 tons to Westbury, slipping a coach or two there, slipping again at Taunton and stopping at Exeter. The train was not scheduled to stop at Newton Abbot but if there were more than nine coaches the driver could stop there for an assisting engine.

In October the directors were applied to by the Organising Committee of the London Olympics for seriously reduced fares for the participants and the staff of the Organisation. The games were to take place at Wembley Stadium starting on 29 July 1948. The GWR directors gallantly volunteered British Railways (Western Region) to sell the participants and staff half-price tickets and free travel if the person applied for a ticket within 15 miles of Charing Cross. All Olympic horses, sports or any other Olympic equipment would also be charged half the usual rate.

With the approach of nationalisation there was a requirement for a standard system of automatic train control for the entire United Kingdom. The most widespread system – almost the only system – was that used on the GWR called 'Automatic Train Control' – ATC. This was patented by GWR signal engineers, Jacobs and Insell, in 1905. It rang a bell if an engine was approaching a Distant signal showing 'All Right' and blew a steam whistle *inside* the engine's cab if the Distant signal was showing 'Caution' (meaning 'Get ready to stop at the next "Danger" signal'). In 1913 the steam whistle was abolished – surely due to furious complaints from the locomen – and instead the mechanism that opened a valve to admit steam to the whistle now opened the vacuum brake pipe to the atmosphere and started to apply the brakes. As the air rushed in it spun a siren to create a screeching sound. The driver would cancel this and take over braking himself.

There was one other system in use, a modern system, using two magnets set in the track. If a Distant signal was at 'Caution' the first magnet caused an alarm horn to sound and the brakes started to go on. The driver cancelled the alarm and the brake released while the 'all black' indicator disc in the cab went to black-and-yellow stripes to remind the driver he had passed a Distant signal at 'Caution'. This was the 'Hudd-Strowger' system, experimented with on the London Fenchurch Street and Southend line from 1930 and brought into daily use on that line in 1937.

The Great Western were very proud of their ATC and wanted it to become the British standard. Since the later 1920s four-aspect colour-light signalling had been installed on some routes of other railways. If the ATC was to be the accepted standard it would have to be able to warn the driver whether he had passed a 'double yellow' or a 'single yellow'. Modifications were made to the system and tests were run at speed.

On 12 October a full dress exhibition was made. The engine chosen was No 5056 *Earl of Powis* with Driver Bill Bateman of Swindon shed. The load consisted of the Dynamometer Car to register the pull on the drawbar and to make a continuous record of speed. Two 'Ocean' saloons, more spacious and comfortable than any Pullman car, were behinf the dynanometer car. Finally, there was a passenger brake van to house the food, drinks and an exhibition of the new ATC system. In the 'Oceans' were the Board of Directors of the Great Western Railway and their most senior officers, plus similar personages from the other railways, Railway Inspectorate Officers, and top people from the Ministry of Transport. It was the GWR directors' last public field day.

The object was to pass over the ATC ramp at 100mph on the approach to Maidenhead and to hear the double hoot indicating the passing of a 'double yellow' signal. The driver would not react to the 'Caution' but allow the equipment to bring the train to a stand, with steam full on, before the Stop signal was reached.

The train would start from Reading on the Up Main and would observe a maximum speed of 75 – which was the usual maximum permitted speed throughout the post-war railway – but, with special permission, would then accelerate to 100mph over the 6 miles remaining before reaching the Maidenhead ramp. I know that Bill Bateman was not happy about working up from 75 to 100 in 6 miles – he said it was 'abusing the engine' – but he was spoken to firmly and said that he would do his best. Twyford was

GREAT WESTERN RAILWAY MAGAZINE

siren for a "Caution" signal; it rings a bell if the signal is "Clear".

On some railway lines in this country (though not at present on the Great Western) another system of signalling is in use which includes two different kinds of "Caution" warning (for there is a double yellow as well as a single yellow light signal). This system, which is known as a four-aspect signalling, uses no semaphore arms. In 1946, Great Western engineers developed for the Automatic Train Control a third aural signal to correspond with this double yellow signal. The new aural signal is a combination of the siren with an electrically operated horn.

As a result of this latest development, it is now possible for Great Western Automatic Train Control to be used in conjunction with four-aspect light signalling. The new four-aspect Automatic Train Control installation is "universal", i.e., it is capable of being fitted to any existing railway track in the British Isles, and a locomotive equipped with it could be driven over any track so fitted in the knowledge that it would respond at all times to whichever of these signalling systems was met with.

A description of the process whereby the two alternative series of signals are repeated on the locomotive is given by diagrams and footnotes on page 216.

To-day there are 2,462 Automatic Train Control ramps in use on the Great Western system, and 3,364 installations on the Company's locomotives.

The Special Demonstration Run

On October 12 a demonstration run was arranged to show how the Great Western Automatic Train Control would function on a track equipped with the four-aspect light signalling system. The train started from Reading, and consisted of a dynamometer car and three coaches, hauled by "Castle" class engine No. 5056, *Earl of Powis*. Aural signals corresponding to the double yellow signals were relayed from the footplate and the dynamometer car to the passenger vehicles on the journey to Maidenhead.

En route the train passed eight Automatic Train Control track installations. Since the demonstration required a clear run as far as the last ramp (where the brakes were to be applied) the signals would normally stand at "Clear"

for each of the first seven ramps. For the purpose of the demonstration, however, ramps Nos. 4 and 6 (as well as 8) were set to give "Caution" signal. The driver of the demonstration train cancelled the first two "Caution" signals, pulling up only on receiving the third (at ramp No. 8). The other ramps (Nos. 1, 2, 3, 5 and 7) sounded the "Clear" signal.

As Great Western track is equipped with semaphore signalling throughout, normally the "Caution" signals on this track would be of the single yellow type. The purpose of the run to Maidenhead, however, was to demonstrate not the familiar single yellow (siren) signal but the double yellow (combined horn and siren) signal, which is a new development. Ramps Nos. 4, 6, 8 had accordingly been specially wired to produce this last aural signal. It should be emphasised that the horn and siren signal given over these ramps was a special signal produced for demonstration purposes, and would normally be used only on tracks where the four-aspect system of light signalling is installed.

Speed, Control and Smooth Riding

The train, the gross weight of which was about 270 tons, accelerated rapidly, passing Twyford, 5 miles from the start, where there was a speed restriction of 75 m.p.h., in 5 minutes 49 seconds. After Twyford the train further accelerated, reaching a speed of 96.4 m.p.h., 1¼ miles from Maidenhead and 19¼ miles from the start in 9 minutes 19 seconds. The speed was steadily reduced from 96.4 m.p.h. and the train was brought to rest at Maidenhead station platform.

Another test was then made when approaching Farnham Road signal box with the distant signal at "Caution" (single yellow). The train passed the ramp at 63.6 m.p.h. and the regulator was left fully open, but the automatic application of the brake brought the train to a stand in 1,505 yards from a maximum speed of 65.5 m.p.h. (the train was accelerating as it passed the ramp).

With a heavier train where the effective tractive effort of the engine is a smaller proportion of the gross weight of the train than of this short demonstration train, the Automatic Train Control application would bring a train to rest from a speed of 60 m.p.h. in about 900 yards.

An incidental observation on the test journey was the wonderfully smooth riding. Even at the peak speed of 96.4 m.p.h. the sensation in the passenger coaches more resembled the swish of a soft brush on the track than the fierce friction of steel against steel. This is a tribute to fine vehicle and permanent way maintenance work.

PRIDE IN THE JOB—9

This month's cover picture introduces another Great Western master man at another type of work, but taking the same traditional pride in the job. Even the dockside crane he captains is more than a machine, really, because other men's "pride in the job" was built into that, too. With our colleague of the Docks Department at the controls, giving it eyes and a brain, the great crane is a vital agency in the process of import and export.

ENGINE NO. 5056, *Earl of Powis*, ON THE DEMONSTRATION RUN.   *Photo. M. W. Earley.*

ENGINE NO. 5056, *Earl of Powis*, ON THE DEMONSTRATION RUN.   *Photo. M. W. Earley.*

passed at the permitted 75mph. At each succeeding mile, speed was: 83.4mph; 87.3; 90.5; 93.3; 95.2 to a maximum of 96.4mph.

One-and-a-half miles from Maidenhead was where the double hoot sounded in the loudspeakers in the train and the brakes went on. The regulator was left untouched and the train was brought smoothly to a stand, steam on, at Maidenhead station platform.[2]

The Strangford viaduct over the River Wye, which had been washed away at the end of March, was brought back into use in an improved form on 13 October. The Chief Civil Engineer decided not to replace the central pier – which was subjected to the strongest flow of the river – but to bridge the gap between the two piers still standing in the water. This would create a clear span over the middle of the river of 91ft 6in. Sheet steel piles were driven into the solid rock bed of the river using a No 7 McKiernan-Terry hammer[3] to form a coffer dam around each pier. Concrete was poured into the space between the old pier and the sheet steel piles but where the sharp cutwaters were to be, wooden formers were used.

Locomotive Department statistics for the month of October were closely similar to those of June, July, August and September. Total coal consumption of all the

GREAT WESTERN RAILWAY MAGAZINE

COFFER DAMS OF SHEET PILING WERE DRIVEN AROUND THE PIERS TO BE ENCASED IN REINFORCED CONCRETE.

TWO SUBSEQUENT STAGES IN THE LAUNCHING OF THE MAIN GIRDERS WHICH WOULD FORM THE NEW SINGLE SPAN.

Rebuilding the Strangford viaduct.

THE BRIDGE TAKES SHAPE. MAIN GIRDERS BEING LANDED ON TO THEIR FINAL BEARINGS BY CRANES.

locomotives in use during the month of October was 50.71lb per mile against 49.38lb for September. Pints of oil consumed in October totalled 7.75 as against 7.78 in September. The number of staff employed by the Locomotive Department in October – 45,046 – was 231 higher than in September.

The directors were 'on top' of all aspects of their railway. They were taking as great an interest in October 1947 as in 1937. The Great Western Railway owned thirty-seven diesel rail cars.[4] The first was put into service in early 1934 and the last in 1942. They were very fast and very comfortable, some of them having a small buffet/bar. Two of them were designed for express parcel delivery. The last twenty were built during 1940–41 and, with the exception of Parcels Car No 34, they were heated by a Vapor-Clarkson automatic steam generator, supplied by Gresham & Craven. Experience with these in service led to the redesign of the water pump on one car's heater. After leaving it in service for four years it was found to be thoroughly reliable. In October 1947 the Directors' Locomotive Committee authorised the expense of fitting the improved water pump to the other eighteen passenger cars' heaters. The cost of this was estimated at £1,785.

Five of the Company's postal sorting carriages which were 41 years old had been condemned and negotiations took place with the Postmaster General as to their replacement by modern vehicles. The outcome was that the Postmaster General agreed that the Post Office would pay the excess cost of building modern vehicles – £1,969 – compared to the estimated cost of those withdrawn. The replacement cost of the five old carriages was £15,250 and the cost of five modern vehicles was £17,219.

In April the Locomotive Committee had authorised the purchase of No 35 Cotham Park, Bristol, for use as a staff hostel. The house was purchased and in October the cost of adapting it to accommodate forty GWR employees was given as £4,970.

The list of improvements for the staff directly or indirectly was long: the replacement of gas lighting by electricity, or a new, easier to use, turntable, or the rebuilding of an ancient engine shed. The list went on: 'Pending the reconstruction of Whitland locomotive depot, now under consideration, it is desired to provide improved staff accommodation. The estimated cost of carrying out the work is £1,155.' Swindon Works' lighting by gas was replaced by electricity between July and October. The estimated cost had been £19,594. The total cost was announced in the October Minutes:

> £22,091 the excess expenditure of £2,497 being due to lighting at the engine weigh table also a certain amount of local lighting in the shops not being allowed for originally and to increases in wages and prices of material. Authority is desired to cover this extra cost.

At the 285¾ mile post between Par and St Austell the line is on an embankment rising at 1 in 64 for Down trains. At the foot of the embankment, there were two open-sided shelters containing bales of hay and farm machinery. On Wednesday 1 October they caught fire. The fire was discovered at 6.15 a.m. The owner, Mr L.A. Smith, a butcher of St Austell, blamed a spark from a locomotive and asked for compensation for his loss. The GWR made enquiries. The Down trains whose locomotives might have thrown a spark were the 4.55 a.m. parcels ex-Par, Driver Trevithick of Truro; 5.41 a.m. goods ex-Par, Driver Dopson of St Blazey; 5.54 a.m. 'light' engine ex-Par, Driver Bartlett, St Blazey; 6.16 a.m. Royal Mail ex-Par, Driver Cuthbert of Laira; 6.20 a.m. ex-Par Harbour, Driver Conibeer, St Blazey.

All these drivers received a form to fill in. None were going to admit to throwing fire on a 1 in 64 rising gradient when two shelters full of winter hay had gone up in smoke. The thought in their minds was probably: 'Why were hay barns built at the very foot of the embankment – why not on the far side of the field far from the line and nearer the gate?' Bartlett, Cuthbert and Conibeer could hardly be bothered to put pencil to form; they had no 'Remarks' to make at all. All they would say was that their engines were in perfect order. Driver Trevithick had No 1023 *County of Oxford*. Everything was in perfect order on his engine, he had his engine 'on the 30 or 35 on the bank and I know nothing of a fire between Par and St Austell'. Driver Dopson had No 5940 *Whitbourne Hall* on the 9.55 a.m. Bristol West Depot–Penzance goods train. He gave the inquiry a sarcastic brush-off disguised as a text book answer. 'I was working my engine in the manner best calculated to take the load economically on the grade and keep time. I had the lever in 30 per cent cut-off.'

What the outcome was I do not know but the company was no pushover. There had to be a good reason for them paying out money and even then they would do their best to undervalue the loss. I have beside me a letter from John Lewis, sent from the Estate Office of the Jenniscombe Lodge estate, Tiverton, dated 2 October, regarding the loss by fire of crops growing by the railway line on Hartnolls Farm, Halberton. This was in reply to the GWR's solicitor's letter denigrating his surveyor's valuation of the damage. Lewis wrote with great indignation:

> I inspected the scene of the fire forthwith and I cannot except [*sic*] your figures, a cheap-jack might but those who know me would know that I should deal with the matter carefully and honestly and yet you say 'and in the view of the company the figure of £8 7s 10d represents a fair valuation.' I do not value the loss in Bristol or London but on the spot and immediately after it took place and in the presence of the Police Constable who made the same return as I did which is the same I sent to you.
>
> I went very carefully into the matter and I arrived ON THE SPOT before the remainder of the corn was burned.
>
> There is the question as well of the farm men who helped to put the fire out and my fees and costs in the matter and but for the efforts of all of us the claim I sent might be £60 or more instead of £17 17s 6d. The yield per acre is more than you are putting it at. I put it at 9 quarters instead of your 6 it was an extraordinary piece of corn and there is plenty of evidence to that fact.
>
> I am therefore unable to except [*sic*] your figures, since the matter is not dealt with by you in a fair and reasonable manner, you have had my claim and I expect you to meet it.
>
> Yours faithfully,
> John Lewis,
> Tiverton.

Again, I do not have any evidence of the outcome. But it is a splendid letter!

Near tea-time on 8 October, the signalman at Moreton-on-Lugg, G.A.J. Davies, had the 2.30 Pontypool Road–Saltney GWR through freight train that was close on the Down Main and the 2 a.m. Guide Bridge–Abergavenny LMS through freight train that was close on the Up. The latter consisted of thirty-four, equal to thirty-seven wagons, 'H' headcode, and was hauled by an LMS 'Super D' 0-8-0 engine No 9369. The train passed Moreton-on-Lugg's (Moreton) Up Main Distant signal at 'Caution' a few minutes before five o'clock. The Moreton signalman had asked 'Is Line Clear?' to Shelwick Junction for the train – 3-4-1 on the bell – and Shelwick had replied with 3-5-5, meaning he was accepting the train under the 'Warning Arrangement'. Moreton would check the train hard and warn the driver – by holding a green flag[5] from the window – to have his train well under control approaching Shelwick and to be ready to stop at the Home signal because the line was clear only that far.

The signals at Moreton were cleared in the Up direction for the Pontypool Road–Saltney train. The Moreton signalman brought the Guide Bridge nearly to a stand at his Outer Home, lowered that, did the same at the Inner Home and displayed his green flag as the engine approached the signal box. The driver of the train responded with a short blast on his whistle to show that he understood. Davies cleared his Starting signal and the driver put on steam.

Standing on the end of the Down platform, Mr G.H. Maysey, a permanent-way man, was watching the approach of the train. He was an acute observer and told the later inquiry:

> The train parted almost opposite the signal box and the leading vehicle of the rear part seemed to turn round by the signal box towards the level crossing gate. The next wagon turned 45 degrees in the other direction, fouling the Up Main. As this happened a GW train was passing on the Up Main. Nine or ten of the leading vehicles of this train had passed before the wagon of the Down train fouled the Up Main and several of the following wagons of the Up train hit the fouled wagon before it was knocked clear.

The driver of No 9369 was looking back as the engine started to accelerate and draw out the slack couplings between the wagons, and he saw the parting take place and the derailment. He brought his part of the train to a stand and went back on foot. There was a terrible mess. The drawbar of an LMS/ex-Caledonian Railway wagon built in 1904 had been wrenched out through the buffer beam and the wagon, deflected from its proper course, came off the road to the left, derailing the following four: the twelfth, thirteenth, fourteenth and fifteenth – two 'bogie bolsters', followed by two ordinary open wagons. They were carrying massive billets of steel. Four wagons of the GW train were derailed and smashed. The Up and Down line tracks were extensively damaged, torn up or pushed sideways. The Down Goods Loop was blocked. The lower part of the signal box was crushed, the signal wires and point rodding broken and twisted. The level crossing gates were smashed.

Signalman Davies did not see the parting or the derailment – he was actually operating the signalling bells. He was at the instrument shelf sending 'Train entering

Section' to Shelwick Junction and Dinmore at 4.59 p.m. when he was thrown backwards as the heavily laden wagons hit his signal box wall.

He had been a signalman for four years. The most perfect knowledge of the Rules and Regulations cannot prepare a man for the shock of an event like that. That has to be an instinctive reaction from the man. He reacted perfectly, and remembered his job. Davies got up off the floor and sent 'Obstruction Danger' – 6 beats on the bell in both directions – called Control, reported the time and the extent of the crash and at 5.04 the Hereford breakdown vans, the Crewe, LMS and the Cardiff and the GWR steam cranes were called out. The Hereford gang arrived at 8.25 p.m., the Crewe crane at 10.40 p.m. and the Cardiff crane at 11.40 p.m.

While the lines were blocked, local passenger trains terminated at Hereford and Leominster and passengers covered the intervening distance by bus. The through expresses, Crewe–Hereford, were diverted via Wolverhampton, Worcester and Ledbury. The skilled gangs cleared the Up Main and the Down Loop at 7.38 a.m. next day so that single-line working could be brought into use over the Up Main. The Down main was cleared and handed back to the Traffic Department at 4.05 p.m. the same day.

Engineman C. Townsend and Fireman G. Lloyd booked on duty at Banbury shed at 3.15 a.m. on 27 October. Townsend was aged 48 with ten years' experience as a driver, and Lloyd was 25 and had been passed as a fireman for six years. The guard of the train was H.H. Croft. They worked a goods train south on the 'New Line' bound for London but were stopped at High Wycombe to change footplates with the men on the 8 p.m. (of the previous night) Old Oak Common to Oxley 'F' headcode freight train. These men had been working for long hours and had to return to their depot, Old Oak Common. The load was '60 equal 68' wagons, including the brake van, and the engine was GWR 2-8-0 No 2883.

The Banbury crew set off with the heavy train at 7.35 a.m. They passed Aynho Junction, 85 minutes from High Wycombe at 9.02 a.m., which indicates an average speed of 25mph. Guard Croft, in his van at the rear of the train, had his handbrake on – just enough to keep the couplings out tight as they passed over Aynho water troughs. These were placed in the 'four-foot' of the Up and Down Main line 550yd north of Aynho Junction and extended for 560yd. The footplate crew lowered their scoop and took water and this had a slight decelerating effect on the engine so that the wagons would close up on it, the wagon couplings would slacken and then, when the drag of the scoop in the water was no longer present, the engine would ease forward and tug on the slack couplings which might cause a break. Croft was applying fine tuning, best practice, which was somewhat ironic in view of what was about to happen.

The thirty-ninth wagon in the train was an LNER open, No 4544, on hire to the GWR. Eleven hundred yards north of the troughs one of the wheels on the leading axle moved – 1½in outwards. It then mounted the rail and ran along the top and eventually dropped outside the rail. The hammering of the wheel over the chairs and sleepers caused the axle to break 14in from the wheel boss. The other wheel, moving inwards, hammering over chairs and sleepers, caused the axle to break off, a clean, shearing break at the wheel boss. The wheels were still held to the wagon by their journals in their axle boxes; the boxes were held by the trunnions and the weight of the wagon above. For half a mile the wheels were sometimes running on the rail top sometimes running on the chairs and sleepers. The train crew had no idea anything was wrong.

Signalman Bill Clarke was on duty in King's Sutton box that Monday morning. He was aged 39 and had been a signalman for twelve years. When the goods was put 'on line' to him from Aynho Junction – 2 beats on the bell – he 'asked the road' from Astrop, got it and pulled off his Down Main line signals. About 5 minutes earlier he had pulled off his Up line signals for the 7.10 a.m. Wolverhampton–Paddington express – as it was passing Banbury South box. He was unable to enter any bell code times in his Train Register because there was no clock in the signal box, but the times could be obtained from the Train Registers in the boxes at Aynho Junction and Astrop.[6]

Clarke was standing by his levers as the train approached. It was travelling at the usual speed for an 'F' headcode. Clarke put his Distant signal back to 'Caution' as soon as the train came in sight. He watched it approaching and crossing the junction which was right outside his box. He saw nothing wrong. He turned as the engine passed and watched it passing through the station, 250yd north of his box. He did not see the upset as the thirty-ninth wagon's displaced wheels encountered the rails of the junction crossing the main line. Only as the wagon passed did he see the danger.

He threw his Starting signal back to 'Danger' – but the engine had already passed that. He sent the 'Emergency Call Attention' to Aynho Junction, Astrop and Adderbury on the Cheltenham line. He pulled over the Up Main detonator lever to place two detonators on the rail top. The Down line detonator placer had been smashed by the derailed wagon. The emergency signal was answered and he sent 6 beats – 'Obstruction Danger' in three directions. He then dashed to the corner window, grabbed a red flag from the stand, waved the flag and yelled at the guard: 'Put your brake on.' The time was 9.06 a.m.

Only then did Guard Croft know that he was in trouble. As the thirty-ninth wagon – LNER No 4544 – went through the station the nearside wheel and axle box was gouging a huge scar along the wall of the platform. The noise brought the Station

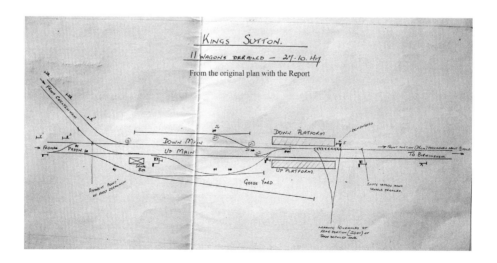

From the original plan with the Report

Master out of his office. When the brake van was opposite the platform ramp the coupling between the thirty-ninth and fortieth wagons broke. No 4544 continued attached to the front part, but now, with no wheels at all, was dragged a quarter of a mile before the coupling broke and left it there. The rear part of the train was brought to a stand when ten of the twenty wagons were derailed by the debris left behind by No 4544. The Up Main was blocked and the Down Starting signal demolished. Guard Croft asked the Station Master to protect the rear of the train while he ran forwards to put down detonators as far north as possible on the Up Main before the 7.10 a.m. Wolverhampton train approached – Croft, the Station Master and the men on No 2883 were well aware of the imminent arrival of the express.

Driver Townsend reckoned he was running at 25mph through King's Sutton station when his fireman called out to him that there was 'a cloud of dust coming out from a wagon'. Townsend stated for the inquiry:

> My mate called my attention to what appeared to be a cloud of dust coming from a wagon about two-thirds back. I stepped across to his side and saw the wagon begin to wobble and immediately other wagons began to pile up. My mate applied the handbrake and shouted to me that the Up fast was coming on the Up road. I immediately blew the brake whistle and my mate exhibited a red flag from the footplate. We had then stopped and the Up fast passed me just then with the brake hard on.

The Astrop signalman, Bert Bevington, was just about to send 2 beats – meaning 'Train entering Section' – for the express when the 'Emergency Call Attention' signal rattled out. The train was passing him at about 60mph. He answered with one beat and received 6 beats in return. He at once threw his Starting signal back to 'Danger' and sent 4-5-5 'Train Running Away on Right Line' to King's Sutton. The engine of the express had passed the signal or was so close to it that the driver, W.L. Jones, did not see it go back and he carried on at 60mph. Ahead, 440yd away, King's Sutton Junction's Up Main Distant signal was showing 'Caution'. Only then would the driver brake.

Driver Jones, a Wolverhampton Stafford Road man, said in his statement:

> I was running at 60mph passing Astrop with all signals 'off'. I received the 'Caution' at the ramp for King's Sutton Distant and I immediately checked my speed. After passing the last overbridge between Astrop and King's Sutton I saw a Down freight train approaching and as I drew level with the engine I heard the brake whistle and saw a hand 'Danger' signal being exhibited from the cab. I could see that the rear part of the train was badly derailed and the Up Main Line was displaced.

The express was brought to a stand alongside the front portion of the derailed train, the express engine 20yd short of the last wagon.

When the train stopped the guard, Stirzaker, 61 years old with thirty-five years' GWR service, walked back in accordance with Rule 179 to protect the rear of his train.

MISHAP AT KING'S SUTTON STATION – 27TH OCTOBER 1947.
SKETCH PLAN OF SIGNALS AND DISTANCES
Re-drawn from the original

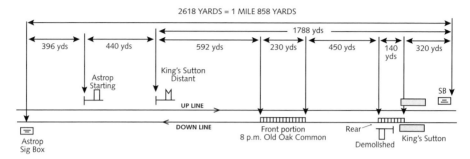

All distances verified 8.11.47

Before going back as far as the full three-quarters of a mile he came to Astrop box – at about 9.30 – and informed the signalman of the situation. Five minutes after he arrived, Inspector Stride arrived on a light engine from Banbury, which had been sent to pull the 7.10 a.m. Wolverhampton train back to Banbury.

Signalman Clarke had informed Birmingham Control a minute or two after he had sent 'Obstruction Danger' and the Controller for the southern section of the area had moved fast, as had the Banbury locomotive foreman and Inspector Stride. The foreman had the crews for breakdown vans assembling when he and Stride left on his engine for Astrop. The Banbury vans arrived at Astrop at 10.15 a.m. The Wolverhampton Stafford Road steam crane was ordered at 9.25 a.m. and arrived at 12.40 p.m.

The 7.10 Wolverhampton train was drawn back, Down the Up Main under the authority of Bevington's issuing Wrong Line Order 'D' to the driver of the engine from Banbury. On arrival back at Astrop, the train was drawn through the crossover to the Down main. The train engine was detached there and the Banbury engine took the train to Paddington via Banbury, Hatton, Stratford-on-Avon, Honeybourne South Junction and Oxford, arriving at Paddington at 3.09 p.m.

Control had been rapidly at work diverting other trains. The 9.10 a.m. Wolverhampton–Paddington train was diverted via Stourbridge, Worcester and Oxford. The 9.5 a.m. Banbury–Paddington train was cancelled and a Midland Red bus (GWR had a 25 per cent share in the Midland Red bus company) left Banbury station at 9.48 a.m., calling at all railway stations to Oxford where a train was waiting for the journey to Paddington. A Midland Red bus did the work of the 11.22 a.m. train from Banbury to Oxford and another bus replaced the 11.25 to Kingham train. A bus from Bicester at 11.30 a.m. went to Aynho station where the 9.10 a.m. Paddington–Banbury via Oxford was waiting. Birkenhead–Paddington (and vice versa) expresses were diverted via Worcester and Oxford or via Honeybourne and the North Warwickshire line.

Meanwhile the local Permanent-way Department was re-laying the damaged portion of the Up Main line, and the crane was clearing the wrecked wagons off the Up Main. At

3.25 p.m. that track was handed back to the Traffic Department and single-line working was instituted between King's Sutton Junction and Astrop. The breakdown vans and the steam crane left at 5 p.m. and, with a speed restriction, the double track was again in the hands of the Traffic Department.

Notes

1   *Rail* 250/469 October.
2   *GWR Staff Magazine*, p. 218. November 1947. I hope that the final stop was not as given in the magazine but at Maidenhead West box Home signal.
3   A product of the USA. According to the company's information its hammer weighed 5,000lb and struck 225 blows per minute. It was lifted up and driven down by steam or compressed air at 100psi.
4   The GWR Locomotive Committee Minutes, *Rail* 250/672, give the figure as 37. The *Encyclopaedia of the Great Western Railway* gives it as 38 as does H.C. Casserley in his 1948 publication *British Railways Locomotives*.
5   A survival from 1840 on the GWR where 'White is Right and Red is Wrong and Green means gently go along'.
6   Signalman Clarke's statement to the Inquiry.

GREAT WESTERN RAILWAY
MAGAZINE

NOVEMBER · 1947

VOL. 59 · NO. 10

Pride in the Job—9
(See Page 218)

PRICE ONE PENNY

NOVEMBER

The directors at the November Board Meeting had only a small amount of business to consider. They agreed that the auditors appointed by the Minister of Transport to oversee the execution and winding up of the GWR under Section 20 of the Act could also undertake the work required by Section 24. They then agreed to the proposed deductions from GWR employees' pensions. The GWR Superannuation Fund was in the red by nearly £2 million and the deductions must have been an attempt to reduce the drain on the indebted fund. The Minister of Transport had given his qualified consent to these reductions – he wrote to the directors – 'on the responsibility of the GWR Board without indicating the consent of the British Transport Commission'.

They then moved on to authorising expenditure on repairs, maintenance, renewals of docks, ships, stations, signalling, track, bridges, viaducts and drains. Some detailed projects included:

> General repair, replacement of boiler and improvement of crew accommodation of steam hopper barge *Sir Ernest Palmer* to be carried out by the Penarth Slipway & Ship Repairing Co. for an estimated £12,500 – the prices to be agreed as the work proceeds owing to wages and materials cost inflation.

Since 1945, prices had risen 10.9 per cent with no sign of abating.[1] Barry Docks were to have £30,000 spent on locks and lock gates, The SS *St Julien*, a Channel Islands ferry, had £9,457 allocated for repairs, and the GWR cargo carrier SS *Great Western*, launched at Cammell Laird, Birkenhead, in 1947, went into Penarth for repairs costing £8,457 and also to be converted to oil burning, with improvements to be made for passengers and crew at a cost of £12,258. The renewal of power signalling cables at Paddington and between Subway and Portobello Junctions was to cost £18,250, power tools for Signal Department gangs came to £10,000, and the re-laying and re-sleepering programme for 1948 was allocated £2,978,690. The renewal of waterproofing on Liskeard viaduct – this meant asphalting over the tops of the arches under the track bed – amounted to £13,600. Repairs to Cymmer tunnel were accomplished for £2,600, and the improvement of drainage of the line at Oldbury & Langley Green came to £2,250. A house was purchased for £3,000 from Mrs H.K. Harris – 21 Oakley Road, Caversham – for a member of the staff. Widening of an overbridge at Churchill & Blakedown required £6,418 (the cost to be borne by Worcestershire County Council). Twelve six-wheeled rail milk tankers were to replace twelve milk churn vans, at a cost of £7,020. Provision of a staff hostel at Old Oak Common and temporary accommodation in the interim came to £236,938. The purchase price paid to T.W. Ward for the tin plate works at Ystalyfera, for conversion to a wagon repair factory, was £16,000. My list is not complete but shows the detailed scope of the directors' supervision.

Lastly the directors turned their attention, as they had done all year, to the business of awarding salary increases to divisional officers and others in that level of management, and a few examples follow. Mr R.B.H. Nichols, Divisional Superintendent Gloucester Division, had his pay raised from £937 to £1,100 a year. Mr Nichols was in charge of the Traffic Division, Gloucester, including supervising the signalmen and their inspectors, the proper carrying out of the Rules and Signalling Regulations and the operational detail of working the trains through the busy junctions, marshalling yards and docks. The equivalent salary of Mr Nichols' £1,100 in 1947, at the officially declared inflation rate of 3,192 per cent, would be £36,212 in 2011. Mr H. Bolton, District Goods Manager, Bristol, rose from £1,373 to £1,550 per year. Other officers' yearly salary increases were: Mr S.E. Tyrwhitt, Divisional Locomotive Superintendent, Cardiff, from £1,173 to £1,350; Mr J.F. Arthur, Docks Mechanical Engineer, Cardiff, from £1,423 to £1,500; and Mr H.N.S. Edwards, Divisional Locomotive Superintendent, Bristol, from £1,323 to £1,425.

The General Manager's report to the Directors' Traffic Committee, dated 27 November, stated:

> The estimated receipts for the four weeks ended November 16th amounted to £4,105,000 an increase of £318,000 or 8.4% compared with last year. Passenger traffic receipts decreased by £75,000 or 4.48%. General merchandise receipts increased by £149,000, 9.65%, and coal traffic brought in an increase of £244,000, a 42% increase. Over the year to date, estimated receipts amounted to £42,112,000 a decrease of £2,442,000 on last year. Passenger receipts were down by 10.73% and all freight train receipts decreased by £522,000 2.34%.

The shortage of all types of freight wagons remained a serious national problem throughout 1947. In November Sir Stafford Cripps, Chancellor of the Exchequer and Minister for Economic Affairs, made a statement on the subject in which he called attention to 'the serious shortage' of railway rolling stock and the extent to which the avoidable immobilisation of wagons is gravely impairing the national effort'. He made 'an urgent appeal to all receivers of traffic by rail to review their transport arrangements and adopt every means of quickening the discharge of railway wagons' and unless a marked reduction in wagon detention was not speedily apparent he would order the railway companies to increase detention charges to a penal level.

The railway companies were asked to intensify their efforts to get traders to empty the delivery wagons quickly so as to make them available for fresh loading. There was so much iron and steel stacked outside the steelworks of the north-east of England that the Railway Executive – made up entirely of the top-class railway officers seconded from the companies – had to forbid the use of bogie bolster wagons for carrying timber, home grown or imported – except where the embargo would delay the unloading of a ship – so that the iron and steel could be taken to the car factories of the Midlands. The wagon shortage was still at crisis level at the end of 1951.[2]

Operating staff at all levels put in long hours to keep traffic moving through marshalling yards and complicated metropolitan railway areas but staff were also leaving for easier – and better paid – work. Influenza, brought on in part by the exhaustion of long working hours, also depleted the ranks of shunters, carriage and wagon repairers, and locomotive crews. By 1950 the railway service as a whole had lost nearly 30,000 men from the operating grades.[3]

'Loaded wagons cleared' was to some extent dependent on the number of wagons loaded by the colliery – and the miners had been working a five-day week since 5 May, a small relaxation in their arduous labours which they richly deserved. In the four weeks ended 14 November the company's staff cleared 155,500 loaded wagons from collieries, which was an increase of 4,481 on the same period in 1946, although since the start of the five-day week there had been a 1.8 per cent decrease in loaded wagons cleared compared with the twelve months up to 5 May 1947. But tonnage in wagons hauled from opencast mining since the start of 1947 had reached 544,200 tons, 12,300 tons more than in 1946. Getting coal into wagons from a coal quarry, open to the sky, was easier than hauling it in tubs from hundreds of feet below ground.

During November 1,853 motor cars were transported from the Morris Cowley works on GWR trains and 564 were moved from Austin at Longbridge for export. This made a total of 24,945 cars hauled for export by the GWR, a 12.6 per cent increase on 1946. One hundred tons of scrap steel went from Swan Village to Belgium, 40 tons of mining equipment was moved from the Mining Engineering Co. of Henwick, and seventy-four BSA motor cycles and 15 tons of malted barley moved from Cardiff docks to Switzerland.

The GWR worked hard all year to extend their 'Zonal' road lorry collection and delivery services and did so on a short ration of petrol. On 1 October the ration was reduced by 10 per cent – 200,000 gallons – but even so, from 1 November the company's Goods Department managed to bring into operation the 'Aberystwyth Zone', working from that railhead with a sub-depot at Machynlleth. The 'Reading Zonal Scheme', covering 580 sq miles, which was brought into operation in 1946 was, in November 1947, extended to 650 sq miles in co-operation with the Southern Railway. This was another very carefully worked out plan to save petrol through co-ordination and co-operation between the companies.

In November the government was considering reducing by another 10 per cent the railway companies' petrol ration. The GWR, in concert with the other railway companies, submitted a report to the Railway Executive for transmission to the Minister, detailing the curtailment of railway road services which would result, and thus on the clearance of traffic from railway wagons which was of such national importance. The companies strongly made the case for the railway road services to be allocated *more* petrol.

One of the vital reasons given for the nationalisation of the railways was that there was a need to co-ordinate road and rail transport. Since 1929 the railway companies had been buying 25 per cent and 50 per cent shares in existing major road passenger companies, improving their buses by bringing in additional investment. From 1930 the GWR and the others were busy developing their road freight 'Collection and Delivery' services. Left to themselves they would have enlarged this policy.

The City of Birmingham transport workers went on strike from 3 November until 9 November. At the end of that week ticket issues from Birmingham Snow Hill and the outlying stations totalled 107,800 compared with 11,100 during the previous week. The General Manager's report stated that the railway carried this huge additional traffic without using any additional trains or staff – although some of the trains were 'overcrowded'. Does this suggest that the GWR Birmingham suburban trains were lavishly provided and normally under-used?

On 3 November the 5.10 p.m. Paddington–Wolverhampton express, which was a new train put on after the war, had a slip coach added to the formation. This was slipped at Bicester and then worked forward at 6.30 p.m., calling at all stations to Banbury.

On 15 November the Ministry of Transport gave up four of the seven permanent reservations of first-class sleeping berths it held on the 11.50 p.m. Paddington–Plymouth train but continued to have permanent reservations on ten first-class berths in the 9.50 p.m. and 12.15 a.m. Paddington–Penzance trains and the 1 a.m. Paddington–Carmarthen train. There were an equal number of first-class berths reserved by the Ministry on Up trains from Penzance, Neyland and Carmarthen.

The Herefordshire and Worcestershire hop-picking season ran through September and October. The GWR had run forty-five special trains, carrying 13,800 hop pickers from South Wales and the Birmingham areas to the hop gardens situated along the Severn Valley and more remote railway byways. Nothing was too much trouble; all traffic was good traffic. However, even the GWR had to draw the line at maintaining stations for no traffic. The Yealmpton branch had just lost its passenger service, and the GWR decided, in November, to close Rhosrobin Halt, between Wrexham and Gresford, 'as from the start of the new timetable in view of the limited use by the public and the road services available in the area'.

During the month ended 20 November, the GWR carried 2,188 cars for export from Morris Cowley and 1,095 cars from Longbridge. Since 1 January 22,528 cars had been 'railed' from these works to the ports, a 24 per cent increase on 1946. Three new factories, producing felt, bacon slicers and plastic materials, had been established, with the assistance of the GWR, in South Wales, bringing the number of factories to thirty-one on GWR territory since the start of the year. A new factory for the Distillers Company conglomerate was nearing completion at Barry where casting resin was to be made.[4] Another Distillers subsidiary, British Industrial Solvents, at Kenfig, would send regular consignments of calcium carbide by rail to the new factory and the outwards traffic from the factory – moulding powder for castings – was anticipated to start at 250 tons a week. The General Manager also gave the good news that another 27 tons of photographic paper was sent from Wooburn Green station, on the High Wycombe to Maidenhead branch, to Dover for export to France, and 6½ tons of pilchards went from Looe to Livorno (Leghorn).

The Station Gardens Competition was held across the company's network. The number of stations putting their gardens forward for the competition since 1945 was less each year and was considerably less than had been the case between the wars. The General Manager suggested that this was because of the cost of seeds, plants and implements. He suggested to the directors that they should make

£400 available so that station staff could apply for a grant to buy material for their station garden.

Eleven prizes of £6 each were awarded for the best garden in each of the traffic divisions of the railway, which were: Cholsey & Moulsford; Swindon Town; Creech St Michael Halt; Symonds Yat; Pontllanfraith; Peterston; Pembrey & Burry Port; Kingham; Leamington Spa; Peplow; Trefeinon.

Prizes, 165 of them, ranging from £1 to £4, were awarded for gardens considered by the divisional officers to be deserving of recognition and £9 10s was made available to be shared by ten stations which had made good use of the hanging baskets supplied by the company.

I have 'Reports of Goods Trains Parting' for twenty-two days in November. This covers the breakaways of sixty goods trains. The vast majority of these were routine, unexceptional, 'all part of the day's work', but one or two are more interesting.

The Worcester–Oxford route has to climb out of the Vale of Evesham with an ascent of 1 in 100 for 4½ miles south from Honeybourne. The last half mile is in Campden tunnel and levels at the south end. A little after Campden station the line falls for 1¼ miles before starting the three steep miles to the final summit just before Moreton-in-Marsh station. Between Blockley and the summit there is a wicked curve and 'pimple'-style gradient around Aston Magna, which was one of the most awkward pieces of railway for a loose-coupled train on the GWR. The Oxford and Worcester drivers had I.K. Brunel to thank for this awful piece of work.

On 14 November the 2 a.m. Rogerstone–Yarnton train broke a drawbar hook. The engine was 2-8-0 No 2877, with Driver Pratley and Fireman Jones of Oxford shed, and Guard Jennings of Oxford was in the brake van. The load was coal, '30 = 49 Class 1' with a 20-ton guard's brake van: a heavy load. They had breasted the long climb out of the Vale of Evesham at Moreton-in-Marsh and were coasting on a breath of steam towards Adlestrop and home. The dawn was breaking, it was 7.45 a.m. and they had been at work all night. There were 26 miles – almost all downhill – ahead of them to Yarnton. There they would run onto the old LNWR connection to the Bletchley line and leave the train for the LMS to collect.

Somewhere in the 3 miles of the gentle downhill journey, a gradient of 1 in 303, after Moreton and before Adlestrop, the draw hook broke on the LMS coal wagon that was coupled to the engine's tender. The engine went through Adlestrop well in advance of its train, the locomen quite unaware of the situation. The Adlestrop signalman sent 'Train Divided' – 5-5 on the bell – to Kingham. A Down passenger train had just passed through Adlestrop and the driver of this eventually saw the rolling wagons of the train. He immediately opened his brake whistle and kept it booming all along the length of the wagons. This brought Guard Jennings from his van in time for the driver to shout to him 'You're divided!' Jennings at once screwed down his handbrake and the 20-ton van was able – with some help from a mile of level track just before Adlestrop – to slow down 500 tons of rolling coal wagons. Jennings was able to bring his train to a stand between the Up Home and Up Starting signals, with the Main to Main crossover conveniently in the rear.

The Distant signal for Kingham was at 'Caution' against the engine and probably the driver and fireman said impatiently, 'Oh blimey – what's up now?' They were stopped outside the signal box by a red flag from the signalman and even then they had not noticed that their train was missing. I can imagine the signalman saying, 'Any idea where your train is?' Their train was 2½ miles behind them – safe and sound. The signalmen 'conferred' and the engine was sent back to Adlestrop over the Down Main, crossed to the rear of its train and from there, under the provisions of Regulation 14A, propelled it to Kingham. There the LMS wagon was placed in a siding and the train carried on to Yarnton.

The GWR report ends with: 'The question of the apparent non-observance of Rule 126 (ix) is being followed up with the Locomotive Department.'[5]

In addition to sixty goods trains, five parcels trains and five passenger trains suffered broken couplings.

Down on the West London line, deep amongst the suburbs, was Shepherd's Bush Yard, situated on the Down, northbound side of the main route. On the afternoon of 24 November a brand new GWR tank engine, No 9754, was marshalling a train in the yard. In the Up Goods Loop, on the far side of the main route, there were ten wagons for the northbound direction. These had been temporarily stabled there as a result of a derailment earlier that day. No 9754 had to collect these and add them to its northbound train. The signalman set the route from the Down Siding across the Down Main to the Up Loop and waved OK to the train crew. The train guard checked the points and waved the engine driver on. The engine was derailed across the Down Main. The signalman sent Obstruction Danger in each direction at 4.35 p.m., and then ordered the breakdown vans. They arrived at 5.46 p.m. The engine was re-railed at 6.35 p.m. and the Down Main was re-opened at 7.10 p.m.

The signaling was under LMS maintenance and there was no signal to detect the correct lie of the points. The LMS Ganger repaired the damaged points the following morning so there was no possibility of determining the cause of the derailment. And there the matter rested.

On 29 November there was a very unusual case of signalmen seeing what was not there on the West London line. The 3 a.m. Norwood (SR) to Temple Mills (LNER) freight train lost the last wagon and the brake van due to a coupling snapping on level track between Viaduct Junction and North Pole Junction – the two signal boxes being 2 miles apart. The signalman at North Pole 'seeing what he believed was the tail lamp of the train' gave 'Train out of Section' to Viaduct Junction at 3.53 a.m. and sent 'Train entering Section' to Mitre Bridge. Mitre Bridge, under the same delusion, sent 'Train out of Section' to North Pole at 4 a.m. Meanwhile the guard of the Norwood train, in the section between Viaduct Junction and North Pole, having screwed down his handbrake tight, was walking back towards Viaduct Junction to protect the stationary wagons from any approaching train.

At 3.53 a.m. Viaduct Junction asked 'Is Line Clear?' for two GWR light engines coupled together bound for Old Oak Common shed. North Pole accepted them and Viaduct Junction signals were cleared. The engines were then passing Kensington.

The 2.55 a.m. Willesden (LMS) to Blackheath (SR) train was running on the Up line from Willesden High Level towards Mitre Bridge. This train passed the broken-away Norwood, moving steadily along on the opposite line. If the Willesden driver saw that it was lacking a brake van he did not stop at North Pole Junction to report it. The Willesden train passed North Pole Junction at 3.55 a.m. and further along the line the driver saw the one wagon and brake van standing all alone on the Down line. Further along he passed what was obviously the guard walking towards Viaduct Junction. The Willesden train stopped at Viaduct Junction at 4.02 a.m. and the driver informed the signalman of the wagon and brake van in the section and the guard walking back.

At 4.03 a.m. the Norwood train passed Willesden High Level signal box. The signalman was properly awake, saw that the train had no tail lamp, and sent 4-5 signal, meaning 'Train Passed Without Tail Lamp' to Mitre Bridge. The Mitre Bridge signalman, now realising that he had not seen a tail lamp, sent the 4-5 signal on to North Pole and the latter, knowing that the Norwood train had been coming uphill towards his place, decided to send 2-5-5 signal: 'Train Running Away on Wrong Line' to Viaduct Junction at 4.04 a.m.

The engines were stopped at Viaduct Junction, and the drivers were informed of the situation and told to enter the section, passing the Starting signal at 'Danger', keeping a sharp lookout for the guard, so they could pick him up, and he could conduct them to the rear of the wagons. The engines left at 4.10 a.m. The engines propelled the wagons through to Mitre Bridge, leaving them to be further dealt with by the LMS while they crossed over and returned to North Pole Junction and so to Old Oak Common. Job done.

I have records for twelve days of November showing forty-four engine failures. For forty-two of them the bare facts are reported. Among those was this entry: 'Monday 10th the 4.55 p.m. Southampton – Didcot failed at Worthy Down. Fresh engine obtained, 54 minutes delay. Thursday 13th. 4.55 p.m. Southampton – Didcot failed at Winchester. Fresh engine obtained. 35 minutes delay.' Maybe these were simple cases of being short of steam or the injectors failing, nothing that was considered to be really serious. However, there were two very serious failures which merited a relatively detailed report.

On his morning inspection of the track on Saturday 8 November the stalwart ganger of the Athelney length found fifteen of the cast-iron, rail-supporting 'chairs' were cracked through the bolt holes on the outside of the rail and thirteen more had their outside corner cracked off and missing. Two sleepers had been smashed by something very heavy. The damage was done 1½ miles west of Athelney and extended for a quarter of a mile. The ganger knew at once how this damage had been done. Athelney was at the end of the long descent from Castle Cary and even in this period of austerity, drivers were permitted to drive up to speeds of 75mph. The strain this put on worn-out engines was considerable and bits tended to fall off.

In this case the 12.15 a.m. Paddington–Penzance 'sleeper' train, consisting of nine cars hauled by engine No 6015 *King Richard III* passed Athelney signal box at 2.47 a.m. and 1½ miles further on one of the coupling rods became detached from one crank pin. This caused it to flail and smash the chairs and sleepers. The driver brought the train to a stand. He and the fireman unscrewed the cap holding the other end of the rod to its crank pin, put it on the side of the line and set off at slow speed for Taunton, 6½ miles away. They were turning in from the Down Main to the Down Relief at Taunton East Junction when the other coupling rod fell off. The engine was brought immediately to a stand, a total failure. No 6015 was uncoupled from its train. The station pilot engine came out on the Up main, crossed to the Down Main, pulled the train back onto the Down Main and propelled the coaches into the station. A fresh engine was found and the train got underway with 89 minutes' delay. The following train, the 11.50 p.m. Paddington–Penzance, was delayed 17 minutes. No 6015 was cleared from the Down Relief at 5.06 a.m.

On 25 November the 1.30 p.m. Paddington–Penzance express, with twelve coaches weighing 489 tons, was hauled by engine No 6018 *King Henry VI*. It passed Curry Rivel Junction at 4.23 p.m., the signalman there sending 'Train entering Section' – 2 beats on the bell – to Athelney. The two signal boxes were 4 miles apart. The express did not pass Athelney after a few minutes more than the usual time had elapsed, and so the signalmen set the provision of Regulation 14A in motion. Athelney had the 9.50 a.m. Laira Junction–Banbury freight train in his Up Goods Loop. He walked across to the Loop, told the driver that the 1.30 Paddington train was in some sort of trouble and asked him to uncouple his engine and go and examine the line through to Curry Rivel. The driver set off with the Athelney signalman's Wrong Line Order 'D' in his pocket, authorising him to return to Athelney Down the Up line.

The driver returned with the news that the engine of the 1.30 Paddington train was a complete failure, 1¼ miles west of Curry Rivel. A fresh engine and the breakdown vans would be required from Taunton. There were going to be heavy delays and so to keep the railway moving, albeit slowly, single-line working would be required over the Up line.

A competent person had to be found to act as pilotman – the Station Master at Athelney appointed himself because he could travel over the Up line without need for any special instructions. He would carry the 'Institution of Single Line Working form' addressed to the Curry Rivel signalman, over the Up line, and when the form was delivered trains could be worked Down the Up line in perfect safety, guaranteed by the presence of the pilotman at the point of departure. A man would be at Curry Rivel and Athelney to clamp the crossover points and hand-signal the trains over those points. A porter from each place could cover those jobs.

A fresh engine, to work the 1.30 p.m. Paddington train forward, No 5924 *Dinton Hall*, arrived at Athelney at 5.44 p.m. The engine off the Laira goods train and engine No 5924 were coupled together, with No 5924 leading. They set off for Curry Rivel at 5.45 p.m. with the pilotman on the leading engine, arriving at 5.58 p.m. Once there, No 5924 went into the Down Siding and the freight engine went out into the obstructed section with Wrong Line Order 'D' to couple to the rear of the 1.30 p.m. Paddington train. The twelve coaches were drawn back to Curry Rivel until they were clear of the crossover road. Then No 5924 came out of the siding, got on the front of the train and left, with the pilotman on the footplate, at 6.43 p.m., bound for Taunton and Plymouth.

The breakdown vans arrived at Athelney at 6.07 p.m. but were not allowed – no reason was given – into the 'dead' (Down) road to sort out No 6018 until 7.10 p.m. The left-hand inside connecting rod big end had shattered, allowing the piston to travel forwards and smash itself against the cylinder head, which was also shattered with the piston protruding. The left-hand inside valve spindle and the left-hand bottom slide bar were bent. The engine was made ready to move and was then towed away at 9.30 p.m. and single-line working was cancelled at 10.20 p.m.

Sixteen trains were delayed for a total of 644 minutes. The 1.30 p.m. Paddington train lost 153 minutes and the other fifteen lost 491 minutes between them. Not included in that was the 4 p.m. Yeovil–Taunton train, which terminated at Langport West, where the passengers continued their journey by bus.

Mr Hawksworth, the Chief Mechanical Engineer of the Great Western Railway, wrote to the General Manager to say: 'My Running and Mechanical Inspectors who examined the rod and its lubricating arrangements are satisfied that the driver who prepared this engine is at fault and this is being followed up personally by my Divisional Superintendent with the man concerned.'

The general public could occasionally be a source of delay. Passengers died of heart attacks on the trains, dead babies were found in lavatories, desperate people jumped in front of trains and killed themselves. I have the reports but just let the bald statement stand for the several incidents.

On 31 November the 5.5 p.m. Paddington–Plymouth train was coming down the bank from Dainton towards Totnes at 10.30 p.m. when the driver felt the brakes being applied gently. The communication cord had been pulled. He at once applied the brake hard and brought the train to a stand. The guard walked through the train until he came to a compartment occupied by two agitated Royal Navy petty officers. They told the guard they had been asleep until they were woken by a strong cold draught and saw that the off-side door of their compartment was open and their companion, another petty officer, was missing. They had then pulled the cord.

There was an urgent need to stop any train or engine coming up the bank from Totnes to avoid running over the missing man. As luck would have it, Driver Bernard Watts of Newton Abbot was on the way up the steep incline from Totnes. He recalls the incident in his own words:

> I was returning light engine ex-Kingsbridge with 4587 and Fireman Discombe. I noticed the 5.5 p.m. Padd. was at a stand and I stopped to see if I could render any assistance. As I was getting down off my engine the guard came up and informed me that a sailor had fallen out of the train and I was just right to go forward to examine the line. I proceeded cautiously and came across him in the 'four foot' near Dainton signal box.

I have to break into Driver Watts' narrative at this point. When the guard of the 5.5 Paddington train had arranged for the line to be examined, he gave a green light to his driver and they carried on down to Totnes, thus clearing the section for the next train. At Totnes the guard informed the Station Master of what had occurred and he called for a doctor and an ambulance and then informed the police. Driver Watts continues:

> I got down and could see he was knocked about rather bad and my mate and I would not move him. I sent my mate to Dainton signal box for assistance while

Dainton signal box, built for the GWR by the Saxby & Farmer signaling contractors of London in June 1884. This ancient signal box was replaced in February 1965 by a 'plywood wonder'. With apologies for the out of period, 1955, photograph. (Peter Barlow/Author's Collection)

Totnes station, seen from a Down express calling at the station in summer 1947. Eight coaches can be seen, new-ish, old and antique. There is an engine standing on the Down Main, tank engine No 3181 on the Up Main and the Ashburton autocar, propelled by No 4813, at the Up platform. (Author's Collection)

I stayed with him. My mate came back on the 2.15 milk and together with the enginemen and the guard we got him into a van and went on down to Totnes.

At Totnes the doctor, ambulance and local constable were waiting. The doctor found that the man was unconscious with severe concussion; in addition he had a broken rib and a serious wound to the back of his head. He was taken by ambulance to Totnes Cottage Hospital. The following afternoon, Totnes Station Master inquired after him and was told he had been taken to the Royal Naval Hospital at Devonport and was still unconscious.

The GWR Carriage & Wagon Department examined the door from which he had fallen – a slam lock door which had been shut when the three men were together in the coach. The lock was found to be working perfectly and the GWR signed the incident off as 'Misadventure'.

Notes

1   House of Commons Research Paper 99/20 of 23.2.99.
2   *Railway Gazette*, p. 675, 21.12.51.
3   Ibid.
4   The Distillers Company started in the nineteenth century making whisky. By 1947 the business was a conglomerate of purchased companies making chemicals, pharmaceuticals, plastics and many other industrial necessities.
5   The driver and fireman must:- ix. In the case of trains not fitted throughout with the continuous brake, look back frequently during the journey to see that the whole of the train is following in a proper manner. GWR 1933 Rule Book.

GREAT WESTERN RAILWAY
MAGAZINE

DECEMBER · 1947

VOL. 59 · NO. 11

PRIDE IN THE JOB

Sir James Milne, K.C.V.O., C.S.I., General Manager, Great Western Railway, 1929—1947

INSURANCE EDITION

PRICE TWO PENCE

DECEMBER

Tackling Practical Problems

The GWR's officers and staff on the ground made great, patriotic efforts to get traders to empty the wagons which delivered their goods. The traders must also have played their part. When the campaign to 'turn round' wagons faster began – on 16 November – 57 per cent of wagons were being emptied and re-used. On 12 December, 70 per cent of wagons were being emptied within 48 hours of their arrival. The number of wagons under load for longer than 48 hours on 16 November was 3,300, whereas on 12 December the figure was 1,890. Overtime working from noon on Saturdays and on Sundays by GWR and traders' staff was partially responsible for the improvement.

The Minister of Transport directed that when wagons were in short supply the first priority had to be 'full load' traffic – coal, coke, 'Calor' and 'Botto' Gas cylinders, and thereafter to the traffic specified, for instance locomotive coal, export traffic, import traffic, grain, flour and foodstuffs for human consumption, coal-mining equipment and so on. The need for a constant supply of rail wagons was a very serious strategic need.

During the three weeks ended 6 December 122,853 loaded coal wagons were hauled from collieries on the GWR system. This was an increase of 4,496 on the same period in 1946.

There was heavy demand for the express freight services and the GWR instituted a better service of fully vacuum-braked express freights. The services were maintained throughout the year in spite of the demands of the government to run more and more coal trains, and the shortage of engines suitable for fast, heavy work. Footplate crews co-operated by learning, and then signing for, greater route knowledge so that they could work through to destination rather than being relieved en route, thus reducing the number of crews needed. There were eight staff hostels at the start of 1947 and six more were added by the end of that year, these being Severn Tunnel Junction (hostel enlarged), Slough, Tyseley, Bristol, Leamington and Southall.

In January the General Manager had informed the directors that the El Oro Mining and Railway Co. had bought a site in the Heathfield and Bovey Tracey districts. The purpose for acquiring it was lignite quarrying, and by December 3,500 tons a week were passing over the Moretonhampstead branch to Newton Abbot and the outside world.

Pilfering from railway goods wagons was always a problem, much more so than it was for road lorries. During the war and in the first few years afterwards, as a result of shortages of food and other things, 'spivs' ran 'black markets' to supply demand – at a price. The Minister of Transport gave the most recent statistics in the House of Commons:

the four railway companies, in 1945, had paid out £2,525,405 in respect of 641,389 claims for goods stolen in transit. In 1938 there had been 151,426 claims costing £180,462. The cost to the railway was not just financial; the exposure to theft meant that traders and manufacturers were discouraged from using railways to carry their wares. The good name of the railways and their employees was besmirched, whether railwaymen were the guilty parties or not. Gangs of children as well as organised groups of 'spivs' raided goods yards. The railway police and railwaymen sometimes managed to catch them at it and arrests were made. Sometimes the villains were killed when they were caught by the sudden movement of wagons, leaving a mangled corpse for a railwayman to find.

During 1947 long-service efficiency medals were awarded. The numbers of these were:

15 years – 79
20 years – 81
25 years – 84
30 years bar to ribbon – 17
35 years bar to ribbon – 4
40 years bar to ribbon – 1

A very important feature of the GWR was their widespread, and very well-organised, St John's Ambulance First Aid movement. Male and female members of staff volunteered for this. There were formal courses of instruction and examinations for competency. In 1947, seventy-one members of staff volunteered for training and 5,048 members of staff passed St John's Ambulance examinations at varying degrees of skill. Women were 'allowed' to be first-aiders (!) and five all-female teams took part in the pan-GWR competition. This suggests that there was segregation in first aid. The Plymouth team won and were presented with the Florence M. Lean Cup.

High standards of medical skill were attained. In 1947 the Gold Medal for exceptionally efficient first aid at the scene of a real injury was awarded to Mr W.E. Morris, Station Master at Llanbedr & Pensarn station, just south of Harlech. Mr Morris was called out of his bed to attend to a motorcyclist who had crashed. He examined the man by torchlight as he lay on the road and treated him so effectively that the doctor who later arrived said Morris had undoubtedly saved the man's life.

A platelayer was struck by an Up express at Wantage Road, resulting in his arm being almost ripped off his body at the shoulder. Porter Walt Binding stopped the bleeding, treated the man for shock and got him removed to shelter. All that remained for the doctor to do when he arrived was to administer morphine and supervise the loading of the patient into the ambulance. For this Mr Binding was awarded the Silver Medal.[1]

Throughout the summer months, eight Inter-Divisional first-aid competitions were held, leading to the final contest for the Directors' Challenge Shield. The finals took place at the Porchester Hall, Paddington, and the Challenge Cup was won by the Swindon team. One of these was my dear old friend Sid Tyler.[2] The Directors' Challenge Shield was presented by the Chairman of the Board, the Right Honourable Viscount Wyndham Portal PC, DSO, MVO.

I have engine failure reports covering twenty days of December. In twenty days fifty locomotives failed on passenger and freight trains. Two engines failed through their inability to maintain vacuum to keep the brakes off – which would have occurred if the engine was short of steam. Several were reported failed 'short of steam'. One train stopped with an overheated axle box on the locomotive. Descriptions are of the briefest nature, the following being examples:

Tuesday 2 December. 11 a.m. Milford Haven to Paddington. Delayed 7 minutes at Stoke Gifford raising steam and 11 minutes at Swindon changing engines.

Wednesday 3 December. 3.18 p.m. Paddington to Wolverhampton. Engine developed defect after leaving shed. Put right by fitters. 29 minutes late start as result.

4 December. 10 a.m Paddington to Swansea. Engine failed after leaving shed. Changed engine. 51 minutes late start; 1.30 p.m. Paddington to Penzance. Stopped 4 minutes at Taplow. Defective spring on engine. 6 minutes delay at Reading changing engines.

5 December. 11.40 a.m. Severn Tunnel Junction to Weymouth. Engine failed at Woodlands signal box (2 miles west of Blatchbridge Junction). Train propelled into the Down Loop at Witham by the 8.50 p.m. Westbury to Weymouth passenger train.

Tuesday 9 December. 3.55 p.m. Paddington to Neyland. Train arrived Swindon 52 minutes late and left 60 minutes late after changing engines.

On 6 December, engine No 2929 *Saint Stephen* failed at Filton Junction on the 6.30 a.m. Swindon–Bristol train. The driver was uncertain of the reliability of the boiler water injectors. He uncoupled from the train and drove to Bristol Bath Road shed, a distance of about 5½ miles. He came back with a fresh engine and the train left Filton only 35 minutes late. This proves that some brisk 'light engine' running was done, with 'box to box' messages applied to get the engine a clear run. An educated guess is that the engine was signalled '4 bells'[3] which was an interesting use of the final phrase of Regulation,

FIRST AID COMPETITION. SWINDON " B " TEAM WON THE DIRECTORS' SHIELD.

The man second from the left is Sid Tyler.

especially since the 'light engine' *was* the disabled train and it *was* going to assist. The Bath Road shed foreman was advised at once and had a fresh engine waiting.

I have a complete record of passenger and goods trains breaking couplings during December. Eight passenger vehicles suffered broken couplings: six GWR carriages and two belonging to LNER. Of the former, two breaks were due to broken hooks or drawbars and four were caused by screw shackles stripping. The LNER coach had its drawbar pulled out.

There were sixty-one breakaways of goods trains involving seventeen GWR wagons, fourteen LMS, five LNER, one Southern and twenty-four Private Owner wagons. Thirty-seven were caused by ordinary three-link couplings snapping. The GWR had four 'Instanter' couplings break, three of them on brake vans. One GWR brake van had its drawbar pulled out of the vehicle.

On 8 December, an hour after sunset, there was a four-way confusion at Merthyr resulting in a sidelong collision. Two passenger trains were waiting to leave the station. At Platform 3 was an LMS train, the 4.43 p.m. to Abergavenny Junction, and on the other side of the same platform, called No 4, was the GWR 4.45 p.m. to Cardiff. The LMS train consisted of three coaches hauled by an 0-8-0 goods engine. There were only three passengers, none in the front coach. The GWR train was formed with four coaches containing fifty-six passengers, hauled by engine No 5601, bunker-first.

In the signal box was Relief Signalman Gould, with Signalman Millin learning the box under Gould's guidance. The LMS train was scheduled to leave at 4.43 p.m., 2 minutes before the GWR train, but the LMS train had arrived at the station late and Signalman Gould doubted that they would be ready to leave at the booked time.

The LMS men were quick with their locomotive turnaround and Gould let them out of the Locomotive Yard at 4.41 p.m. It was a reasonable guess that they would not be ready to leave at 4.43 p.m. so Gould told Millin to 'get the road' from Brandy Bridge for the GWR train. But the LMS men were very quick and at 4.43 p.m. they whistled-up 'ready to leave'.

That was just as Millin had received 'Line Clear' from Brandy Bridge and had lowered the signals for the 4.45 to Cardiff. Just then, at 4.44 p.m., the Platform Inspector telephoned to say that the LMS train had been ready to leave for a minute, or a minute-and-a-half, and to let it go. Millin threw back the signal on Platform 4, got 'Line Clear' from Rhydycar Junction on the LMS, and lowered the No 3 Platform Starting signal. It was 4.45 p.m.

But the guard of the GWR train had seen the signal 'off' at the end of his platform and gave a green light to the fireman on No 5601 without looking again. The GW fireman did not look at all and the train started, but so had the LMS train. They had been hurrying to leave ever since they had arrived and they came along the platform at a cracking pace. The GWR train was moving slowly because it was on time, and to the LMS driver it looked stationary.

The two trains merged together, sidelong. The leading LMS and GWR coaches overturned, others were severely scraped and the trains stopped. No-one was hurt. But it is a very good cautionary tale to warn footplate crews to check their signals.

On 11 December Signalman Bert Harris booked on duty in Fawley signal box at 6.45 a.m. to work until 2.45 p.m. He was aged 26, had been on the GWR ten months and a signalman at Fawley for eight of those. At 9.55 a.m. ganger John Tinton arrived at Fawley driving his motorised trolley from Rotherwas Junction, Hereford. He was aged 47 with seventeen years' GWR service, and had been Ganger of the Motor Trolley Length for five years. He had been issued with a motorised four-wheeled, roofed in trolley since the start of 1947. He came to the box and asked for the ganger's occupation key so that he could occupy the single line towards Ross-on-Wye. He intended to put the key into the instrument at Hut 14 and thus reopen the single line for paying traffic. Bert Harris turned the key out of the instrument and gave it to him.

Bert then went to write the occurrence across the page of his Train Register, and John Tinton went back to his trolley, started up and drove away. The signal was at 'Danger' and the points were not set for him to leave the passing loop. Tinton went straight past the signal and hit the point blades from a 'trailing' position. His trolley was very light and instead of forcing its passage by bending the blade sideways, the vehicle was lifted up over the rail and landed 'on Olde England'. No harm was done to anything except, maybe, John's pride.

The GWR inquiry into this took place eleven days later. The conclusion was:

> The seriousness of Ganger Tinton's lapse is aggravated by the fact that his attention was drawn, by his Inspector on 6th November, to a circular issued by the Divisional Engineer about a similar mishap which occurred at Speech House Road on 15th October. Furthermore Ganger Tinton signed to say he had been shown the circular.
> Remarks and Recommendations
> NIL.

On 15 December the 7.35 p.m. Hereford–Worcester local goods train was hauled by engine No 2241, with Driver Hunt of Worcester. There were thirty-one wagons behind the engine with a GWR hand winched crane (No 191) marshalled next ahead of the guard's brake van. Ahead of the crane was the 'runner' wagon – on which the jib of

The Ledbury banker. (Author's Collection)

At Ledbury, the 'train engine' is facing up the 1 in 80 towards the single-track tunnel as the banker is brought onto the rear of the train. (Peter Barlow/Author's Collection)

the crane rested. At 10.43 a.m., as the train was stopping at Ledbury's Up Main Inner Home signal (on a 1 in 70 rising grade), the screw shackle coupling between the crane and its runner stripped its thread. The crane and the brake van promptly started moving backwards down the steep gradient. Without the 'runner' to support it, the jib dropped below horizontal and the chain and hook eventually became entangled with the track, anchoring the crane solidly to the Up Main track.

The Ledbury signalman sent signal 2-5-5 'Train running away in wrong direction' to Stoke Edith, Ashperton being switched out.

Guard Merriman of Worcester was in the van and he was injured when the breakaway took place. His injury was enough to prevent him from using his handbrake to stop the wagons and the train finally came to a stand in the dip between the 1 in 70 falling from Ledbury and the 1 in 150 rising towards Ashperton. Whether Merriman carried out his protection of the obstructing wagons is not stated.

The Station Master at Ledbury commandeered the Ledbury banking engine. The number is not reported, but these engines had to be very powerful and were usually 2-8-0 tank engines. He obtained 'Wrong Line Order Form D' ('Signalman to Driver. I authorise you to travel with your train on the Up line in the wrong direction to this signal box') from his signalman, and, riding on the footplate, he entered the section to Stoke Edith on the Down Main, under Regulation 14A, to examine the line. The Ledbury Station Master saw that the hand crane jib and chains had become so entangled that only the breakdown vans could free them, but there had been little damage to the track. He returned on the engine to Ledbury, running Up the Down line by virtue of Wrong Line Order 'D'.

While the Station Master was away the signalman informed Control of the need for breakdown vans to come from Hereford, and made arrangements to find staff to institute single-line working and a signalman to open Ashperton signal box. He would have done this by recruiting the staff on his station and, to get a signalman, telephoning the District Inspector at Hereford. Single-line working was ready for use at 1.19 a.m – all trains over the Down line. The breakdown vans arrived at Ashperton from Hereford at 1.57 a.m. and went into the obstructed Up Main.

The first train over the single line left Ashperton at 2.30 a.m. on 16 December. This was the 5 p.m. Llandilo to Newland train worked by engine No 6806 *Blackwell Grange*, with Driver F. Verden and Fireman D.J. Flynn of Cardiff. This train had been waiting at Ashperton for 4 hours. They had thirty-four wagons, with Guard C. Smith in the brake van, and they left at 2.30 a.m. The engine worked hard up the 1 in 70 hill approaching the crossover points from the Down to the Up Main at Ledbury station. The points were clamped and the hand signalman gave them a green light and the train came to a stand at the Up Main platform at 2.45 a.m. to allow the pilotman to get off the engine. As the train stopped the wagons ran back against their couplings. A three-link coupling snapped between the third and fourth wagons and at once started to run back, through the crossover onto the single line. Guard Smith screwed down his brake, but the wagons rolled, being far heavier than the 20-ton van. However, he could slow them down, and they stopped alongside where the first breakaways had stopped. The Ledbury banker, with the pilotman on the footplate, went into the single line and brought the wagons back, arriving in Ledbury at 3.34 a.m.

The breakdown gang untangled the crane jib and chains and the engine and vans propelled the brake van and crane through to Ledbury, arriving at 4 a.m. The Ledbury gang got up very early on 16 December. They repaired the damage to the Down Main and handed the track back to the Traffic Department at 5.45 a.m. Single-line working was withdrawn when the train occupying the section cleared and normal working resumed at 6.06 a.m.

On Christmas Eve a collision occurred at 8.26 p.m. on the Up Main line at Neath East box. The evening was very dark and no-one was aware of the obstruction. Shunter Barnes was marshalling the wagons for the 6.55 p.m. Neath train in the Up Sidings – which were connected to the Up Goods Loop No 2, which was on the Downside of the line (see diagram). When the train was formed, there was one LNER wagon standing against the buffers, behind the brake van of the train.

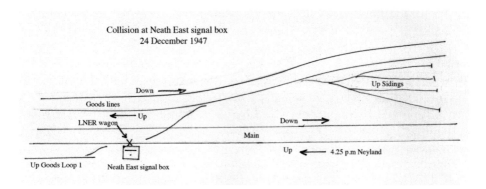

Collision at Neath East signal box
24 December 1947

Barnes told Signalman Powell that the 6.55 train was ready to leave at 7.46 p.m. The train had to come out of the sidings, along the Up Goods, cross over the Down Main, join the Up Main and then enter Up Goods Loop No 1, running towards Neath Engine Shed box. Powell asked 'Is Line Clear?' to Neath Engine Shed box on Up Loop No 1 at 7.46 p.m., set up the route and cleared the signals. The goods train entered Up Loop No 1 at 7.49 p.m. and Powell restored the junction for normal 'straight up and down' running.

Next on the Up Main was the 4.25 p.m. Neyland–Cardiff passenger train. Neath West 'asked the road' from Neath East at 8.20 p.m. and Powell 'gave the road' and 'asked on' to Neath Engine Shed box Up the Main. The train passed Neath West at 8.25 p.m. It was close to Neath East at 8.26 and Powell was just about to send 'Train entering Section' to Neath Engine Shed box when there was a terrific bang outside and he sent the signal '6 bells' (meaning 'Obstruction Danger') in both directions.

The LNER wagon that had been against the buffer stops in the Up Siding had followed the 6.55 goods train out and rolled across the tracks, coming to a stand right outside Neath East box, on the Up Main. It was invisible unless one leaned out of the window. The 4.25 p.m. Neyland train was running at about 20mph, having just left Neath station, so no-one was hurt, but Signalman Powell and Driver Phillips both had an almighty shock. The LNER wagon was not derailed but was considerably entangled with the front of the engine, which was No 4927 *Farnborough Hall*.

The train, pushing the wagon, had passed over the facing connection to Up Loop 1. After the wagon was disentangled from the engine, the train set back and went on its way via the Up Loop 1. All Up trains were diverted around the smashed wagon on the Loop until 11.5 p.m., when the wagon was removed and normal working resumed.

Time for reflection

On 19 December fifteen of the eighteen GWR directors met in the venerable Board Room at Paddington for their final meeting as directors of the Great Western Railway Company. They were: Viscount Portal, (Chair); Lt Col the Hon. J.J. Astor; the Hon. Sir Edward Cadogan; A.W. Baldwin; W.M. Codrington; Sir Charles Hambro; Cyril E. Lloyd; G.F. Luttrell; the Rt Hon. Harold Macmillan; J.V. Rank; Sir William Fraser; Sir W. Reardon-Smith; Capt. Hugh Vivian; Sir George Harvie Watt; Col Sir W. Charles Wright. The most senior officers of the company were in attendance, as they always were.

Viscount Portal's first utterance was:

As this is the last occasion on which the Board meet before the Great Western railway undertaking vests in the British Transport Commission I would like, on behalf of all the directors to thank the officers attending the Board, for the help which they have at all times given to the directors over such a long period, and for the skill and ability which they have displayed in carrying out the responsibilities entrusted to them in connection with the company's business.

The severance of the old associations is keenly felt by many and the officers who continue under the Transport Commission will carry with them the best wishes of the Board for success and happiness in their new sphere. To those who retire this year I wish them health and good fortune and trust that there will be occasions in the future when all could meet together again and recall pleasant memories of the past.

The General Manager, Sir James Milne, who was retiring at the end of the month, thanked the Chairman and directors on behalf of the GWR officers for his kind words.

During the six years of war and into 1947 GWR Headquarters staff had been evacuated to Aldermaston and district at the start of hostilities, but were gradually being brought back to Paddington during 1947. The station had suffered bomb damage and office accommodation was limited. To increase office accommodation and to improve facilities £160,000 was being spent on buildings, alterations, renovations and better furniture and equipment, and improved heating, lighting and telephone systems. Nos 121 to 141 Westbourne Terrace were being converted for use as offices, and £115,600 was to be spent on the necessary alterations.

The directors approved spending on thirty-five projects. Included in these were dock improvements at Weymouth, including £10,800 for the provision of a new 5-ton crane and the transfer from Swansea docks of two 3-ton cranes. No 10 Florence Road, Ealing, was purchased from 'Homes for Motherless Children' for conversion to a hostel for GWR police. At Aynho, £2,645 was paid to the War Department for some sidings. Six Hillman 'Minx' 10hp saloons were bought from Rootes Ltd for use as company cars, at a cost of £2,968 13s 6d. There was additional payment to Cammell Laird for the construction of the SS *St David*, amounting to £169,994. The SS *St Andrew* was refurbished after the Royal Navy had finished with it at a cost of £56,000, and £7,450 was to be spent with Philip & Son for the reconditioning of the Kingswear–Darmouth ferry – *The Mew*. The list goes on. The directors looked after the railway as if there was no such thing as nationalisation.

Thirty to forty salary increases had been awarded to clerks and superintendents all around the railway at every board meeting. Thirty-one men got their rise at this board meeting. Among them was Mr A.W.H. Christinson, Divisional Locomotive Superintendent, Newton Abbot. He was 'advanced' from £1,373 to £1,500 p.a.; the equivalent money in 2011 would be £49,389.[1] Divisional superintendents were paid according to the size of their division; for instance Mr Rendell, in charge of the Neath Locomotive Division, was raised from £1,173 to £1,350 p.a. (2011 equivalent: £43,092). Mr A.G. Pollard, Assistant Chief Accountant, was raised from £2,350 to £2,500 p.a. (2011 equivalent: £79,800). A male 'clerk' in the Chief Goods Manager's office at Paddington earnt £625 p.a. (2011 equivalent: £19,950). A female 'Chief Clerk' with twenty-six years' service was paid £431 18s (2011 equivalent: £13,789). This woman was aged 56, and was retiring on a pension of £150 p.a. (2011 equivalent: £4,788) and a female 'shorthand secretary' with fourteen years' service received a salary of £315 18s (2011 equivalent: £10,086). Her pension was £75 p. a. (2011 equivalent: £2,394).

On the labour question, the National Union of Railwaymen and the Transport & General Workers' Union submitted claims on behalf of the men employed in loading ships with coal, for increased pay from the existing £4 14s a week to £5 4s 6d as well as for two – instead of one – weeks' paid holiday. The claims were 'under consideration' by the soon-to-be-abolished railway companies.

The General Manager

SIR JAMES MILNE, K.C.V.O., C.S.I., ANNOUNCES HIS RETIREMENT

SIR JAMES MILNE

AT the close of this month we shall regretfully take leave of **Sir James Milne**, K.C.V.O., C.S.I., our General Manager for the past eighteen and a half years (next to the longest tenure of that office in the Company's history), who has recently announced his decision to retire on December 31.

Educated at Campbell College, Belfast, and Victoria University, Manchester, Mr. Milne joined the Great Western Railway in 1904 in the Chief Mechanical Engineer's Department, Swindon, as a pupil under the late Mr. G. J. Churchward. He came to London in 1908, enlarged his experience in various sections of the Traffic Department and entered the General Manager's office. In 1912 he took charge of the Passenger Train Running Department in the office of the Superintendent of the Line, and four years later became chief clerk to the divisional superintendent, Pontypool Road.

Subsequently appointed Assistant Divisional Superintendent at Swansea and Plymouth in turn, Mr. Milne became, in 1919, Director of Statistics in the Ministry of Transport. After the passing of the Railways Act, 1921, he assisted the Geddes Committee on National Expenditure. In 1922 he became Assistant and, later, Principal Assistant to the General Manager, and in the following year he visited India with Lord Inchcape's Indian Retrenchment Committee—a

service for which the honour of C.S.I. was conferred on him in the King's Birthday Honours of that year. Appointed Assistant General Manager in 1924, Mr. Milne gave evidence before the Railway Rates Tribunal and the Joint Select Committee of the House of Lords and House of Commons on the Railway (Road Transport) Bills of 1928.

In July, 1929, when Sir Felix Pole relinquished the General Managership, Mr. Milne was appointed to succeed him. In the New Year Honours of 1932 he received a Knighthood; and in 1935, in recognition of the Centenary of the Great Western Railway Company, the further honour of Knight Commander of the Royal Victorian Order was conferred on him.

Sir James Milne has been Chairman of the General Managers' Conference on eight occasions since 1931, and Deputy Chairman of the Railway Executive Committee since its formation, when war was imminent, to operate the railways as agents of the Minister of Transport. In February of the present year Sir James was appointed a member of the Special Fuel Committee set up by the Cabinet to deal with the coal crisis. In chronicling a Great Western career of such distinction, it is natural that our thoughts should turn once again to the theme of our popular series of cover pictures: here at leadership level is "Pride In The Job."

A FAREWELL MESSAGE FROM THE GENERAL MANAGER

DURING the eighteen years for which I have had the honour of being General Manager of the Company, many changes of a wide and varied character have occurred in almost every branch of the Company's activities, and thanks to the co-operation of all concerned they have been met satisfactorily.

We are now faced with the greatest change of all, i.e., nationalisation; and, as a consequence, the Great Western Railway Company, which has existed for 112 years, will cease on January 1, 1948, to have a separate entity.

When this momentous change takes place I am confident that all members of the staff will make an important contribution to the well-being of the country. Every possible effort will be needed to make the new administration a success, and I know that, in the duties entrusted to you, you will worthily uphold the traditions which have so long been associated with the name of our great Company.

Although I shall no longer be with you, I shall always remember with gratitude and esteem the loyal co-operation and support which I have at all times received from the Officers and the staff in the good and bad periods through which we have worked together.

I extend my warmest thanks and good wishes to you all and I trust that the future may bring prosperity and happiness to you.

The General Manager's final report to the directors stated that the estimated receipts for the three weeks ended 7 December amounted to £2,940,000, an increase of £328,000 (12.56 per cent) on same period in 1946. Passenger traffic fell by £25,000 (2.21 per cent). General merchandise receipts rose by £176,000 (17.2 per cent) and coal traffic receipts rose by £177,000, which was 38 per cent up on the same period in 1946. Over the whole year to 7 December 1947, estimated receipts amounted to £45,052,000, down by £2,636,000 as compared to 1946. Passenger receipts were down £2,467,000 (10.33 per cent), and general freight receipts showed a decrease of £169,000 (0.71 per cent).

In October the government had ordered the railways to issue tickets at workmen's rates to any 'artisan, mechanic or labourer' at any time of the day or night because of the 'staggering' of working hours in order to avoid 'peak' demands for electricity. In December the Government wanted these cheap tickets to be issued 'to all categories of workers whose hours have been so changed subject to the proviso that they were entitled to workmen's ticket within the normal hours of issue'. I wonder how the booking clerks would know that the person was one who was so entitled. Sir James Milne reported that the new regulations would come into force on 1 January 1948.

During the full year of 1947, with steel and other metals in short supply, Swindon Works craftsmen constructed fifty-five new engines: ten 'Hall'; seven 'County'; ten 2-6-2T ('41xx'); eight 0-6-0 (3210-17); and twenty 0-6-0T ('94xx'). This was twenty-two fewer new-builds than in 1946, but in 1947 priority had to be given to repairing the large backlog of engines awaiting light and heavy repairs. So, besides building new engines, the Works staff gave a heavy repair to 727 engines and light repairs to 330. The figure for heavy repairs included twenty-four 'Austerity' engines loaned by the government to the GWR, which had to be thoroughly repaired before they could be used. Taking all GWR workshops around the system the number of locomotives being given heavy repairs throughout 1947 was 1,085.

Fifty-six locomotives were scrapped during the year: three 'Bulldog' class 4-4-0s; two heavy goods engines of Great Central Railway design, purchased from the War Department after the Great War; four 'Aberdare' 2-6-0 goods engines; and forty-seven others, mostly tank engines of antique vintage, including some from the Welsh railways absorbed in the 'Grouping' of 1921.

Swindon Works 'A' shop for locomotive under repair. (R.M. Casserley)

During the war Swindon Works built eighty 2-8-0 heavy freight engines for the government to the designs of the Chief Mechanical Engineer of the LMS, Sir William Stanier – who had been Works Manager at Swindon from 1920–1931. These engines were based at depots around the GWR until late July 1947, when they were handed over to the LMS.

Oil firing was fitted to twenty-one engines, five of them being of the 'Castle' type, and eleven being 'Hall' engines; twenty were '28xx' class 2-8-0 engines, as well as engine No 6320, a 2-6-0. No 6320, when fitted for oil burning, was the equal of a coal-fired 'Hall' in climbing Sapperton bank, according to E.J. Nutty, Chief Assistant to S.O. Ell at Swindon Research & Development Department. In 1947 a new design of steam superheater and regulator valve was designed at Swindon and during 1947 the devices were being fitted to the boilers of No 5049 *Earl of Plymouth* and No 6022 *King Edward III*.

Oil-burning engine No 3904 (changed to No 4972 when coal fired) *St Brides Hall* was fitted with a Metropolitan-Vickers air-turbo electricity generator to power head and tail lamps, cab and inspection lights. A steam ejector created a vacuum into which, via the generator turbine, the atmosphere rushed.

Engine No 5978 *Bodinnick Hall* was fitted with an experimental rail de-sanding device. At stations where there was power signalling and 100 per cent track circuiting of the rails it was vital that sand, dropped to assist adhesion as the locomotive pulled away, did not become encrusted on the rail top and thus insulate the engine from the rail, which would prevent the track circuits from working to lock points and signals.

A general purpose weed-killing train and another specifically to work on dock quays were both built at Swindon.

English Electric were in the process of building six 350hp diesel-electric shunting engines for the GWR.

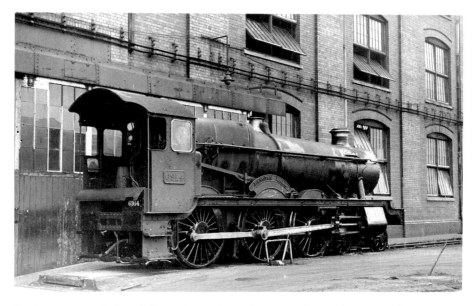

No 6914 *Langton Hall* ready for work outside 'A' shop, 4 April 1947. (H.C. Casserley)

No 2947 *Madresfield Court* passing Hayes on the Down Main with empty milk tanks from Wood Lane, on 30 June 1947. This engine had its tender punctured by Luftwaffe machine-gun fire in 1942 near Westbury, Wiltshire. (Peter Pescod/Transport Treasury 335)

Metropolitan-Vickers (M-V) were working as contractors to the GWR for the construction of a gas turbine locomotive. This was being built on licence from the Swiss patent holders, Brown-Boveri. M-V were making the wheels and chassis frame plates, but construction of transmission and other mechanical parts was delayed by a shortage of draughtsmen at Brown-Boveri.

Swindon Carriage Works built 118 vehicles during the year, and ten Corridor Thirds were built for the GWR by the Gloucester Carriage & Wagon Co. The vehicles built at Swindon were:

Corridor Composites	3
Corridor Thirds	30
Corridor Brake Thirds	22
Non-Corridor Thirds	31
Post Office Van	1
Rail Milk-tank Trucks	26
Fish Vans	5

The corridor coaches were 8ft 11in wide at the waist, and 64ft long over the ends. The non-corridor coaches for both branch and suburban services were the same width and 1ft shorter.

With the restoration of Restaurant Car Service the GWR set about renovating all their cars – in the year before nationalisation! Truly, the GWR directors were an honest bunch of real railwaymen. Ninety cars were involved. They were stripped bare internally at Swindon and sent to Messrs Hampton & Sons for rebuilding and re-equipping. By the end of 1947 forty-four restaurant cars had been refurbished, or were undergoing reconditioning. Swindon Works converted fifty-eight coaches for use as wartime ambulance trains. They all came back to Swindon in 1947 and thirty-five were still in a condition suitable for re-conversion into ordinary carriages.

During the year this great company built 1,506 goods wagons, as detailed below:

Open goods 13-ton vacuum braked	206
Open goods 13-ton non-vacuum braked	523
Covered goods 12-ton vacuum braked	123
Covered goods 12-ton non vacuum braked	93
Covered car carrying 'Mogo' 12-ton vacuum braked	100
Goods brake vans 20-ton	79
Loco coal wagons	7
Ballast wagons 20-ton	75
Ballast wagons 14-ton	27
Ballast wagons 10-ton	50
Container carrying flat wagons	177
Tube wagons 21-ton	45
E.D. 'Loriot' 20-ton	1

In addition, thirty-nine 20-ton ballast hopper wagons with bodies built by Fairleede Engineering Ltd were released to traffic, making a total of 1,545 new wagons for 1947. And in addition to that, Swindon Carriage & Wagon Works repaired 13,945 wagons and scrapped 1,080 wagons.

At the end of 1947, the Great Western Railway was a solvent business. Since their inception in 1835 they had never received a subsidy from government[2] – but the company had subsidised the nation. The government never fully repaid the GWR for the war work they had undertaken during 1914–18, when they were under government control. The company had to carry the huge costs of restoring the sixty small railways they had been forced to take over under the 1921 Railways Act. They were then never allowed by government to charge the fares and rates which, by the 1921 Act, the company was entitled to charge. They had not received their legal due from the government under the wartime control established in 1939. In spite of all those disadvantages – and the lack of legal restrictions on the competing road hauliers – the GWR so managed their affairs that they completed their 110-year history as a profitable, dividend-paying railway.

The directors paid tax to the British Inland Revenue on their attendance fees; they even donated a little of them to the Staff 'Helping Hand' fund. They received no bonuses for doing what they were paid to do. They got no 'golden handshake' for their loss of office at nationalisation. The company ended the year with £705,000 in their current accounts with various banks and £4 million in deposit accounts. Against that background, the weekly wage bill was £720,000. They had short-term investments amounting to £28 million, of which £15,700,000 was invested in government bonds and £3,600,000 was held in Tax Reserve Certificates, which was the equivalent of paying their taxes to the nation in advance. The £954,000 the GWR received as debenture loan stock to mature in 1951–52 was invested with the Railway Finance Corporation. All year there were about £1,100,000 of GWR cheques issued or shortly to be issued but not yet cashed by the recipients.

GREAT WESTERN RAILWAY

MAGAZINE

| December · 1947 | Vol. 59 · No. 11 |

The Chairman

THE RIGHT HONOURABLE VISCOUNT PORTAL OF LAVERSTOKE, P.C., D.S.O., M.V.O.

READERS of the farewell message from the Chairman of the Company, the **Rt. Hon. Viscount Portal**, which appears on the next page, will regret the severance of the association with the Company's affairs of such an eminent public man whose services to the Country have been both distinguished and outstanding.

Born in 1885, the eldest son of the late Sir W. W. Portal, 2nd Baronet, who was Deputy Chairman of the old London and South Western Railway, Viscount Portal was educated at Eton and Christ Church, Oxford. He commanded the dismounted Regiment formed from the Household Cavalry during the European war of 1914–1918, and in 1918 was awarded the Distinguished Service Order for services at Passchendaele.

Viscount Portal joined the Board of Directors of the Great Western Railway in 1927, and took an active part in the Company's affairs, especially in connection with the schemes for the rehabilitation of the Special Areas in South Wales. He was made Chief Industrial Adviser to the Government for the four Special Areas, South Wales, Durham, Lanarkshire and Cumberland. He was Chairman of the Treasury Fund, Special Areas Reconstruction Association Ltd., and one of the Nuffield Trustees. He was also Chairman of the Bacon Development Board; of Wiggins Teape & Co. and for several years a Director of the Commercial Union Assurance Company, Ltd.

Viscount Portal, who was created a Baron in 1935 and a Viscount in 1944, is still Chairman of the Disabled Persons Corporation, Chairman of the National Camps, Vice-Chairman of King George's Jubilee Trust, President of the XIVth Olympic Games and of Portals Ltd., his own family business who make the Bank Note Paper for this Country and many other Countries and which has been in existence for 236 years.

He is Vice-Lieutenant for the County of Hampshire and has been given the Freedom of the City of Cardiff and the Borough of Merthyr Tydfil.

On the outbreak of the recent war, Viscount Portal became Regional Commissioner for Wales under the Civil Defence scheme, and then served as Chairman of the Coal Production Committee. He resigned his Directorship of the Great Western Railway Company in 1940 on appointment as an additional Parliamentary Secretary to the Ministry of Supply. He held that post until 1942, when he was appointed Minister of Works and Planning and First Commissioner of Works and Public Buildings, and became a member of His Majesty's Privy Council. After a distinguished term of office during one of the most difficult periods in the Country's history, Viscount Portal resigned the office of Minister of Works in the latter part of 1944, when he succeeded Sir Charles Hambro as Chairman of the Great Western Railway Company in March 1944.

Viscount Portal is keenly interested in transport problems and social questions, particularly where the welfare of the staff is concerned, and his knowledge of public affairs, gained through many years of varied experience, is probably unique. His election to the Chairmanship of the Great Western Railway Company came at a critical time in the history of the Country as a whole, and of the railway industry, when post-war problems demanded close and constant consideration, and the Great Western Railway was indeed fortunate in possessing such an able and experienced leader.

On behalf of our readers, we tender grateful thanks to Viscount Portal for all he has done in promoting the Company's interests and the welfare of the staff, and we hope he may long be spared to carry on his public work.

VISCOUNT PORTAL

GREAT WESTERN RAILWAY MAGAZINE

CHAIRMAN'S ROOM
PADDINGTON STATION

On the 1st January next the Undertaking of the Great Western Railway Company becomes vested in the British Transport Commission, and the change of ownership brings to an end the administration of the Company's affairs by a Board of Directors, a system which has operated continuously for 112 years. In that long period, which has witnessed both good and bad times, the Company has established honoured traditions which have earned for the Great Western the respect and affection of many.

Perhaps what we cherish most is the reputation associated with the Company for courtesy to the public, fostered from the very earliest days by those responsible for guiding the Company's destinies, and put into practical effect by generation after generation of the staff whose helpfulness in difficult conditions is now a by-word.

In matters affecting the welfare of the employees, the policy of the Directors has always been to show practical sympathy, and the Board are gratified to know that their pension and other similar arrangements were inaugurated long before the State schemes were introduced.

I myself naturally feel the forthcoming changes, as I am the third generation of a family which has been intimately connected with Railway affairs, and I know these sentiments are shared by my colleagues on the Directorate and by many others.

The heartfelt wishes of the Board for success and future happiness go to all members of the Company's staff, and I am confident that in the new Organisation they may be relied on to give of their best as they have always done in the past.

Portal

At the end of 1946 the company carried forward £845,514 of their profits into 1947. Of that the company paid £269,305 to the British Transport Commission; there is no explanation for this in the GWR Accounts. The carry-forward from 1946 added to the earnings of 1947 made a gross profit of £8,115,980 – and that was the end of the road for the GWR. Debenture holders were paid £1,649,855, leaving £6,446,125 for Preference and Ordinary shareholders. £2,528,552 was paid out at the mid-year dividend, which left £2,528,552 for the end-of-year dividend.

The last General Meeting of the Great Western Railway Company proprietors and directors was held in London on Friday 5 March 1948. An account was published in *The Times* on 6 December, beginning with Viscount Portal's address to the gathering. Here it is:

For 112 years these meetings have been held continuously in good times and bad and even in the face of enemy action. They have on occasion been the scene of conflict of opinion between individual stockholders and the Board especially in times of industrial crisis but I think I am justified in saying that at by far the greater number of meetings the atmosphere has been most cordial and the efforts of the directors to expand the Great Western Railway's undertaking in the interest of those it serves have invariably been met with encouragement and enthusiasm when the support of the proprietors has been sought.

Today's meeting is unique in that there are no resolutions requiring the stock holders approval but the directors felt that it would be the wish of many proprietors that they should have the opportunity of meeting together once more before the Company with its proud record ceases to exist. The Transport Act received the Royal Assent on 6th August and I feel sure you will all know the efforts which were made to obtain more favourable terms for the stock holders. The fundamental principles of the Bill remained unchanged, however, and on January 1st the undertaking of the Great Western Railway passed into the ownership of the British Transport Commission.

As the Accounts no longer need the approval of the proprietors they have been circulated in abbreviated form and they explain how the directors have decided to distribute the amount which is in accordance with the provisions of Section 20 of the Transport Act in respect of the years 1946–7.

This amount is made up of the main sources of revenue of the Company during the period of government control, which were:-

1. The fixed, annual, adjustments for interest on capital.
2. The net revenue arising from undertakings excluded from government control consisting largely of dividends on the Company's investments in omnibuses and carriage companies.
3. Profits on realisation of investments.
4. Additional revenue arising from the exact ascertainment of the Company's revenue previously estimated for years prior to 1941 when the Control Agreement was amended to provide a fixed annual sum.

The net revenue from the first of these two sources for the two-year period has been certified by the auditor appointed under the Act. The first item is not variable except to the extent of a minor adjustment for interest. The second item has a substantial increase in 1947 compared to 1946 due to additional and increased dividends in respect of road undertakings.

The Transport Bill as originally drafted precluded the Company from distributing amongst the stock holders the proceeds of profit on realization of investments an amount attributable to pre-1941 financial adjustments. £542,540 was brought into our 1946 accounts in this respect but was not then distributed and a further sum of £31,460 arose in 1947. We were, however, ultimately able to convince the Minister of Transport of the justice of the stockholders' right to these moneys and sub-section 8 of Section 20 was embodied in the Act providing for the additional payment to the Great Western Company of £574,000.

I should like here to mention that several stockholders have been good enough to suggest that a resolution should be submitted to this meeting asking for approval to the payment of a reasonable sum to the members of the Board in consequence of their loss of office and I hardly need say that this was a gesture greatly appreciated. The Board feel that any payment of this nature could quite properly have been paid out of other assets but as the Act does not permit this the Directors preferred not to accept any compensation, since the alternative would have been to reduce the final payment to the stockholders, many of whom are, as we know, persons of limited means whose income will already be cut as a consequence of the conversion of their holdings into the British Transport Commission 3% stock.

After providing for the final dividend on the Preference stocks and the interim dividend of 2% already paid on the Consolidated Ordinary stock, the balance for distribution amongst the holders of the Consolidated Ordinary stock is £2,267,616 and it permits the payment of a final dividend of £5.282% making £7.282% for the year.

I should like to pay a tribute to the services rendered by Mr. C.R. Dashwood, now Chief Accountant of the Western Region who was Chairman of the Railway Accountants' Committee throughout the war period. Mr Dashwood was made a Commander of the Most Excellent Order of the British Empire in the Honours list of June last and I am sure you would wish me to extend him hearty congratulations.

Our auditors, Sir Alan Rae Smith and Sir Lynden Macassey, will, I know, endorse my remarks in this respect and as the old audit arrangements no longer operate I should like to express to those gentlemen and to the members of the Audit Committee, our appreciation of the useful functions which they have performed. The firm of Messrs Deloitte, Plender, Griffiths & Co., of which Sir Alan Rae Smith is a partner, have been connected in a professional capacity with the audit arrangements of the Great Western Company almost since its inception and we owe a great deal to the wise counsel and expert advice which we have received from past and present members of the firm over that long period.

The transfer of the railway undertakings to the British Transport Commission has inevitably brought about many changes in personnel. Sir James Milne who was General Manager of the Great Western Company for over 18 years retired on December 31st after serving the Company and the State with great ability throughout some of the most difficult times in our history and the Board would like to take this opportunity of putting on record their appreciation of his services.

Mr. F.R.E. Davis, who was Secretary of the Company for nearly 22 years and assistant Secretary before that, also retired towards the end of last year. As Secretary for this exceptionally long period he worked in the closest association with the Board, whose full confidence he enjoyed and to him too, the directors are glad to pay a tribute to his outstanding services. He is with us today in a voluntary capacity because he has acceded to the wish of the Directors to act for them in connection with the winding-up formalities.

Mr. K.W.C. Grand, who was Assistant General Manager to Sir James Milne, now holds the responsible position of Chief Regional Officer under the Railway Executive and I am sure you would like to offer your congratulations to him on being selected for this important appointment. Those of us who have an intimate knowledge of his capabilities and his practical experience in railway matters have every confidence in his ability to deal with the wide variety of problems which will no doubt arise under the new organization and to him and to all the other members of the Great Western staff who are now numbered amongst the employees of the British Transport Commission and the Railway Executive we extend good wishes for their future happiness and success. We feel sure they will carry out their duties in their new sphere with the efficiency and courtesy which characterized their service with the Great Western Railway Company.

I cannot close the proceedings without thanking the proprietors for the kindness and consideration they have always extended to the Directors and to me and my predecessors who have occupied this chair. To many of us the well being of the railways has been part of our heritage almost from boyhood days and whatever changes the future may bring we shall always remember with pride and affection the part we were privileged to play in dealing with the administration of the company's affairs and the many friends we made amongst all classes of the community whilst acting in that capacity.

Proprietors Thanks and Appreciation

Mr W.J. Stevens.
My Lord Chairman, Ladies and Gentlemen. At this final General Meeting of the Great Western Railway Company the proprietors desire to place on record their grateful appreciation of the loyalty and devotion of the Chairman and the Board of Directors, the Officers and the entire Staff of the company and to the nation throughout the history of the great company.

Before submitting this resolution I should also like to thank you, Sir, for your very dignified speech.

Our company has a history of over 112 years and though our future is snatched from us, we may dwell with gratitude and pride on a long period of great achievement. After all the GWR is the only leading railway company which has maintained its individuality throughout and may yet be said to be '112 years young'. I am glad to have been a shareholder for over 40 years. Regarding compensation to directors, we note your decision with great respect and it is characteristic of the dignified way in which you have always conducted the company's affairs. (Hear! Hear!) My comment is brief: So shines a good deed in a naughty world.

So may we let pride in its long and honourable history and gratitude to those who have served it so well be the keynotes of the Meeting.

I beg to move accordingly.

Mr J.E. Palmer Tomkinson seconded the resolution which was carried with acclamation.

PADDINGTON'S LAST GREAT WESTERN TRAIN. *Engine* 5037, " *Monmouth Castle* ".

NIGHTS OF THE WESTERN ROAD. SIR JAMES MILNE MEETS HIS " NAMESAKE " ENGINE AND ITS CREW.

The 11.50 p.m. Paddington, hauled by No 5037 *Monmouth Castle* was the last Great Western Railway train to leave Paddington.

No 7001 *Denbigh Castle* was renamed *Sir James Milne* in February 1948. Sir James Milne is seen here standing beside his locomotive namesake.

The very last engine to be built under the auspices of the old Company was No 7007 *Ogmore Castle* – seen coming out of the Works in July 1946. It was renamed in January 1948. (H.O. Vaughan)

Mr K.W.C. Grand, Chief Regional Officer:- My Lord Portal, Ladies and Gentlemen. This is indeed a sad moment for those of us who have spent the whole of their business career in the service of the Great Western Railway Company. As this is the last occasion on which I shall see you, Sir, I should like, on behalf of the Officers and Staff to thank you, Sir, and the other members of the Board, for the kindness and consideration which we have received at your hands during the many years we served the Great Western Railway Company.

If I may say so, I think our company was unique inasmuch as the officers looked on the directors as personal friends. At the same time, we of the Western Region will give of our best to the new administration and our efforts will be inspired by the tradition which has been handed down from generation to generation throughout the long history of the Great Western Railway Company.

This is the last occasion the proprietors, directors and officers will meet but I hope it will not mean the severance of the many friendships we have made with those with whom we came into contact all over our great system. (Applause)

The Chairman: I should like on behalf of the Board to thank Mr Stevens and Mr Tomkinson for the kind words that have been said about the Board which we do appreciate and it is also my wish that we should express our warmest thanks to Mr Grand for what he said, not only on his own behalf but on behalf of the other officers and staff.

This is a very sad day for us all but we took the view that things must be carried on in the most efficient way possible and so we wish everyone well in whatever takes place in the future. (Applause)

Gone With Regret

Notes

1   *Great Western Railway Magazine*, July 1947, p. 144.
2   Sid Tyler volunteered for the army in August 1914, aged 14, and was accepted into the cavalry. He was transferred to 4th Bn Wiltshire Regiment in March 1916 and went 'over the top' at the opening of the Battle of the Somme on 1 July. He survived unscathed until the Third Battle of Ypres, July–November 1917. In 1920 he joined the GWR. He said to me in 1965: 'If there was any good that came out of that war it was that it gave me a life-long interest in first aid.' He served Swindon Junction first-aid team for 45 years. He was captain of the winning team in 1965.
3   Express passenger train, newspaper train, or breakdown van train or snowplough going to clear the line, or light engine going to assist a disabled train.

APPENDICES

Appendix I

The Board of Directors of the Great Western Railway in 1947
The year(s) each person was appointed and/or served follows the name in italics

Chairman Appointed to the Board
Viscount Portal (1885–1949) PC, DSO, MVO, GCMG, *1927 to 1938*
Served in the Devon Yeomanry and Lifeguards in the First World War.
Parliamentary Secretary to Ministry of Supply 1938.
Minister of Works and Planning 1942–44.

Formally Appointed Chairman
Friday 28 March 1947 by Minute 1 of that date. See *Rail* 250/63.
Annual fee as Chairman £6,000.[1] After tax £3,975.
Directors' fees, see *Rail* 250/782.

Deputy Chairman
William Ward MC, 3rd Earl of Dudley (1894–1969), *1936*
Described as 'The greatest land and factory owner in West Midlands'. Owner of the
Round Oak steelworks and Baggeridge colliery.
Annual fee as Deputy Chairman £3,000. After tax £1,650.

Directors
Sir Charles Hambro KBE, MC (1897–1963), *1930*
Coldstream Guards 1916–18. Military Cross for 'conspicuous bravery'.
Director of Hambros Bank, 1922. Director of the Bank of England, 1930.
Deputy Chair of GWR 1934–40. Succeeded Viscount Horne as Chairman in 1940 but
    secret war work took up much of his time.
Awarded KBE in 1941 for his work with the SOE. He was Head of Sections dealing
    with Resistance Groups in Norway, France, Belgium and Germany.
He guided the financial affairs of the GWR from 1934. The GWR was the most
    successful of the four. (*Oxford Dictionary of National Biography*)
Annual fee £1,091 8s 9d. After tax £491 1s 3d.

Lt Col J.J. Astor (1886–1971), *1929*

Country gentleman.
Served in the Life Guards in the First World War.
Held several Honorary Colonelcies.
Director of Hambros Bank and Barclays Bank.
Owner of *The Times*, 1922–66.
Annual fee £918 0s 6d. After tax £505 9s 6d.

The Honourable A.W. Baldwin (1904–76), *1937*

Stourport Foundry. Son of thrice Prime Minister Stanley Baldwin.
Annual fee £1,151 9s 8d. After tax £904 1s 0d.

The Honourable Sir Edward Cadogan KBE, CB (1880–1962), *1929*

Officer in Suffolk Yeomanry 1914–18. Served at Gallipoli and in Egypt.
Barrister.
Conservative Party MP until 1945. A benefactor to the underprivileged.

W.M. Codrington Esq. CMG, MC, *1944*

Annual fee £1,212 18s 6d. After tax £878.

Gilbert Wills, Lord Dulverton, OBE (1880–1956), *1927*

W.D. & H.O. Wills, Bristol cigarette manufacturer.
President of Imperial Tobacco.
Annual fee £819 13s 0d. After tax £369 17s 0d.

Sir William Fraser CBE, *1944*

Annual fee £819 13s 0d. After tax £369 17s 0d.

Cyril E. Lloyd Esq., *1923*

Annual fee £1,209 8s 0d. After tax £544 4s 0d.

C.F. Luttrell Esq., *1930*

Dunster Castle, landowner.
Benefactor, Minehead and Somerset.
Annual fee £977 2s 0d. After tax £440 3s 0d.

The Rt Honourable Harold Macmillan PC, MP, *1929–40* and *1945–47*

Thrice wounded in the First World War.
Director Macmillan publishing company.
British government representative in North Africa during 1944.
Working closely with Dwight D Eisenhower, 1942–45.
Annual fee £1,054 0s 10d. After tax £579 14s 5d.

J.V. Rank Esq., *1942*
Business executive with interests in flour milling.
Annual fee £982 1*s* 0*d*. After tax £540 3*s* 0*d*.

Sir William Reardon-Smith Bt, *1943*
Shipping line owner.
Annual fee £1,013. After tax £611 13*s* 4*d*.

Captain Hugh Vivian MICE, *1944*
Industrialist and marine engineer.
Annual fee £778 13*s* 10*d*. After tax £418 7*s* 10*d*.

Sir George Harvie-Watt Bt, KC, MP (1903–89), *1943*
Soldier, barrister, businessman, politician, PPS to Winston Churchill 1941–45.
Annual fee £689 14*s* 10*d*. After tax £379 8*s* 10*d*.

Colonel Sir Charles Wright CB, CBE, *1936*
Annual fee £838 13*s* 8*d*. After tax £461 6*s* 0*d*.

Notes

1   The chairman's annual fee was £6,000 in 1923. According to HMRC's inflation factor Viscount Portal's 1947 fee had the purchasing power of £191,520 in 2011.

Appendix II

Officers of the Great Western Railway in 1947
(from *Rail* 250/125)

General Manager:	Sir James Milne KCVO, CSI
Assistant General Manager:	K.W.C. Grand
Company Secretary:	F.R.E. Davis CBE
Joint Assistant Secretaries:	S.B. Taylor; S.G. Rowe
Registrar of Stocks:	A.C. Barnes
Chief Cashier:	J.A. Ralph
Registrar of Deeds and Records:	J.W. Griffin
Solicitor:	M.B.H. Gilmour
Assistant Solicitor:	R. Chitty
Chief Conveyancing Solicitor:	A.E. Bolter
Chief Accountant:	C.R. Dashwood OBE
Assistant Accountant:	H.T. Forth
Assistants to Chief Accountant:	A.G. Pollard; J.W.J. Webb; A.W. Tait
Superintendent of the Line:	G. Matthews CBE
Assistant Superintendents of the Line:	S.G. Hearne; H.H. Phillips (Cardiff)

Operating Asistant: Leslie Edwards
Commercial Assistant: L.W. Conibear
Staff Assistant: K.C. Griffiths
New Works Assistant: H.G.W. Gaunt

Divisional Traffic Superintendents

Birmingham   A.V.R. Brown
Bristol   R.G. Pole
Cardiff   H.H. Swift
Chester   N.H. Briant
Exeter   H.A.G. Worth
Gloucester   R.H.B. Nicholls
London   C.T. Cox MBE
Newport   W.R. Stevens
Swansea   C.W. Powell
Worcester   J.F.M. Taylor

Chief Engineer: A.S. Quartermaine CBE
Assistant Engineer (General):   C.H.T. Morgan
Assistant Engineer (New Works):   H. Savage MBE
Assistant Engineer (Maintenance):   M.G.R. Smith MBE
Bridge Assistant: P.S.A. Berridge MBE, FICE
Staff and Office Assistant: A.T.F. Waple

Divisional Engineers

Bristol   H.A. Alexander
Cardiff   A.W. Hollingdale
Gloucester   T.C.B. Davies
London   E.T. Davies
Neath   M.A. Henry
Newport   E.C. Cookson
Oswestry   C.A. Neale
Plymouth   N.S. Cox
Shrewsbury   J.A. Denney
Taunton   F. Holland
Wolverhampton   R.F. Wilson

Divisional Docks Engineers

Barry, Cardiff, Newport, Penarth: R.H. Edwards
Port Talbot and Swansea: T.H. Dovell

Chief Mechanical Engineer: F.W. Hawksworth
Principal Assistant: F.C. Hall
Loco Running Superintendent & Outdoor
  Assistant: W.N. Pellow

Staff Assistant: W.H. Bodman
Electrical Assistant: M. Macdonald
Locomotive Works Manager (Swindon):   K.J. Cook OBE
Carriage & Wagon Works Manager (Swindon):   H. Randle
Office Assistant: H.W. Gardner

Divisional Locomotive Superintendents

Bristol   H.N.S. Edwards
Cardiff   S.E. Tyrwhitt
London   H.G. Kerry
Neath   H.T. Rendell
Newport   C.L. Simpson
Newton Abbot   A.W.H. Christison
Oswestry   A.G. Snell
Wolverhampton   V.J.H. Webb
Worcester   L.G. Morris

Dock Mechanical Engineers

Barry, Cardiff, Newport and Penarth: J.F. Arthur
Port Talbot and Swansea: D.E. Cameron

Chief Docks Manager: L.E. Ford OBE
General Assistant: W.H. Victory
Assistants to the Chief Docks Manager
   (London and Provinces):   W. Jeffers and L.G. Taylor

Dock Managers

Barry   T. Carpenter
Cardiff and Penarth   D.G. Hopkins
Newport   L.T. Edmunds
Plymouth   J.H.L. Lean
Port Talbot   R.H. Rice
Swansea   E.V. Swallow

Signal & Telegraph Engineer: F.H.D. Page OBE
Chief Assistant: G.H. Crook
Assistants to Chief S&T Engineer: A.W. Woodbridge (Mr Woodbridge
                                         became Chief in April 1947)
                                         and R. Hodges

Stores Superintendent: Vacant
Assistant Stores Superintendent: H.R. Webb
Assistants to Stores Superintendent: C.F. Faith and A.G. Roberts
Architect: Vacant
Road Motor Engineer: A.E.C. Dent

Chief Medical Officer:	H.H. Cavendish-Fuller MD
Stationery Superintendent:	H.W. Croft
Chief of Police:	A. Lane
Chief Goods Manager:	David Blee
Deputy Chief Goods Manager & Mineral Manager:	C. Furber
Principal Assistant to Chief Goods Manager:	G. Cornish
Assistant to Chief Goods Manager:	A. Bond
General and Staff Assistant:	T.H. Hollingsworth
Rates Assistant:	C.H. Coe
Claims and Salvage Agent:	H.A. Sims
Road Transport Controller:	H.H. Starr
Assistant to Chief Goods Manager at Cardiff:	A.C.B. Pickford

District Goods Managers

Birmingham	J.A. Warren-King
Bristol	H. Bolton
Cardiff	C.E. Shaw
Exeter	D.H. Hawkeswood
Gloucester	W. Lampitt
Liverpool	W.M. Hitchcock
London	H.J. Hoskins MBE
Newport	R.P. Davis
Shrewsbury	J.F. Anstey
Swansea	R.A. Ryan
Worcester	C.H. Adey

District Traffic Managers (Goods and Passenger functions combined)

Plymouth	J.S.P. Pearson
Oswestry	T.C. Sellars
Traffic Manager for Ireland:	F.S. Veltom (11 Nassau Street, Dublin)

Appendix III

Sample of Locomotive statistics
(from *Rail* 250/282)

For the four weeks ending 22 February 1947

1. Locomotive fleet total	3,932
2. Locomotives available daily	2,994 (76.14 per cent of total fleet)
3. Locomotives in use daily	2912 (97.26 per cent of those available)

4. Average engine miles per day   94.69 per engine in use
5. Average engine hours per day   12.6 per engine in use
6. Passenger* train miles   2,011,161
7. Goods train miles   1,602,207

For the four weeks ending 9 August 1947
1. Locomotive fleet total   3,937
2. Locomotives available daily   3,110 (78.99 per cent of total fleet)
3. Locomotives in use daily   3,004 (96.59 per cent of those available)
4. Average engine miles per day   93.21 per engine in use
5. Average engine hours per day   11.00 per engine in use
6. Passenger* train miles   2,828,446
7. Goods train miles   1,610,875

Consumption of coal and oil per engine mile
Pounds of coal used per engine mile
For the week ending 9 August 1947
Passenger*   46.34
Goods   47.82

For the week ending 12 July 1947
Passenger*   48.09
Goods   49.62

Pints of oil used per engine mile
For the week ending 9 August 1947
Passenger*   8.04
Goods   7.73

For the week ending 12 July 1947
Passenger*   7.75
Goods   7.45

* Includes parcels and empty coaching stock trains

Appendix IV

Locomotives converted to oil firing
The numbers in brackets are those carried after conversion

The twenty '28xx'

2872 (4800)	10/45 to 9/48	2853 (4810)	8/47 to 6/49
2854 (4801)	11/45 to 2/49	2847 (4811)	9/47 to 6/49
2862 (4802)	2/46 to 9/48	2888 (4850)	11/45 to 9/48
2849 (4803)	5/46 to 4/49	3865 (4851)	12/45 to 4/49
2839 (4804)	5/46 to 10/48	3818 (4852)	1/46 to 9/48
2863 (4805)	5/46 to 5/49	3839 (4853)	5/47 to 11/49
2832 (4806)	5/46 to 4/49	3837 (4854)	6/47 to 8/49
2848 (4807)	6/47 to 7/49	3813 (4855)	7/47 to 6/49
2834 (4808)	7/47 to 1/50	3820 (4856)	7/47 to 6/49
2845 (4809)	8/47 to 12/49	3831 (4857)	8/47 to 5/49

The five 'Castles'

100A1	1/47 to 9/48
5039	12/46 to 9/48
5079	1/47 to 10/48
5083	12/46 to 11/48
5091	10/46 to 11/48

The eight 'Halls'

4968 (3900)	5/47 to 3/49
4971 (3901)	5/47 to 4/49
4948 (3902)	5/47 to 9/48
4907 (3903)	5/47 to 4/50
4972 (3904)	5/47 to 10/48
5955 (3950)	6/46 to 10/48
5976 (3951)	4/47 to 11/48
6957 (3952)	4/47 to 3/50

The one '63xx'

6320	3/47 to 8/49

Source: Railway Correspondence and Travel Society, *Locomotives of the Great Western Railway* Parts 8 and 9

Appendix V

Engine Failures, as far as known, August–December 1947

August – nineteen days recorded

Passenger	52
Freight	nil
Total failed	52

September – twenty-nine days recorded

Passenger	63
Freight	13
Total failed	76

October – twenty-four days recorded
Passenger   54
Freight   8
Total failed   62

November – twenty-two days recorded
Passenger   44
Freight   12
Total failed   56

December – twenty-one days recorded
Passenger   59
Freight   5
Total failed   64

The grand total of failures over 115 days is 310, working out at 2.7 failures per day

Appendix VI

Best Kept Length of Permanent-way for 1947

London Division
Hungerford
Ganger: W.J. Huntley, Sub-ganger: L.J. Philips. Lengthmen: F. Jessett, C.H.J. Suter and F.G. Smith.

Bristol Division
Dauntsey
Ganger: C.W.R. Newth, Sub-ganger: C. Ovens. Lengthmen: A.E. Gingell, W.H.C. Gingell, C. Hatt and R.G. Bubb.

Taunton Division
Exeter St Thomas
Ganger: F.J. Yandell, Sub-ganger: H.J. Denyer. Lengthmen: J.H. Caniford and S.J. Beer.

Plymouth Division
Truro
Ganger: F.B. Coplin, Sub-ganger: G.H. Watson. Lengthmen: G.H. Wason, S. Andrew, R. Hawke and E. Woolcock.

Newport Division
Pontypool Road Depot
Ganger: S. Worboys, Sub-ganger: S.J. Tasker. Lengthmen: E. Philips, R.J Dobbs, H. Thomas, W.J. Harvey, J.O. Joy, H. McDonough and A.J. Roberts.

Cardiff Division
Pontypridd

Ganger: G.S. Austin, Sub-ganger: I.M. Pugh. Lengthmen: F. Banfield, A.J. Bailey, C.E. Godfrey, A.W. Stevens and W.V. Owen.

Neath Division
Clarbeston Road

Ganger: O. Thomas, Sub-ganger, G.H. Morris. Lengthmen: J.H. Saies, J. James and L.J. Evans.

Gloucester Division
Broadway

Ganger: W.E. Andrews, Sub-ganger: W. Horne. Lengthmen: F.J.T. Kirby, H. Clay and H. Holmes.

Wolverhampton Division
Rowley Regis

Ganger: H.T. Biles, Sub-ganger: W. Gummery. Lengthmen: F.J. James, E.S. Harrold, L. Arnold, A. Withers and T.W. Round.

Shrewsbury Division
Hodnet

Ganger: L.G. Wyn, Sub-ganger: H. Billington. Lengthmen: J.R. Williams and D. Manning.

Central Wales Division
Lynclys

Ganger: A. Hughes, Sub-ganger: G.R. Roberts. Lengthmen: R. Drayton, C. Mills and C.W. Hughes.

Sources

The Great Western's Last Year: Efficiency in Adversity has been written entirely from research into GWR official records and from reports in the *Great Western Railway Magazine* – which was the company's own journal and carries great authority – and from GWR internal reports on collisions, derailments, passenger and freight train breakaways for 1947 which I have in my collection. As a one-time steam-age signalman I have not been able to resist the temptation to make two or three 'educated guesses' as to the 'why' of some part of a sequence of events and I have occasionally used my own experiences of steam railway work – such as foot-plating through the Severn Tunnel – to describe conditions, but whenever I have descended into educated guessing I have made it clear that this is my opinion rather than fact.

Documents consulted:

At The National Archives, Kew
Rail 250/62 Minutes of Board meetings 12/1945–2/1948.
Rail 250/282 Minutes of Directors' Locomotive, Carriage & Stores Committee 1947.
Rail 250/469 General Manager's Fortnightly Reports to the Directors' Traffic
    Committee 1947.
Rail 250/482 General Manager's Fortnightly Report on Labour Matters 1947.
Rail 250/782 Directors' Attendances 1926–1947.
Rail 937/194 GWR Working Time Table Sections 1, 3, 4, 5, 6, Summer 1947.
ZPER 19/60 and 61 *Great Western Railway Magazine* 1947 and 1948
Unless otherwise stated all illustrations are scanned from the 1947 and 1948 *Great*
    Western Railway Magazines – the publication was still entitled *Great Western*
    Railway Magazine in 1948.

At my Home
GWR Rule Book 1933.
GWR General Appendix to the Rule Book 1936.
GWR Signalling Regulations 1936.
A Pictorial Record of Great Western Engines, Vol. 2, Jim Russell/OPC.
A Pictorial Record of Great Western Coaches: Vols 1 and 2, Jim Russell/OPC.
Locomotives of the GWR, Parts 8 and 9, Railway Correspondence and Travel Society.
British Railways Locomotives (1948), H.C. Casserley/Ian Allan.

INDEX